COMFORT ZONES

A Practical Guide for Retirement Planning

ELWOOD N. CHAPMAN

Canadian Edition by
Charles T. Ormrod, C.A.

Reid Publishing Ltd.
Oakville, Ontario

COMFORT ZONES
A Practical Guide for Retirement Planning

by Elwood N. Chapman

Originally published 1985.
Crisp Publications, Inc.
95 First Street
Los Altos, CA 94022

Canadian Edition by Charles T. Ormrod, C.A.
Published 1987.
Reid Publishing Ltd.
Box 7267
Oakville, Ontario L6J 6L6

ISBN: 0-921601-00-X

Printed in Canada.

Cover design by Carol Harris.

Acknowledgments

One cannot complete a book of this nature without a human support system. When you take five years to research, review, write and rewrite a manuscript, your support group becomes even larger. It would be impossible to individually thank the preretirees, retirees, and personal friends who, through formal interviews and casual conversations, provided me with insights and case studies. I would, however, like to thank the following special people for their critical reviews of the original manuscript.

Dr. Mary Carmen
Director of Aging Services
Prairie View Hospital
Newton, Kansas

Dr. Richard H. Davis
Leonard Davis School of Gerontology
University of Southern California
Los Angeles, California

Florence S. Gross
Articles Editor, *Modern Maturity*
American Association of Retired Persons
Long Beach, California

Roland M. Jones, A.E.P.
Jones Associates
Santa Rosa, California

J. G. Parkel
IBM Director of Personnel Services
Armonk, New York

Carl Shafer
Director of SERV, Dow Chemical
Midland, Michigan

Roland Jones deserves special mention for introducing me to the "comfort zones" concept.

Also, my sincere thanks to the personnel and training staff of Bullock's Department Stores, Los Angeles, California for permitting me to test material in this book in a series of preretirement seminars.

There is no way I can fully thank my friend and publisher Mike Crisp who not only suggested the original work but has supported and advised me through the entire effort.

I wrote *Comfort Zones* during the period when my wife, Martha, and I made our own passage into retirement. Although we sometimes find it difficult to live up to the standards presented in the book, we acknowledge that writing it has better prepared us for retirement and enhanced our lives.

Martha not only helped with the editing and typing, but also provided me with the comfort zone I needed to finish the project. Because of this and other reasons too numerous to mention, this book is dedicated with love to Martha Chapman.

Preface

Comfort Zones is a practical, learn-as-you-go guide to a better retirement. Designed with you in mind, this book's primary objective is to help you plan for retirement in a thoughtful, logical, yet manageable way. To accomplish this, each chapter includes self-assessments that will tell you how prepared you are for the factual material that follows. An abundance of practical activities allow you to directly apply the information presented to your personal situation. Throughout the book there are cases and examples to think about—and compare your thoughts and solutions with mine. You can also measure your progress by answering questions at the end of each chapter.

Consider *Comfort Zones* to be a guide rather than a book to be read once and then tucked away on a shelf. A preliminary version has been used very successfully by several companies in their preretirement training programs as well as by individuals involved in their transition to retirement. It can help make your personal journey into a more rewarding retirement. Good luck.

Elwood Chapman

ABOUT THE ILLUSTRATIONS

We are not always conscious that we show our attitudes to friends and associates. So that we may become more aware of this (and have some fun, too) all illustrations in COMFORT ZONES have been drawn to resemble the tiny amoeba, which makes comments the author might be reluctant to make himself.

To refresh your memory, the microscopic amoeba is grey in color, constantly changing size and shape and often referred to as the lowest form of life.

"After all, I'm just an amoeba."

Contents

To know how to grow old is the master work of wisdom, and one of the most difficult chapters in the great art of living.

Henri Frédéric Amiel (1821-1881)

I

TAKING CHARGE

This section will help prepare you for your retirement adventure. After completing the first five chapters, you should be able to: live with more style before retirement; make a smoother, more succcessful transition when retirement arrives; recognize and adjust to the myths and misconceptions about retirement; and make better retirement decisions.

1

Your Attitude Toward Retirement

Some years ago, before my retirement, I visited a small mining museum in northern Ontario. A friendly woman greeted me as I entered. She was so polite, helpful, and enthusiastic that we soon struck up a conversation. She told me she was a volunteer for the museum. I subsequently learned she had recently celebrated her eightieth birthday. Her eyes sparkled as she talked. Today, I only faintly recall the museum, but I still have a clear picture of this delightful person. I felt at the time that, with an attitude like hers, retirement could be exciting.

Attitude is simply the way you view things mentally and emotionally. If you want to see the beautiful and humorous side of life, you can focus on these positive factors, and that is primarily what you'll see. If you want to see the unpleasant side, all you need do is let your mind dwell on the negative aspects. This is true all through life, but accentuating the positive is immeasurably more important as you approach retirement. To be negative then can be disastrous.

* Mrs. Branson looks only to the past. She has never accepted the challenge of retirement. Two comments she often makes are: "Without work, I feel unchallenged and useless" and "The good part is over—only the day to day remains." Mrs. Branson views retirement as hanging on until she can no longer function. Her complaints have driven most of her friends away. Her children make duty calls only. She has elected to write off what could be the best part of her life.

* Mrs. Jordan is in the same general situation as Mrs. Branson, but she has accepted the challenge. She makes an effort to bring good things out of retirement. Here are two comments she makes: "I have a new role to play, and I'm eager to get on with it" and "I'm free to enjoy new adventures." Mrs. Jordan has disciplined her mind to focus on the positive side. Her attitude shows she has decided to get the most out of retirement.

Measuring Your Own Attitude

What about you? Which route will you take? To measure your attitude toward retirement, complete the following assessment by circling the appropriate number. Circling number 10 means you believe the statement in the left column is completely true for you; circling number 1 means you believe the statement in the right column is completely true for you. If neither extreme fits, select the number that fits you. Once finished, total your score and write it in the box provided.

If you scored 80 or higher, it appears that you will make the most of retirement. If you were between 50 and 80, you are less enthusiastic but should be able to create a rewarding retirement. If you rated yourself under 50, I hope you will fill out the scale again after you have completed this book.

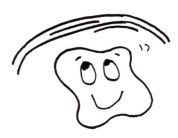

Creating Your Own Rainbow

Some people see retirement as a low-fun, low-excitement, low-happiness period. They expect so little that when the time arrives, little is what they get.

Dean's Attitude

Dean was eager to leave his career, but he had heard so many negative stories about retirement that he didn't expect much. All he really anticipated was a time to relax. He didn't mentally expect or plan for much. Although Dean lived 18 years after retirement, he accomplished little. His retirement years lived up to his low expectations.

ATTITUDE ASSESSMENT

Retirement is going to be the most exciting part of my life.	10 9 8 7 6 5 4 3 2 1	I dread every hour in the future.
There is an abundance of exciting opportunities after retirement.	10 9 8 7 6 5 4 3 2 1	After retirement, everything is downhill. Opportunities disappear.
I want to stay in charge and be an active, involved retiree.	10 9 8 7 6 5 4 3 2 1	I just want to withdraw from it all.
I will turn changes into opportunities.	10 9 8 7 6 5 4 3 2 1	I am not up to coping with changes.
I intend to expand my sense of humor.	10 9 8 7 6 5 4 3 2 1	What's humorous about getting older?
Retirees have advantages over others in our society.	10 9 8 7 6 5 4 3 2 1	Retirees have no advantages; society is cruel to them.
I can make new friends of all ages.	10 9 8 7 6 5 4 3 2 1	Nobody wants to know me. I'm obsolete.
Retirement is the best time of life to have fun and take new risks.	10 9 8 7 6 5 4 3 2 1	This is the time to draw back.
Now I can use my creative talents and contribute.	10 9 8 7 6 5 4 3 2 1	I have nothing left to give.
It's possible to have a positive attitude even with a physical problem.	10 9 8 7 6 5 4 3 2 1	People with physical problems should give up. Why fight an uphill battle?

Total Score _____

Others, unlike Dean, decide in advance to take a positive attitude and squeeze every possible joy out of retired life.

Jason's Attitude   Jason wanted everything: international travel, creative accomplishment, time with grandchildren, cultural events, more golf, and some new adventures. His retirement expectations were so high it worried his wife. She was certain there would be a letdown. It never happened. Jason lived 20 years beyond retirement and was totally involved for 18 of them. His retirement lived up to his expectations.

The Human Life Cycle The accompanying diagram of the human life cycle demonstrates the basic challenge that all retirees face. As you study it, three things become obvious:

* Next to the mature adult phase, the retirement period is usually the longest.

* Because childhood and adolescence are growing periods, and both adult phases are working periods, retirement is the phase that is most free for creative and leisure activities.

* If a person wants to complete the life cycle in a positive manner, the retirement years are by far the greatest challenge.

TYPICAL HUMAN LIFE CYCLE

CHILDHOOD
(age 0–12)
Heavily protected period

ADOLESCENCE
(age 12–18)
Shortest, most traumatic period

RETIREMENT PHASE
(50–55–60–65 to ?)
Most challenging phase

YOUNG ADULTHOOD
(age 18–35)
Most difficult passage

MATURE ADULTHOOD
(age 35 to perhaps 65)
Longest, most productive period

A Realistic Note We should not anticipate dramatic changes after retirement. Most of us will retain the same personality characteristics and coping skills we developed earlier. If you have a positive outlook on life, retirement should be easier for you. The pattern is already set. Naturally there will be a challenge, but it will be easier for you than for a pessimistic person. This doesn't mean behavior and attitude are impossible to change. Sometimes people with a negative outlook earlier in life "come into their own" after retirement. They find a way to make up for things they didn't accomplish earlier. But becoming a "late bloomer" is not easy. The opportunity is present, but it takes determination and self-discipline to change.

The Detachment Syndrome As you prepare for a new stage of life, you have a natural tendency toward withdrawing from the reality of your environment. Retirement has always had an escape connotation. We have been conditioned to expect our later years to be free of hassles. We anticipate a quiet, peaceful, wind-down period. We sometimes dream about the day we leave the "rat race" behind.

Yet we know that the further from reality we get, the sooner we will become dependent on others. So we have a problem. On one hand we want the relaxed environment we anticipated. On the other, we want to stay independent and free. A real dilemma!

If we do not stay in charge by maintaining our health, protecting our living environments, and managing our money, we will ultimately fall victim to the detachment syndrome. We will be enveloped in a retirement marshmallow where everything at first seems soft and delightful but later turns out to be sticky and uncomfortable. We can lose our flexibility and find ourselves in a state of semidepression. Retirement may mean leaving work behind, but it does not mean leaving reality behind. Retirement should be an opportunity to replace a work-oriented lifestyle with a new, equally exciting one. The detachment syndrome is a trap we should learn to recognize and avoid.

Taking Charge The Canada Pension Plan (CPP), Old Age Security (OAS), provincial health insurance plans (PHIP), and other programs were designed to provide financial and medical support to people when they need it the most. Too often, however, many make the mistake of interpreting these important benefits to mean that society will take care of other matters as well. This is nonsense. The moment you receive a seniors card, you must take more responsibility for yourself, not less. For example, if you work for a large corporation or the government, you have all kinds of built-in financial and human support. The moment you retire, this support (or much of it) is gone forever. You may have government pensions and health plans, and benefits from your former company, but you have lost other support items. Ask a person how it feels to retire from an organization. Most will describe some feelings of insecurity or emptiness, especially at first. Minimizing these feelings means *you* must take charge.

What does "take charge" mean? Basically it means that you accept the responsibility for your retirement lifestyle. You provide the direction for your new life. It means if you don't take charge of yourself, you may become another victim of the detachment syndrome. Face it! Nobody is standing by to take you to retirement heaven. Nobody can help you as much as you can help yourself.

Taking charge means facing decisions—not backing away from your problems, not relying on others, staying in control. You have the choice of either crawling through retirement, hoping others will give you a push, or experiencing it under your own steam, holding your head high with style.

The Delayed-Action Strategy

Most people looking at retirement say that more than anything else they want to maintain their freedom. "I've worked hard all my life to achieve a degree of freedom, financial and otherwise. I don't expect to give it up lightly." Bravo!

Staying free means staying in charge. It means keeping control of the money you have as long as possible. If you give your money away, you will lose certain options that can help ensure freedom: the freedom to live where you want, how you want to live, and taking part in the activities of your choice. It means you should postpone, as long as possible, the time when others step in to help. If you are happy living where you are now, *delay* moving. Do not give your estate away until you are sure it is not required for your own happiness. Avoid handing problems and responsibilities to others if you can still deal with them yourself. There may be circumstances that make it difficult to follow this strategy; but, generally, the longer you take charge the better. The longer you maintain your freedom the happier you will be.

Using Special Circumstances as an Excuse

You may have a chronic health problem that convinces you it's impossible to accept the challenge of being a creative, happy retiree. You may wonder why you should enter a race if you're handicapped and can't win.

Ralph's Problem

Because of injuries suffered in an automobile accident as a young man, Ralph is seriously handicapped. As a result his work was so tiring he had little energy to enjoy his leisure hours. You might expect that when Ralph finally retired he would simply rest. Not so. Ralph anticipated retirement as an opportunity to do something that would provide personal rewards he was unable to enjoy earlier because of his work. He became interested in a telephone "crisis center" and now works there every day as a volunteer. He told me: "These are the best days of my life because the pressure is off. It is almost as if I had to serve an apprenticeship between the ages of 30 to 60 so I could become involved in real life."

Ralph could have withdrawn and allowed others to take charge. Instead, he is maintaining his independence through choice. He does not use his special circumstances as an excuse.

Keep Your Sense of Humor

The best way to make the most of almost anything, including retirement, is to maintain a sense of humor. The ability to see the funny side of things helps people over some rough spots. When your retirement arrives, you will need your sense of humor more, not less. If you have always been a "tease," keep it up. If you like jokes, keep telling them. If you have the ability to look at the light side when things go wrong, work to maintain this trait. Switch your positive attitude into high gear and protect your priceless sense of humor.

Mr. Dreyfus

Mr. Dreyfus, a successful retiree, has a refreshing perspective. "The longer I live, the less I intend to take setbacks seriously. Major problems in my past seem far less significant today because I can see them in perspective. Most problems blow over. It is easier to adjust because previous problems normally were not that important in the total scheme of things. My priorities have changed, so now I can laugh at some of the things that used to make me an emotional wreck. Without a sense of humor, it would be easy to become a sad, lonesome person."

Make a Contract with Yourself

If you are less enthusiastic about retirement than you feel you should be, you can decide to move to the brighter side. One way to do this is to make a personal contract to do a better job with this phase of life than any previous period.

Summary

A key to your retirement happiness is your attitude.

You have a choice. You can take charge, accept the challenge and make the most of your opportunities, or you can coast through retirement and never know what you have missed.

To make the most of retirement, take your sense of humor with you.

PROBLEM TO SOLVE   **Retirement Remorse**

Hilda is not adjusting well to retirement for some good reasons. First, she quit work prematurely because of a personality conflict with her superior. She continues to resent what happened and maintains a negative attitude toward the organization where she spent 35 happy years. She is having a hard time accepting a fixed income. She feels insecure because she is not getting all the benefits and protection she formerly took for granted. Finally, Hilda is having trouble because she didn't take any time to plan for retirement. Believing she would work longer, she did not attend the retirement seminars offered by her firm. Most of her friends still work and are not available during the day. Hilda is nervous about spending money to travel, and she has not developed any serious activity

After eight months of retirement, she asked her older sister to pay a visit. Jane, her sister, arrived and found Hilda in a depressed mood. After a few days, Jane decided to confront the situation. She told Hilda: "Here you are with the advantages of retirement and you are making yourself miserable. You should either change your outlook or go back to work until you are ready to make the most of retirement."

Do you agree or disagree with Jane's approach? Think about how you would approach the problem. (Compare your answer with that of the author in Appendix C.)

SELF-QUIZ

True	False	
_____	_____	1. Retirees have less control over their attitudes.
_____	_____	2. Making the most out of retirement is not much of a challenge because there is so little you can do about it.
_____	_____	3. The average person has more time as a retired person than as a child.
_____	_____	4. Most retirees are "late bloomers."
_____	_____	5. The delayed-action strategy says to postpone turning things over to others as long as possible.

(Answers in Appendix C.)

2

Making the Transition

To be able to fill leisure intelligently is the last product of civilization.
Arnold Toynbee

Although your retirement date may still be years off, it's not too early to start your preparation. Experts agree the more advance planning you experience the better. If your retirement is close—or already under way—retirement seminars or books like this one can be helpful. The transition to retirement is not always smooth. It can be a period of emotional ups and downs and psychological detours.

Because this period can be unsettling, I refer to it as a passage—like taking a ship through rough waters. Making the transition is like an unpredictable voyage from one safe harbor (mature adult) to another (retirement).

Needed: A New Retirement Identity

Passage means to leave one place for a new one. Those who retire find their personal passage is not over until they have found a comfortable place in a new environment.

13

The new roles of retirement fall into three major categories. I call them Plans A, B, and C. *Plan A* is leisure. You choose not to work (either for money or as a volunteer). You assume a role with social or leisure implications. *Plan B* involves working for money, either for someone else or in your own business. Often Plan B is done on a part-time basis. You expend some of your leisure time, but not all of it. *Plan C* involves volunteer work, usually through an organization. It also replaces some of your leisure time. These plans will be discussed later.

As an adult you established yourself as a unique individual and probably felt good about it. You knew who you were. You had an identity. To make a safe passage into retirement, you will need to establish yourself as yet a somewhat different person. One identity will be left behind, and you will not be totally comfortable until you have established a new one. You can't carry your previous identity indefinitely. You need to find a new "self" you are comfortable with.

Jake's Identity

Jake was a respected corporate lawyer, well known both in legal circles and in his community. He was pleased with his identity and the status it brought. Although he knew it would be hard to leave, he looked forward to retirement and more time to himself. It was a reward he had earned.

In time, however, Jake discovered that playing more golf was not as challenging as he had expected. Working on his mountain cabin did not provide the psychological rewards he had anticipated. Taking it easy became a bore. He increasingly found himself in periods of depression. He knew retirement would require an adjustment, but he felt he could work it out.

Jake eventually did work things out, but it was not an easy passage. "I refused to accept that something could happen to me psychologically when I retired. I had worked so hard for it, I thought the adjustment would be a pleasure. I never realized how much personal attention and status my job offered. After retirement, I had to rebuild a new identity pretty much from scratch. I feel okay now because I am consulting, writing, and learning some new skills, but it would have been easier if I had planned better for retirement."

Previous Experience Only Limited Help

You always know when you have a good identity because you have confidence in what you are doing. Others recognize and admire the role you play. You feel your life has meaning and purpose.

You have a lack of identity when you do not feel positive about the role you are playing. When you start to feel life has little purpose, and your goals are out of focus, you do not feel good about yourself. Often your relationships with others are not satisfying. This is typical for anyone going through a temporary loss of identity. Time seems to drag, and there is a loss of motivation. During this period there is often a great deal of self-assessment.

Moving from one phase of life to another can cause individuals to temporarily lose their identity. As a young person you may have struggled to "find yourself." You may have experimented with more than one identity during your life. Your "adult identity" may have come later. Even after finding a mature, adult "self" and feeling good about it, you may have lost it once or twice through a career change, marital change, or psychological trauma. For most people searching for an identity is not new. These earlier searches can help you as you search for a retirement identity.

There is one big difference in making the transition to retirement—a difference that makes adjustment more difficult. As a mature adult, there were normally standards and expectations provided by the environment. There were acceptable work-oriented models. Success was more easily measured. You normally knew when you were on the right track and what to expect. By contrast, retirement takes you into a kind of no-man's-land. There are few reference points; everything must come from within. You decide on your own postretirement activities. Your expectations are often your own, and there are few guideposts. You need to reach a destination to find a new identity, but don't know how far it is or when you will reach it.

Retirement into What?

Too many people retire to nothing and then wonder why they are empty and disenchanted. They never sit down ahead of time to determine what they want from retirement. It's important to retire to something. The more you know about what you really want, the easier and faster your passage will be. You will have a safe "identity harbor" in which to anchor. You will have a destination.

Without effective planning, it is possible to become stranded between the last two phases of the life cycle. Some people are no longer effective or happy as mature adults, but they refuse to move on. They are dissatisfied with what they are, yet they reject what they could be. They lose one identity but do not see the need to find another. Many in this situation fear retirement. They believe it will shorten rather than lengthen their lives. They see only the disadvantages. They refuse to accept the notion that there is a point where moving ahead makes sense.

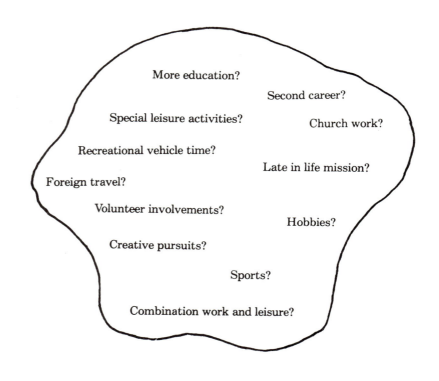

More education?

Second career?

Special leisure activities?

Church work?

Recreational vehicle time?

Late in life mission?

Foreign travel?

Volunteer involvements?

Hobbies?

Creative pursuits?

Sports?

Combination work and leisure?

Sam's Situation

Sam retired at 60 so he could travel, pursue his hobby, and reflect on life. For the first three months (honeymoon period), all went well. Then he began to feel dissatisfied. He wanted to be involved with younger people. He missed the rewards he enjoyed in the past, but he found it difficult to come up with replacements. He wanted a new lifestyle, but he couldn't discover the right blend.

Sam had no way of knowing it, but he was in limbo between a used-up lifestyle and a fresh one he could have in the future. He was stranded on one shore but refused to undertake the trip to a new identity.

There is a point in everyone's life when the advantages of the future outweigh the present. It's often difficult to know when this occurs, but a primary signal is an uneasy feeling something has ended, that a role has been played out, and to hold on to the past will prevent enjoyment of the future.

How to Make a Successful Passage

Let's assume it is time for you to retire. How can it be accomplished with the least disruption? First you need to recognize the advantages of a new identity. Next you must recognize and accept the disadvantages and learn to adapt to them in a graceful manner. These

EARLY VERSUS LATE RETIREMENT
(for those working full time)

Unless you are forced to retire for medical reasons, you normally have some control over when you start your passage. This is true even if your company should offer you a tempting incentive for early retirement. Some prefer to stay in their mature adult roles longer than others. Others decide, because of special circumstances, to make their passage early.

Mabel had been raised by her grandparents who were outstanding role models. After they were gone and she had also lost her husband, she moved into a retirement center. It wasn't that she was abdicating her mature adult responsibilities ahead of time; it was a phase of life she looked forward to. She started her passage at age 55.

Jack, with a different view, decided to stretch his adult period as long as possible. It was a good time of life for him. He owned his own business, and had a young wife and family (second time around). He had a negative image of inactive men. He knew he would eventually make the move but wanted to postpone it as long as he could. He started his passage at age 69.

One advantage of early retirement is that once you have made the transition (found a new identity) you have more time to enjoy it. Please think about other advantages.

Other than the financial one, a danger in early retirement is that you will not find an identity as good as the one you left behind. What other disadvantages can you think of?

_____   _____

_____   _____

_____   _____

My choice would be to:

Retire as soon as conditions allow. ☐

Delay retirement as long as possible. ☐

two steps add up to the word *adjustment*. Capitalize on the good things and minimize the bad. Instead of resenting where you are in the life cycle, learn how to enjoy it.

Eliminate Excess Baggage

When you elect to make the move, you should leave behind many of your previous responsibilities. It is time to leave certain parts of your old lifestyle to others. You should not take excess baggage on your journey. Excess baggage can be wanting to retire and work full time too, or needing the status of your previous role. Also included is holding on to activities you no longer enjoy and refusing to leave certain work-oriented roles behind so you can assume new, more rewarding ones. Excess baggage results in an inability to change your former lifestyle.

Recently I drove past an old recreational vehicle that had the personalized license plate FREE. Down the road at a highway rest stop, I introduced myself to the occupants of this vehicle and told them that I enjoyed their license plate. They offered me a cold drink and, before we got back on the Trans Canada, shared their thoughts about retirement with me. They were struggling to make the transition because it was difficult to leave certain things behind, but this was why they were on the road. They were trying to travel lighter and to learn the process of being free.

Learn to Use Your New Freedom Wisely

Adults often have trouble making a good transition to retirement because they fail to understand the dimensions of their new freedom. They have enjoyed so little freedom in the past because of responsibilities that they are often overwhelmed. Instead of taking advantage of freedom, they flounder because there is so much of it. A few are destroyed by it.

Because we are so programmed in the first four phases of our lives, we are not taught how to use freedom wisely. Nobody tells us it must be tempered with self-discipline. To be enjoyed, freedom must be respected and channeled.

In making your transition, you will have more freedom than you have ever had before. You can get up early in the morning or sleep late. You can read the entire newspaper or watch several TV news programs. You have more options than ever before—an opportunity to cut loose, fulfill dreams, and do some of those crazy things you talked about before retirement.

Freedom is beautiful! It's also a trap.

If you're not careful, freedom will swallow you like quicksand. It's important not to lose control. You make the most of freedom only with self-discipline. It is not an open door to unlimited pleasure but an opportunity to use time wisely.

Marie's Freedom

Marie retired after 40 years as a dedicated church secretary and office manager. She was highly disciplined and respected. During her tenure, she worked with a dozen ministers. She was especially good at time management and follow-through—a structured person running an efficient office. Soon after retirement, Marie fell into a total collapse. She relaxed so much and did so little that she soon didn't attempt anything. This lasted six months. Then, with some help from one of her favorite ministers (retired), she learned she needed her old discipline to pull herself back and use her freedom with a purpose. It took time for this to happen, but now she's doing some significant volunteer work. She also edits books for pay (using the income to take trips). She has joined two social groups, and her new life is full and exciting.

Before you get freedom, you should think about it. How should it be used? What are your leisure priorities? Do you want to read more? Socialize more? How you use your time will determine the quality of your retirement life.

Once you have completed this chapter, please turn to Appendix A and complete the IRA (Inventory of Retirement Activities).

Use Your Natural Talents

Your transition will be more successful when you make use of your talents and skills in new ways. It is through the utilization of your unique abilities that you find new roles.

I know a former school superintendent who began his career as a zoology teacher. Following retirement he brought his previous knowledge of animals back into play by starting a wild animal museum. Similarly, a former mathematics teacher now holds private art shows. A retired executive is using his mechanical skills to repair boats. You can probably find similar examples among your acquaintances.

Everyone has skills and talents that have not been fully used because of limited opportunity or too little leisure time. These talents can be dusted off and put to use in retirement roles that are both exciting and fulfilling. Those who do not wish to utilize old talents can always go back to school to develop new ones.

Minimize Disadvantages

It would be deceiving to suggest there are no disadvantages in retirement. In the following exercise, the left column contains five typical disadvantages you may face after retirement. It is only a partial list. The second column lists ways these disadvantages can be minimized. If one applies to you, and you are willing to make efforts to compensate for it, place a check in the box on the right.

TYPICAL RETIREMENT DISADVANTAGES

Disadvantages to retirement	Ways to minimize or compensate	Applicable to me
1. Possible loss of energy, endurance, agility.	Build physical stamina through more exercise and better diet.	☐
2. Reduced income.	Learn to spend money more carefully; get a part-time job.	☐
3. Loss of recognition from previous roles.	Find some role replacements; get recognition from new involvements.	☐
4. Decision-making becomes more difficult.	Take time to improve decision-making ability; learn when to seek help; listen better.	☐
5. Possibility of more down periods; coping is increasingly difficult.	Learn more about mental health; discover what you can do to prevent or get out of such periods.	☐

You may not be able to eliminate all the disadvantages you face in retirement, but you can make progress with most. The more you try, the better things should be. This understanding on your part is significant. Your strategy should include making the most of your once-in-a-lifetime advantages and slowing down or eliminating the disadvantages. If you accept this premise and start to do something about it, you will be ahead of the game.

How Can You Tell When Your Passage Is Over? When you begin to feel good about being a retiree, and when you have learned to capitalize on your advantages, you'll know you've made progress. When you look back at your preretirement phase of life and are happy with where you are now, you have made the passage. When you think less about retirement because you are too busy enjoying the day-to-day adventures of your new role, you have made the transition.

Ethel's Adjustment Ethel unexpectedly lost her husband. Her adjustment was traumatic, for he had been the "take charge" person of the family. For almost two years she didn't live; she merely existed. Finally things began to clear. She started waking up with more enthusiasm. Her self-confidence returned. She joined a bridge group, learned to play golf, and took her first trip to Mexico. She began to feel good about herself. Four years after losing her spouse, she was a different person. She was relaxed, yet motivated; content, yet involved. She made the most of her advantages and down-played her disadvantages. She was proud of her passage even though it took four years to accomplish.

Timing and the Likelihood of Making a Plan Work

A realistic retirement plan can influence how you age. It can determine your "happiness factor" once the step has been taken. A plan, however, does not have an automatic success warranty; it must be implemented carefully. Many retirees spend hours rehearsing their plans only to let them atrophy once the day arrives. In addition to designing a good plan, you must make it work. Let's discuss some phases most individuals experience as they approach retirement.

Phase I: Preretirement

Gentle but increasing anxiety occurs as you approach retirement. This anxiety can be healthy if it produces sound planning. The more planned changes the better, so long as you do not lose interest in your work role and become less productive.

Phase II: Retirement

Psychologists claim people are capable of showing improvement during crisis periods. In this respect, the passage to a new lifestyle can be considered something of a crisis period. This is the best time psychologically to make changes. Although some significant positive changes can occur shortly before retirement (especially during the last few months), they are more likely to occur after retirement. For most retirees, the first year is critical. Some seem to extend the "honeymoon period" and make their major changes after the euphoria disappears. Eventually the impact of retirement will be realized. Phase II is the best opportunity to make measurable changes.

Phase III: Postretirement

Sadly, the longer you wait after retirement the less likely change will occur. The habits and behavioral patterns you establish soon after retirement often "lock in" and determine the quality of retirement living for the rest of the journey. Making necessary changes close to your retirement day will usually be easier than a few years later. This does not mean that an 80-year-old retiree is incapable of making positive behavioral improvements; it's simply less likely.

This points to the need for solid preretirement planning. Design a good retirement plan during Phase I and make it operational during Phase II. If you wait until Phase III, it may be too late.

This book will help you prepare and execute a plan that takes these timing factors into consideration. It should help you achieve your retirement goals.

Summary The passage between adulthood and retirement is difficult.

One must retire to something.

Part of the process is learning to use freedom.

The passage is complete when there is a comfortable identity and a rewarding lifestyle.

PROBLEM TO SOLVE **Honeymoon Period**

Marge is disturbed because her husband retired six months ago and is having trouble adjusting. Still employed, she returns home at night to find him glued to the television set. Frequently he is in a bad mood. Although their marriage had been happy, there is more bickering between them now. She is aware that, even though he spends time working in the yard or fixing his car, his heart is not in it. She has tried to get him involved in social activities with little success. When she finally mentioned her concern about his inactivity, he said: "I had my nose to the grindstone for 40 years, and I'm going to sit back and enjoy the leisure. I've earned the right to do nothing. I want my work ethic to disappear. Once this has happened, I'll start making plans."

In discussing the problem with a friend at work, Marge received this advice: "Don't worry, he's just living through a typical retirement honeymoon period. He has been looking forward to retirement for so long, he wants to savor it. When he gets tired of sitting around, he'll bounce back and become involved. You'll see."

Is Marge's concern justified? Do you agree with her friend? Think about your answer and then compare it with that of the author in Appendix C.

SELF-QUIZ

True	False	
_____	_____	1. The transition to retirement is easier than other phases of life.
_____	_____	2. Most retirees are well prepared to make their passage.
_____	_____	3. The older you become, the less freedom you have.
_____	_____	4. Most people who start their passage have no trouble leaving excess baggage behind.
_____	_____	5. The disadvantages of retirement far outweigh the advantages.

(Answers in Appendix C.)

3

Living with Style

Whatever you are, as you get older you become more so.
Betty Broach

Years ago my favorite feature in *Reader's Digest* was "The Most Unforgettable Character I Ever Met." These short articles often portrayed retirees who defied conformity. They were unforgettable because their lifestyles made them stand out in a crowd. They were intriguing because they had the courage to be different. After reading one of these articles, I would say to myself: "When you get to that stage of life, be a character."

As you approach and enter retirement, you should find ways to be different. Up to a point, of course. You should not act younger than you feel. You should, however, be free to be different the way younger people are different. You should resist pressures that push you into a form of rocking-chair conformity. You should march to your own drummer more than you did in the previous phase of your life, not less.

Join the Parade A new generation of retirees is emerging. They are defying the traditional images so frequently portrayed. They refuse to accept the old stereotypes. They are creating new, more active lifestyles. Instead of sitting back and watching things happen, they make things happen. Instead of accepting the traditional roles that await them, they create new ones. Some of this is happening because medical advances help extend the active years. More, however, comes from the fact that they see themselves differently. As a result, they are more individualistic and diversified. They are creating a new kind of retiree.

Today, for the first time, you see conservative retirees who still have their traditional values but live with a modern, upbeat style. They kick up their heels more. They spend money with more abandon. This may not fit the mold their adult children anticipated, but these "new retirees" know they are not being ignored or taken for granted. You hear them say: "If other generations have the freedom to be different, so do we. We can design a new, more exciting lifestyle."

Most would agree that whatever the financial circumstances or state of health, simply surviving is not enough. Nobody wants to drag themselves through retirement. If the hours sacrificed to achieve this stage of life are to be worthwhile, they must be lived with some vigor, humor, and style.

Style Defined *Style* means living with some flair. It means doing unusual and unexpected things. It is staying involved with current changes, speaking up, and proudly defying the norm. Style means communicating a lively, positive image to others. It means looking and acting the part of a confident, involved person. People with style are noticed.

Style is an individual matter. You don't copy a style from another; you create your own. If you want to break out of your previous routine and be outlandish, do it. If you want to withdraw for a while to lead a quiet, creative life with fewer outside contacts, do so. But whatever direction you take, do it with conviction.

You may even decide to be anachronistic.

To me, an anachronistic person is one who can maintain values and style from an earlier period but survive successfully in today's world. So, if you believe in certain standards that no longer seem to fit younger generations, keep them—but not to the extent of being distant and negative. Defend your values but participate. Anachronistic people may hold onto parts of the past, but they never let others put them on a shelf. They have a style that may shake others up, but one that earns respect.

Mrs. B's Style Mrs. B is a high-powered executive who chose not to retire at 65. She is effective in her specialty and respected because she accepts most change gracefully. She fights like a tiger, however, those changes she does not believe in. Some feel she is recalcitrant and dogmatic, but all she is doing is being what she wants to be. Mrs. B. feels she is free to defend what she wants to preserve in our society. A student of history, she wants to save what she feels should be saved. She does not accept change for change's sake. One thing is certain—if you met her, you would not forget her quickly. She has style.

Of course, you don't have to have anachronistic tendencies to have style. Everyone can develop his or her own.

Joe Harvey Joe Harvey, age 72 and a widower of 10 years, lives in a retirement center and makes the most of it. He doesn't like the word *retire*. He interprets it to mean withdraw, retreat, and give up. As a result, he refuses to use it. He refers to his retirement as his "new phase." His friends are amazed at his behavior. He spends money freely, dresses with care, and has diversity in his life. He is always organizing pleasure trips for others in the center. Instead of waiting for his environment to make him happy, he does something about it. Joe has style.

Melinda and Warren Melinda and Warren watched their parents age in the old-fashioned manner: little activity, little involvement. They decided when the time came for them to retire, they would break the mold. Although they stay close to their home town, they spend money to look sharp. They are very active. They play important roles in their church, belong to volunteer organizations, and attend many social and community events. Each day and week has outside commitments. They are not sitting back watching the parade; in their own way they are leading it. They have style.

Sitting on the Sidelines There are newly retired individuals who contribute to the stereotype of the passive, discarded, negative retiree. These folks disengage themselves upon retirement and become grouchy, defensive, unchanging, and unhappy. They often look bored, act bored, and are bored. They fall into the "waiting mold." They permit themselves to be pushed into old-fashioned retirement patterns because they refuse to seek new roles. They refuse to join more dynamic retirees. They seem to believe that the best retirement is to get away from the mainstream.

Identity, Image, and Style

If you have a good feeling of self-worth, you probably enjoy who you are—the way you look, talk, and act. You like being unique. You have a good identity. Great!

Image is how others view you. The impression others have of you constitutes your image. How do others see you? Do you fall into the preconceived "waiting mold" they have in their minds or are you different and upbeat? Do other think you have style?

The image you transmit to others will determine the quality of the relationships you have with them. You cannot ignore your image. It is more important to you now than ever before. The way others perceive you will determine the way they interact with you. This includes everyone you come in contact with—doctors, lawyers, neighbors, friends, and family.

Communicating a Negative Image Is Easy

A few retirees do some unnecessary things that create a negative image. Although young people also display these negative behaviors, unfortunately they are associated more often with retirees.

The accompanying checklist describes five of these traits. All show an absence of style. Only retirees with physical problems or very advanced age should be excused or given special understanding. If you check the square next to the trait, you agree that it is damaging and should be avoided when you retire.

What Others Want Retirees to Be

Younger people want those nearing or already retired to live with style. This will help them to view retirement positively. They want upbeat models so they will understand that the last phase of their lives can have excitement, pleasure, and fulfillment. Adults still far from retirement want to destroy the image that retirees are simply "waiting things out." They are saying: "Show us through your actions that we can be effective and happy when we get there. Convince us that retirement is worth working for."

Become a Good Role Model

Retirement is an excellent time to be proud of what we are and become good models for younger people.

Ms. Armour

Ms. Armour was always a strong person. She was attractive, successful, and popular during her working years. Yet, when she retired from her role as an educational administrator, she started to feel less and less confident. She spent more time looking in the

```
┌─────────────────────────────────────────────────────────────┐
│                    POOR IMAGE CHECKLIST                       │
│                                                               │
│   ☐   1.  Expecting or demanding courteous attention from     │
│           others because you are retired instead of earning   │
│           such attention through your own courteous behavior. │
│                                                               │
│   ☐   2.  Looking sloppy and unkempt.                         │
│                                                               │
│   ☐   3.  Moving dejectedly as though life is over instead of │
│           walking with a spry, positive gait.                 │
│                                                               │
│   ☐   4.  Constant and unnecessary complaining about the trib-│
│           ulations of being a retiree; repeated references to │
│           poor treatment you receive from others.             │
│                                                               │
│   ☐   5.  Expressing unjustified disdain toward the behavior  │
│           of younger people; becoming an "old grouch."        │
│                                                               │
└─────────────────────────────────────────────────────────────┘
```

mirror. She became more critical of her hairdresser and too aware of her neck wrinkles. She knew she was going through a transition, but she didn't know how to deal with it. Finally, she decided to come up with a new image. She lost some weight, changed her hair style, and bought some new clothes. Then she took a real vacation. When she returned, she had a new spring in her step. Her confidence was back, and she felt good about herself. What caused the change? She discovered she could not continue with what she was in the past, but it took time to discover what she wanted to be in the future. She had to become proud of her new self before she could communicate a new, satisfying image.

Image and the Aging Process

There's nothing wrong with trying to look younger than the phase of life you are in. Many retirees look like they belong in an earlier period. Many mature adults work to look like young adults. The younger you look to yourself (identity) and to others (image) the better, but don't overdo it to the point of becoming absurd. There is another danger. You may try so hard to look younger that you subconsciously reject the phase of life you have reached in other ways—emotionally, physically, and psychologically. Some people stay in one phase of life longer than others, but there comes a point of diminishing returns. When we talk about image, we are talking about appearance, not lifestyle. You can be retired, accept a new lifestyle, and still look like a mature adult. Good! Looking younger chronologically is worth the effort, but rejecting a phase of life that is better for you may create conflicts that you would be better off without.

A Good Image

A close friend is envied because he is over 80 but looks 60. He was born with the right genes and has always taken good care of himself. Long ago, he accepted the life of a retiree and loves it. He doesn't deny where he is. In fact, knowing where he is and enjoying it makes looking younger all the better. The fact that he has accepted his age may be partially responsible for the young image he communicates. He is comfortable with his style. He does not fight so hard to stay in a previous phase of life that he loses friends.

Resisting the Steep-Decline Syndrome

The better you look to yourself and others, the more involved you will probably be in activities. But some retirees, at the point in life where they have some excellent cards to play, have a tendency to quit the game. Instead of hanging in there and creating a new lifestyle, they take retirement literally and fall back too far.

It is certainly appropriate to enjoy a slower, less hectic pace, but not to the point where we let down and lose our spirit. If this happens, we permit the last phase of life to escape without providing the rewards we have earned.

This is the "steep-decline syndrome". Unfortunately we've been programmed to believe that retirement is the beginning of the end—that when we qualify for CPP and OAS everything moves quickly downhill. The accompanying illustration provides perspective.

We glide through childhood, survive adolescence, struggle through young adulthood, and then finally arrive at mature adulthood, which we hope is a long, productive stretch. Then comes retirement. At this critical point we should discover a new, less demanding tempo, accept new roles and challenges, and work to improve our

RETIREMENT

MATURE ADULTHOOD

YOUNG ADULTHOOD

ADOLESCENCE

CHILDHOOD

lifestyles (note the dotted lines of the diagram). We often relax so much that everything slides too soon (solid lines). We fall into a decline that does not exist except in our minds.

A few years ago my publisher shared a quotation from an 85-year-old woman reflecting on her life. In my opinion, she describes a style she might have had, and one still possible for the rest of us. I have benefited from reading it. It is entitled "Traveling Light."

Traveling Light

If I had my life to live over, I'd dare to make more mistakes next time. I'd relax. I would limber up. I would be sillier than I have been this trip. I would take fewer things seriously. I would take more chances. I would take more trips. I would climb more mountains, swim more rivers. I would eat more ice cream and less beans. I would perhaps have more actual troubles but I'd have fewer imaginary ones.

You see, I'm one of those people who live seriously and sanely hour by hour, day after day. Oh, I've had my moments, and if I had it to do over again, I'd have more of them. In fact, I'd try to have nothing else, just moments, one after another, instead of living so many years ahead of each day. I've been one of those persons who never goes anywhere without a thermometer, a hot water bottle, a raincoat and a parachute. If I had it to do again, I would travel lighter than I have.

If I had to live my life over, I would start barefoot earlier in the spring and stay later in the fall. I would go to more dances. I would ride more merry-go-rounds. I would pick more daisies.

Anonymous

Summary

A new retiree is emerging—more active, more involved, and with more style.

These retirees are communicating a new image that younger people appreciate.

Retirees should resist falling victim to the steep-decline syndrome.

PROBLEM TO SOLVE   **Farewell to Challenges**

Everyone is worried about Henry. He spent most of his life being a "good person." He did this by fulfilling the expectations established by his parents, his wife, and society. He has been a good son, husband, and father. Last year Henry retired with anticipation. He wanted to tinker in the garage, relax in old clothes, and get away from all the standards that others (and life) had imposed on him. So far he has been able to relax, spending each day at his own tempo. He told his wife: "Hazel, I feel life imposed upon me from the start. I forced myself to live with goals and standards I really didn't want. Now it is my turn to be free; and freedom is doing what I want to do. I do not feel any further obligations. I've paid my dues. Please do not expect me to accept other challenges. Just let me be."

Hazel has discussed Henry's attitude with their children. They are all worried he will turn away from reality on a permanent basis.

Is their concern justified?

Compare your thoughts with those of the author in Appendix C.

SELF-QUIZ

True	False	
_____	_____	1. Style means living with flair.
_____	_____	2. To be anachronistic means to live gracefully in two worlds at the same time.
_____	_____	3. Younger people want us to behave as our parents did.
_____	_____	4. Identity is feeling confident and good about yourself; image is how you appear to others.
_____	_____	5. Many retirees needlessly taper down too fast, too soon.

(Answers in Appendix C.)

4

Decision Making and Comfort Zones

As I grow older I pay less attention to what people say. I just watch what they do.
Andrew Carnegie

As chief of police for a large community, Mr. Jackson spent most of his adult life on the hot seat. His basic reason for early retirement was to get away from what he called the "pressure cooker." He wanted to free himself and protect his health. He figured he had made enough decisions to last a lifetime.

How did it work out for the chief? He got rid of his job decisions, but he picked up almost as many personal ones. Some were more difficult to make than those he previously was paid to make.

Retirement doesn't mean floating into a euphoric world where decision making is unnecessary. Often it is just the opposite. There are as many personal decisions to make, and they can be more difficult because they have greater consequences. This is true because there is less time to recover from a mistake. If you make a poor

31

financial investment and lose some of your nest egg, you don't have the same chance to recover the loss as previously because your earning opportunities are fewer. If you prematurely sell your home, it may be impossible, because of financial and other complications, to buy it back or purchase a similar one.

Another complication is that, at the very time when mistakes are more serious, we seem to make more judgement errors. We get a double whammy when we least need it. Why?

We are mentally as capable as ever, and we certainly have more experience upon which to base good decisions. But there may be certain subtle, psychological forces at work during retirement that mitigate against us. If we know about these factors ahead of time, we can offset them.

Take fear for instance. Fear is anxiety caused by anticipated danger, pain, evil, or the unknown—real or imagined. It is this anxiety—usually caused by a long list of retirement unknowns— that causes us to make poor or incorrect decisions. We get upset and take the wrong direction.

Assume a widow, soon to retire, is thinking about selling her home. This is a home she dearly loves. Logically, if her health remains good, she could live there for another 20 years or so. But fear begins to creep into her thinking. She worries about the possibility of robbery. She frets over the possibility of losing good neighbors. She fears she may run out of money. She reasons that a move to a less expensive retirement home would allow her to sell her car and cut down on expenses. Selling her home now means she can get a high price with tax advantages. The list continues. You can see the risk of making a fear-dominated decision that could cause regrets.

Fear Versus Logic The simple illustration below shows how fear constantly pushes toward the surface and how logic pushes in the opposite direction to keep fears under control.

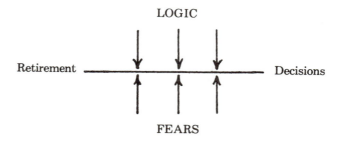

As we move into retirement, fear of the future can increase. More than ever, we must control and rely on our rational powers.

A Lady Driver

I know a lady of 70 who is an outstanding driver. She is capable of many more years of safe driving. Not long ago, she pulled into a service station for gas. When she paid the bill, the young attendant said: "I wouldn't go on the highway with those tires, ma'am." This single sentence caused fears to pop to the surface. Her logical mind soon caught hold, however, and she drove to her regular mechanic to get his opinion. He said: "You still have a good ten thousand miles on those tires. Don't let those kids get to you." Her logic prevailed. She got a second opinion and her confidence was restored.

Most people approaching retirement begin taking precautions, which is often good. But becoming more cautious does not always eliminate fears. More often these precautions are symptomatic of our fears getting stronger.

What is the answer? The philosophy expressed by Carl should be helpful.

Carl's Confidence

Carl, a widower of three years, has retained his ability to make sound decisions. When he makes a mistake, he can pass it off quickly without losing confidence. Asked about his ability to do this, he replied: "I recognize the need to keep my confidence and stay in charge of my mind. If I lose that ability, I lose my freedom. I discipline myself not to agonize over decisions. The consequences of most decisions are seldom as severe as one anticipates. I have always made mistakes and will make more in the future. I must not let one or two force me to lose my confidence. To let fear take over at this stage of my life, when I have less to lose, would be ridiculous."

Improve Your Decision Making by Using a Logical Process

Following an easy-to-remember, logical procedure is an excellent way to improve decision making. This procedure causes the mind to follow logical steps that should produce better decisions. It also saves time and helps the individual to make up his or her own mind.

You might consider adopting the procedure on the following page when you are faced with a difficult decision.

The simple, logical procedure can improve the quality of your decisions. You will no longer vacillate so much between alternatives. Once you have gone through the process a few times, you will develop confidence in it.

DECISION-MAKING PROCESS

Step 1   Write the desired outcome as you perceive it. Spell out what you hope happens as a result of the decision you make.

_____

_____

Step 2   Write alternatives that are open to you (limit to three if possible). If you have only one alternative, it is a "yes" or "no" problem.

Alternative 1   Alternative 2   Alternative 3

_____   _____   _____

Step 3   List the facts (advantages and disadvantages) under each alternative. This may require some investigation.

_____   _____   _____

_____   _____   _____

_____   _____   _____

Step 4   Consult others for their opinions and suggestions. Make sure these people are knowledgeable and have your best interests at heart. Write their opinions under the appropriate alternative.

Opinion 1   Opinion 2   Opinion 3

_____   _____   _____

Step 5   Based on what you have written above, make your decision and write it in the space provided. Do it immediately and consider the process completed.

Decision: _____

_____

As you anticipate the decisions ahead of you, keep these additional tips in mind.

Believe in Your Mental Capacity   A procedure is nothing more that a tool designed to help you think logically. If you lose confidence in your mental abilities, no procedure can come to your rescue.

Recognize That Giving Up Decision Making Is Giving Up Freedom

The longer you make your own decisions, the more freedom you will keep. Even those who love you and have your best interests in mind cannot make your decisions unless you give up enough freedom to allow them to do so. Consider the advice of others and keep those close to you informed, but make your own decisions as long as you can.

Remember That a Bad Decision Can Often Be Corrected

If you dwell on the consequences of a decision too much, it may keep you from making a good one. Those leaders who are outstanding at making good decisions acknowledge that they often make poor decisions but don't dwell on them. They also mention that most bad decisions can be corrected quickly if one is willing to admit that a mistake has been made. Even a very serious mistake can be corrected, as shown in the following example.

Mary's Decision

Mary met Allen when she first moved to the retirement center. An attractive woman of 71, she quickly made friends with other women. They kept telling her how lucky she was to have Allen's attention and that he was the most eligible bachelor in the center. Their relationship grew and eventually they married and moved into Mary's home. After the first weekend, Mary sensed she had made a mistake. Allen was an alcoholic. He soon tried to take over certain areas of life that were important to Mary. How could she face her friends? Her family? To make such a stupid mistake. Humiliating! Fortunately she got hold of herself. She contacted her lawyer and an annulment was arranged. Mary soon recovered her normal life, thankful that she had had the courage to face a major mistake and not let it eventually destroy her. She did not fall into a pit of remorse. She not only recognized that she made a mistake, but, best of all, she did something about it.

Making Decisions Within Your Comfort Zones

More than any other single factor, you should ensure that your decisions fit within your personal comfort zones. A comfort zone is a range within which your personal values and beliefs fall. You have accumulated your values over many years, and chances are good that they are more important to you now than ever before. They constitute your standards and principles. When you take them into consideration, you are likely to stay within your comfort zone. When you ignore them, you move into a new territory where you may be uncomfortable.

If you make a decision that falls within your comfort zone (fits into your lifestyle), chances are good that it will not cause remorse. It will reflect what you are used to and what you really want.

If a decision falls outside your comfort zone, it will probably cause internal conflict. We are frequently tempted, or persuaded, to make decisions outside our respective comfort zones in the hope that we will adjust. We seldom do.

* Charlie and his wife moved from a home where they had chickens and a garden into a fancy condominium. Charlie never adjusted because living so close to others was not in his comfort zone.

* Mrs. Q had always wanted a Cadillac, so she bought one. Six months later, she sold it and bought a less ostentatious automobile—one more within her comfort zone.

* Mr. and Mrs. James saved for three years to take a fancy cruise. Although they made the most of it, they never took a second one. Why? They discovered that formal dinners, formal clothes, and considerable drinking were not in their comfort zone.

You may have heard people say: "I don't like the decision, but I can live with it." All of us must learn to live with decisions we can't avoid or control; but, when we are in charge, we should choose those that fit into our comfort zones. Roland Jones, a financial planning consultant, maintains that comfort zones become more fixed as we reach retirement age; if a decision falls outside of our zone, we become unhappy.

Assume that you live alone and one of your young relatives (perhaps a grandson or granddaughter), whom you love, gets into financial trouble. You want to help. Assume further that this person is unmarried and lives with a person of the opposite sex. Perhaps the only way for you to help is to invite them to stay with you. Because of your views on marriage, such an arrangement does not fall within your comfort zone, but you feel you can handle it. Will it bother you if they sleep together under your roof? If you will be uncomfortable, won't you be doing everyone a disservice with your invitation? Helping them some other way may be a better solution.

Comfort zones are critical to good decision making. That's why it's difficult for others to make decisions for you. They may know their zones but not understand yours.

Adapting to change, being flexible, however, and staying in charge is the key to success at any age. It is not a good idea to violate comfort zones, especially during retirement. It took years to build our standards; we should live within them comfortably.

When faced with a decision, it's best to ask yourself these questions. Will the decision reflect my values or someone else's? Will I be comfortable with the decision or will it cause me regrets? Will the decision enhance the kind of retirement lifestyle I have planned or detract from it? Will it simplify my retirement years or make them more confusing?

If you take time to ask these questions, you will sense whether the decision is within your comfort zone. Once you know where it fits, you can make the decision with confidence. You can relax because you know you are being true to yourself.

Summary   Retirement does not provide an escape from decision making.

Retirees should maintain their decision-making capabilities as long as possible.

Using a written decision-making procedure can improve the quality of decisions.

Decisions should always fall within an individual's comfort zone.

PROBLEM TO SOLVE   **Decision-free Retirement**

Mrs. Henderson is a much-loved widow who intends to retire in June. She has been an elementary school teacher for almost 30 years. Her students look forward to her classes and work hard to please her. She has many friends in the community; and, because of her positive attitude, she is considered an asset at any social function or party.

Mr. Henderson, who owned his own business, left his wife financially comfortable. With the help of her son, she maintains two rental units and some other good investments.

Recently her son, also a teacher, proposed that he take over the management of the properties so she could more fully enjoy her retirement. He would take care of everything and report the results to her each quarter. For this service, he would take 20 percent of the income after expenses. Everything would remain in her name.

Mrs. Henderson is tempted. She doesn't like dealing with business matters and really doesn't like to think about money. Also, she does not feel she is good at those types of decisions. She hopes to spend her retirement time traveling, playing bridge, and keeping busy with other activities. She also feels it would be good for her son to take over because whatever is left will be his later anyway.

The only thing that bothers her is that her son's wife, Shirley, seems overly assertive and money-oriented. Mrs. Henderson is not sure, but she is suspicious that the idea came from Shirley and not her son.

What would you advise Mrs. Henderson to do? Compare your thoughts with those of the author in Appendix C.

SELF-QUIZ

True	False	
———	———	1. The more you use your mind, the longer you will keep it.
———	———	2. With good mental discipline, retirees should be able to keep fears from surfacing and continue to make the same quality of decisions they made before retirement.
———	———	3. Following a logical, written procedure is a good way to prevent bad decisions.
———	———	4. Comfort zones are based on significant, long-term values.
———	———	5. When possible, decisions should fall within one's comfort zones.

(Answers in Appendix C.)

5

Myths and Misconceptions About Retirement

Some people spend more time planning a two-weeks vacation than they do their retirement.
Anonymous

Retirement is a passage from one lifestyle to another. Those who take the voyage seriously and do the right kind of planning usually have a smoother trip—and more fun when they arrive.

Discussions with seasoned retirees, who have come through the voyage successfully and are now living with style, indicate that there are many myths and misconceptions about retirement. If you listen long enough, you'll hear these myths stated as fact. Here are some of the most common ones.

The Female-Exclusion Myth Some people, often women themselves, continue to believe that only men retire. This misconception ignores career women who have the same retirement adjustment problems that men have. Also, it falsely assumes that women not holding down 9-to-5 jobs cannot retire. This may stem from the old saying: "A man's work is from sun to sun, but a woman's work is never done." Homemakers often have a more difficult voyage than those who retire from a job. Women who have been homemakers all their lives need to insist on being a full partner when their spouses retire.

One reason the myth may continue is that women sometimes lose their spouses early. The transition to widowhood is so traumatic that it hides the equally important second passage they must make.

The Piece-of-Cake Myth

Retirement should be the dessert that follows the full-course meal of earlier life. Perhaps this is why preretirees view the transition as a piece of cake. Instead of thinking ahead to retirement, they make comments such as:

* "My retirement plan consists of putting all of my work problems in my briefcase and presenting them to my boss as a farewell gesture."

* "Retirement is a pot of gold at the end of the rainbow. You don't have to plan for something that beautiful."

Many preretirees are so occupied with getting out of their career traps that they seem to care little about what happens when they leave their jobs. Despite the fact they have planned other phases of their lives, they seem to feel retirement will take care of itself. The opposite is often true. For example, many retirees go back to work because they cannot handle leisure time.

Learning to live with style after retirement does not necessarily come easy.

The Honey-Do Myth

The word has been out for years that some men put off retirement because they fear their wives will control their free hours. It will be "Honey, do the dishes," "Honey, do the windows," and "Honey, take the dog to the vet." Normally these individuals need not worry because most women don't want someone underfoot, monitoring their activities and invading their space. One wife expressed it well: "The only time you will ever hear me use that honey-do expression is when I say 'Honey, do something on your own, away from the house, so we can both have room to breathe.'" Spouses need the same autonomy after retirement that they did before.

The Hobby Myth

A friend tells the story of a man so concerned about retirement that he experimented with hobbies in advance. By the time he retired, he had run through his hobby possibilities and had to find something more substantial to occupy his time. The same thing can happen after retirement. Don't get me wrong—hobbies are a great idea.

Those who can derive satisfaction from photography, gourmet cooking, stamp collecting, and so on are lucky. But hobbies must continue to be fun and interesting or they quickly become unsatisfying. Few people create a complete new lifestyle around hobbies. A few will be able to convert their favorite hobby into a small business or lifetime artistic involvement, but most are not this fortunate.

The Retirement/ Early-Death Myth

We have all known people who were not around long after their retirement parties. The unhappy news causes strange reactions.

* "It's too bad Joe didn't work longer."
* "The moment people retire, they grow old."
* "I'd still have Fred if he hadn't retired so early."

Retirement can be painful, but it is not lethal. It is, rather, a change not unlike those earlier in life. Most people who die shortly after retirement probably had health problems before they stopped working. Retirement had nothing to do with their demise.

The only connection between retirement and early death may be that some retirees fail to keep active. They relax to the point that their bodies self-destruct. They give up. They fail to stay in charge. There are many reasons for retiring early, and there are just as many for retiring later. But staying on the treadmill because you fear that retirement will cause early death should not be one of them.

The Prior-Success/ Easy-Passage Myth

It's not difficult to see why this misconception persists. It stands to reason that those people who were successful before retirement should find retirement easier to cope with than those who did not do as well. Success breeds success; failure breeds failure. Translated this means that corporate presidents should have an easier retirement than custodians. Professional ball players should make smoother transitions than the vendors who sold hot dogs in the stadium. Nursing superintendents should adjust better than orderlies. True? Absolutely false! In fact, it often works the other way around. Those who earned high psychic rewards from their careers may have trouble finding replacements after retirement. It may be difficult to find a retirement role that provides enough ego satisfaction. All retirees can build a better lifestyle.

The Paid-Up-Dues Myth

Some conscientious individuals who have worked hard all their lives feel that they are home free when they retire. They say:

* "I've done my bit for society; now it's society's turn."
* "I've paid my dues through church work for 30 years. Now the church can take care of me."

These people operate under the premise that you pay your dues during working years and then draw interest. A pretty dream but, sadly, life doesn't work that way. In fact, happy retirees often pay more dues, not less. They contribute more to charitable organizations and communities than when they were working. Perhaps the most successful retirees are those who have an opportunity to repay society by sharing their talents.

The Odd-Job Myth

If you ask friends who plan to retire in the next few years about their expectations, some will reply: "There are enough jobs around the house to keep me busy for at least 10 years."

These well-meaning individuals, without knowing it, are using odd jobs as an excuse. They think about how satisfying it will be to catch up on all the little chores they have been avoiding. It usually takes only a few weeks to discover the truth. Having more time doesn't make a job any more fun to do. In fact, some retirees hate them so much they return to work to earn enough money to pay the plumber, gardener, and painter. All probably wish they had done more serious preretirement planning.

The Sell-a-Little-Real-Estate Myth

Retirees are attracted to real estate like children to a candy store. You hear this expression over and over: 'I'm working on my real-estate license to supplement my retirement income by working a few hours a week. All I need to do is sell a few homes each year. Best of all, it won't interfere with my leisure activities."

Those who know better find it difficult to keep quiet when we hear this dialogue. Professional realtors chuckle because they know they will not receive any serious competition from this quarter. At best, a part-time realtor will make very few sales. Selling real estate is not a part-time, few-hours-per-week career. It is difficult and time-consuming. The professionals say you have to be in the field seriously or you should get out. Many retirees attempt real-estate careers for a while and then painfully lower their sights or give up. A few invest the time required to become successful.

The Your-Money-Will-Go-Farther Myth

Inflation should have exploded this myth years ago. Not so. You still hear:

* "Think of the money I'll save doing repairs myself."
* "We will buy less meat and improve our health."

* "My pension contributions will begin to flow back."
* "The age exemption after 65 will be a windfall."
* "Senior discounts are all over the place."

Although there are financial advantages after retirement, certain factors continue to be ignored. What about the problem of having more time to spend less money? What about increased expenses for home, car, and medical insurance? Utility bills? Unfortunately people don't have trial retirements to test how far their money will go. They would discover that retirement dollars do not stretch any farther than preretirement ones, and there are usually fewer of them.

The Stay-Busy Myth

Keeping busy is a great idea after retirement, providing you are doing what you want to do. But if you keep busy simply to be busy, you are falling for the myth. Some people think that if they stay busy enough, their retirement problems will go away and they will be happy ever after (see Appendix A). Others stay busy to anesthetize themselves against thoughts of aging or living alone.

These individuals seem willing to trade a life of potential contentment (which comes from contemplation, planning, searching, and taking time to "smell the roses") for a frenzied existence. Instead of slowing down to design a rewarding retirement strategy, they spend time and energy on meaningless tasks. They visit the supermarket daily when once or twice a week would do. They accept social invitations knowing they will be bored. Worst of all, they stretch dull chores around the house. You get the feeling these retirees are avoiding retirement. Are they afraid to face a new, more mature identity? Has life been so disappointing that they dare not hope for anything better? Are they afraid to get off the treadmill and search for late-in-life happiness?

The Big Time Misconception

Most retirees grossly underestimate the amount of time they will have on their hands following retirement. We live within a 24-hour time box. Yesterday is gone, tomorrow is pending, today is center stage. To be happy, both before and after retirement, we must deal effectively with each time block—every day.

Actually, time relates to our waking hours. Retirees often do not understand how large a block of time 16 hours is. You can fly to London from Vancouver and still have time for a stage play in 16 hours—or drive across two or three smaller provinces. During this time period, it is possible to play 18 holes of golf, take a good swim, have dinner with friends, go dancing, and still read a few chapters before bed.

Yet, if it is not filled with meaningful activities, 16 hours can be forever. Compare the statements in the first column with those in the one on the right.

"The days get longer and longer."	"The days get shorter and shorter."
"Time weighs heavily on my hands."	"I need more time to achieve my goals."
"I'm climbing the walls."	"I need to squeeze out more time."

These contrasting expressions indicate that some retirees not only treasure their time but know how to convert it into excitement. Others permit time to bore them to death. What is the difference?

The answer may lie in planning. Some retirees keep something planned to maintain their excitement and motivation. Others, with the same opportunity, have no special events to fill the time and stretch uninteresting tasks just to get through each day.

John Copeland's Day

John Copeland awakens as late as he can, gets up, and reads the sizable morning paper from start to finish—hoping it will keep him occupied until 10:00 a.m. He then shaves and works in his shop for a while, but he often does not have a project and soon loses interest. He is pleased when his wife asks him to take her shopping—it's something to do. When they return, it's time for lunch. Good! More time will disappear. After lunch he may sweep out the garage or talk to a neighbor. When he comes back in the house, he is disappointed because it's only 3:30 p.m. He was hoping it would be later so he wouldn't have to wait so long for the 6 o'clock news. He watches an old movie until 6:00 and then watches an hour and a half of news—much of it news he has already seen. His wife joins him for part of it. Then comes dinner, followed by more television. Finally, at 9:00 p.m., he is happy to go to bed—because he has been able to stretch out another day.

The tragedy of retirement for Mr. Copeland is that he did not create enough activity interests ahead of time. He was so anxious to get to retirement he didn't realize just how much time there was to spend.

If you do not take charge of your retirement time, you might look back and say: "I squandered my retirement hours and was unhappy doing it."

There are other myths, misconceptions, and misunderstandings. The challenge is to recognize them for what they are so that you can go to the heart of what retirement is all about—finding a new, rewarding lifestyle.

Summary   Women have their own retirement considerations; often these are more difficult than those of men.

Knowing the myths and misconceptions about retirement helps an individual avoid foolish, unnecessary mistakes.

The challenge of retirement is knowing what to do with your time.

PROBLEM TO SOLVE   ## Retirement Attitudes

Major Valor, Mrs. Jason, Mrs. George, and Mr. Shaw find themselves in the same preretirement discussion group, sponsored by their organization. Their assignment is to discuss their personal philosophies on how to enrich their retirements through the best time utilization. Each has three minutes to talk.

Major Valor: "I'm a strong preparation person. I believe there is a high correlation between planning and success. Those who do not design a detailed, structured plan usually fall apart and miss the purpose of retirement. You may think that my military background conditioned my response, but it is more than that. I retired once and know what I am talking about. This time I'll have a blueprint and wake up each morning to a 'do list'; I'll know in general terms what I want to do six months along. My experience tells me the more planning the better."

Mrs. Jason: "The Major and I disagree. I believe in the day-at-a-time approach. Live every day as though it is your last. Don't make plans because they may lead to disappointment. Get up in the morning and let it happen. This way you are free; this way you don't frustrate yourself needlessly. I believe in the hedonistic philosophy, especially after retirement: enjoy hour by hour. Planning only makes life more complicated."

Mrs. George: "I'm a little like you, Mrs. Jason. I too am enthusiastic about the free-spirit approach. On the other hand, some planning is necessary. For example, I'll plan vacations and things like that, but deliver me from making lists and scheduling my time into blocks. I like to follow my whims on a day-to-day basis, but I also like to know the general direction I am going. Live each day at the time, but each day should be a part of a bigger plan. I haven't worked all my life to retire and put myself in a straitjacket. I'm tired of having so many responsibilities. All I want is freedom to be good to myself."

Mr. Shaw: "The only way to make retirement work is to find a mission and let it fill your life. If you are so inclined, give your life to God, and he will tell you what to do with your time. Retirees need something to consume them, something that will lead to new horizons. The only happy retirees I've found are those with a late-in-life mission—a cause that provides them with a sense of purpose, meaning, and fulfillment. All that planning seems to do is put people in their little narrow time boxes where they have been all their lives. No thanks!"

Which attitude do you support, if any? What modifications would you make? Would you combine aspects of any in your own? Compare your thoughts with those of the author in Appendix C.

SELF-QUIZ

True   *False*

_____   _____   1. Men have more retirement problems than women.

_____   _____   2. After retirement, most women like their spouses around home all day.

_____   _____   3. People who refuse to retire live longer.

_____   _____   4. Hobbies need to be balanced with other kinds of activities.

_____   _____   5. It is not unusual to find a retiree who stretches tasks to fill time blocks.

(Answers in Appendix C.)

II

UTILIZING YOUR TIME

If you have not already done so, before reading this section, turn to Appendix A and complete the Inventory of Retirement Activities (IRA). Once this has been accomplished and you have read the chapters in this section, you'll be able to: compare your high, average, and low retirement interest activities; decide if Plan A (leisure), Plan B (leisure plus a part-time money job), or Plan C (leisure plus a volunteer activity) is best for you.

6

Plan A: Pure Leisure

A perpetual holiday is a good working definition of hell.
George Bernard Shaw

Leisure! To lounge and spend time in idleness . . . to slow the pace . . . to throw off responsibilities . . . to relax . . . to play. These are the rewards of retirement—the big payoff for working all those years.

Pure leisure (Plan A) is keeping all your retirement hours for yourself. It is refusing to work for money or running your own business or accepting a time-consuming volunteer job. It is tending to the business of living (household chores, shopping, etc.) and then devoting the rest of your time to planned leisure activities. It is being free of entanglements with organizations.

No guilt feelings, please.

Some retirees react to total leisure as a selfish way to live—self-gratification without concern or compassion for others. Not so. You can adopt Plan A as your retirement lifestyle and still make contributions to the lives of others on a personal, one-on-one basis. You can

49

continue to pay your human and social rent. It is just that you refuse to have organizational connections that require responsibilities. Participate in church life, but refuse to assume a leadership role. Be a member of a fraternal organization, but refuse to accept an office. Enjoy country-club life, but back away when it comes to being in charge of anything. You have reached a stage in life where it is time for others to carry organizational responsibilities. You paid your dues. You carried the load long enough. It is time to enjoy.

It all sounds idyllic—the way retirement should be. But don't expect it to be easy; few people can pull it off. Many want Plan A but eventually settle for B or C. A Duke University Center on Aging study revealed that more than half of 200 men (52 percent) said they got more satisfaction from work than leisure. And 55 percent of 200 women surveyed said they enjoyed working more than free time.

Can you make pure leisure work? Can you take full advantage of the opportunity? Can you use your retirement freedom without becoming so involved in a creative pursuit that it either turns into a business or becomes an obsession? Some signals will come from your activity profile (Appendix A). If you scored low in both working (15) and volunteer work (16) and your leisure activities were high, Plan A may be your best bet. Give Plan A careful consideration. Also complete the following Preference Scale. After doing this you should have considerable insight into what is best for you.

If you scored above 80, you have an excellent chance of making pure leisure work successfully. If you scored between 80 and 60, you may need a job of some type (Plans B or C). Additional signals on this will become available after you complete scales in the following chapters.

Learning Not to Work

Many retirees have the work ethic so ingrained that no matter how hard they try, they cannot escape it. Work is what life is all about. Many may dream of a leisure lifestyle—they have earned it and have all the money they need—but pure leisure provides too much time. Without work they will feel frustrated.

Can people successfully learn not to work? What kind of retiree can wrap the work ethic into a neat package and leave it behind forever? Such individuals normally have one or more of the following characteristics:

* They have exhausted their capacity to work. They have been at it so long and so hard that there is no motivation left. Work has become repulsive. The farther it is behind them, the better. Usually these people never liked the work they chose.

PURE LEISURE PREFERENCE SCALE

Most people cannot handle a life of leisure because they have trouble using all of the time available. This scale is designed to help you discover how you might cope. Circle the number that indicates where you fall in the scale from 1 to 10. After you have finished, total your score in the space provided.

I am worked out. When I retire I never want a job of any kind.	10 9 8 7 6 5 4 3 2 1	I admit I have the work ethic. I will always need to work.
After retirement I'll have all the money I'll need to live a life of leisure	10 9 8 7 6 5 4 3 2 1	It will be necessary for me to work and supplement my income.
I will never be a volunteer.	10 9 8 7 6 5 4 3 2 1	I look forward to volunteer activities.
I can organize my leisure time completely. Time will not be a problem.	10 9 8 7 6 5 4 3 2 1	I cannot plan or discipline myself. Too much time is my greatest worry.
It won't bother me to spend my life pleasing myself. I've earned it.	10 9 8 7 6 5 4 3 2 1	I'll never be happy in retirement without doing something in an organized way for others.
My psychological makeup is such that I can relax for days without any self-pressure.	10 9 8 7 6 5 4 3 2 1	Two days of relaxation and I am climbing the walls.
I enjoy sports both as a participant and as an observer. This will use a lot of my time.	10 9 8 7 6 5 4 3 2 1	I've never been much on sports. It's too late to get involved now.
I would like to spend at least half of my leisure time traveling. I have the money to do it.	10 9 8 7 6 5 4 3 2 1	I'm a homebody. I've seen all of the world I want to see. Besides, I don't have the money.
I can think of 10 leisure activities that I will enjoy.	10 9 8 7 6 5 4 3 2 1	I can't think of any leisure activity I would enjoy.
I'm positive about my ability to cope with the leisure life.	10 9 8 7 6 5 4 3 2 1	I'm negative about making leisure work.

Total Score _____

* People claim they no longer need a feeling of accomplishment. They have fulfilled career and money goals. Except for a few humanistic desires, entertaining themselves is what retirement is about.

* Some insist a lifestyle of leisure does not provoke guilt feelings. In fact, Plan A gives them a feeling of pride and satisfaction.

Leisure Is Not Inactivity

The first thing successful Plan A people recognize is that leisure does not mean inactivity. Sitting around doing nothing or just taking care of the business of living is not their strategy. Leisure is not idleness, although some time will be set aside for total relaxation and meditation. Leisure, in a practical sense, is being able to choose among a variety of pleasures, such as those enjoyable, exciting activities in the Inventory of Retirement Activities.

Plan A retirees have the unique capacity to substitute leisure activities for work activities. Do not think they turn golf, reading, creative efforts, or other activities into work. They do not. What they do is schedule their pleasures in such a way that these continue to remain pleasurable. Once an activity begins to feel like work (pressures are mounting), it is discarded and another takes its place. There is always an activity they want to spend time on—one that will challenge their minds and keep them involved.

Wide-Variety Theory

Some experts maintain that the broader one's leisure activities are, the more chance that Plan A will work. In other words, if you have a variety of activities, you will spice up your lifestyle and keep from becoming bored. Here are some thoughts:

* Switch from physical activities (running, golf, tennis, walking) to mental activities (bridge, reading) and back.

* Move from an activity where you are happy alone (working on a craft) to a social activity (dancing, bingo).

* Have something new on the back burner, an activity you have always wanted to try if you had time.

Coming Up with the Right Activity Mix

Each person must design his or her own activity mix. Experimentation will probably be necessary, and the right balance may not surface immediately. Some people make Plan A work with three or four activities; others need more. Some can spend a majority of their time on one activity (travel), but others cannot. It boils down to interests and aptitudes. One naturally spends more time on high-interest activities. As interests change, so should activities. Keeping the right mix so the mind is challenged is the key to success with Plan A. Only a few people do it convincingly.

The Leisure Activity Tree, on page 54, is designed to help you explore the activity mix that will bring you the greatest happiness. The various activities (leaves) are located on six limbs. Although you may wish to concentrate your activities on one special limb, at least one activity on each limb is recommended. Starting from the bottom, climb out on each limb and mark at least one activity. If you do not find a favorite activity, write one on the blank leaf. After completing this, compare your results with those in your IRA profile.

Quality Levels of Leisure Activities

Some retirees claim Plan A works for them when it does not. The quality of their leisure is such that a great deal is left to be desired. They occupy time but their personal satisfaction is low. They are bored with certain activities. They seem to have excessive down periods. Some would be much happier with Plan B or Plan C, but they do not seem to realize it.

What is a satisfactory quality level? How do you know when the level is sufficiently high to make a Plan A lifestyle effective? Here are some ideas:

Signal 1   Plan A is working when your leisure activities keep your mind challenged and you want to spend more time on them rather than less.

Signal 2   You receive satisfactory rewards from activities. They make you feel good. Competitive people often have good luck making Plan A work because they often win at the games they play—tennis, golf, bridge. Winning can be stimulating.

Signal 3   You keep in contact with the kind of people you enjoy. Good communication takes place. Your social contacts make you feel good about yourself.

Signal 4   Your creative nature is satisfied. You feel achievement even if you do not share what you do with others.

Signal 5   Your activity mix provides you with a sense of exuberance and richness.

Following are profiles of retirees who have made Plan A work.

The Model Plan A

You might consider Mr. P as something of a model when it comes to Plan A. After a 45-year career with Canadian Pacific, he designed a leisure program that he has no intention of deserting. One reason is that he literally worked himself out. He worked very hard, and the considerable overtime and rotating shifts took

LEISURE ACTIVITY TREE

an additional toll. If anyone earned retirement, he did. He started working when he was 12 and stayed with it until age 65.

He has diversified his leisure activities into a pattern that meets his personal desires. Mr. P is a good golfer and thoroughly enjoys playing. He also loves to gamble and plays poker one night each week plus two or three afternoons at his club. He and his wife take advantage of travel privileges earned while with Canadian Pacific and take two or three transcontinental trips each year. He reads mysteries, enjoys social activities with his wife, maintains regular communication with his friends, and does a little professional loafing. "I've tried to design a lifestyle that makes me feel retired. We live in a condominium, so—thank goodness—there are few odd jobs to keep occupied. We don't have enough capital to be overly concerned with our investments. I'm not tempted to fill my days with much besides pleasurable activities."

You can tell he has a good Plan A attitude. His lifestyle fits into his retirement income. Beneath everything, he works to make his time satisfying. "Sure, I get a few guilt feelings at times because my life does not seem to have a great purpose, but I'm not the type to do volunteer work or get involved in some cause. It's not my thing. My retirement is not perfect. I have problems—including a few down periods. But, by and large, it's what I want."

Tornado Trouble

Driving across Manitoba one spring afternoon, I stopped at a public rest area. As I pulled up, a couple was getting out of a large recreation vehicle pulled by a camper-truck. I introduced myself and made an interesting discovery. Although they did not look it, she was 82 and he was 80. They told me they had lost their home in the Barrie tornado four years earlier. Following this traumatic event, they bought a trailer and started travelling, never purchasing another home. If they want to settle for a while, they find a park where the climate is warm and stay for a few weeks. They describe themselves as nomads who discovered their current lifestyle by accident. They plan to celebrate their sixtieth wedding anniversary by flying to Paris for two weeks. During our time together, they made some interesting comments. The husband said: "There is a whole society like us. None of us works. None is connected with any organization. We are currently on our way to the Bay of Fundy but it doesn't matter when we arrive. Someday we will probably settle down for good in the best park we can find. When this happens, we will be among friends. Friendly seniors are easy to find."

Ruby's Ability   Everyone comments on Ruby's ability to have a leisure lifestyle with her modest income. She lives alone in an apartment and is in total charge of her finances. She does her own chores. When she is not traveling, she visits grandchildren, goes out socially with men, plays bridge, walks, dances, and reads. She has been invited to participate in many kinds of volunteer organizations but declined because she is not interested. Her attitude toward retirement is expressed in these words: "My husband worked hard all of his life and had precious few leisure moments before I lost him. I had to work for a few years and disliked every moment. All I thought about was my retirement. Now I am intent on making the most of it. Frankly, I have a lot going for me. I'm as free as a bird, not indebted to any person or organization. I can vary my activities according to my own desires. I keep my schedule where I have all the time I need for myself. Retirement, for me, is beautiful.

You may know people who have been successful in a quality leisure retirement. Talk to these individuals about how and why it works for them. Learn from their experiences. The more research you do, the more you will learn that Plan A is usually the most difficult of all. Very few can retire to pure leisure with style. Many try it, but few make it work. Those who do have a right to be proud.

Before you can make your best decision, you need to consider the two alternate plans—B and C. Follow these basic rules:

Rule 1   *Keep an open mind.* If preconceived ideas dominate, you may wind up with the wrong plan and get less from your retirement than is possible. For example, you do not abandon leisure activities if you accept Plan B or Plan C.

Rule 2   *Be true to your desires.* For most of us, retirement is the last chance to fulfill dreams. You have lived long enough to know yourself, so be honest. Remorse can occur when you look back and realize you spent your available time the wrong way.

Rule 3   *If you are married, work out a plan that will be best for both parties.* An open discussion of all three plans is the way to accomplish this. It is possible for one spouse to employ Plan A and the other to employ Plan B or Plan C. To succeed requires discussion ahead of time, and each person must have enough space in which to operate.

Summary   Plan A means devoting retirement years to pure leisure. Except for routine living tasks, no work or major organizational commitments are involved.

Some retirees who try Plan A fail and move to Plan B or Plan C. Others operate at a low-quality level.

Those who can make Plan A work for them at a high level have accomplished a great deal.

PROBLEM TO SOLVE　**Plan A Success Formula?**

Malcolm and Jean Payne can hardly wait for retirement because they have been workaholics—Malcolm as a sales representative and Jean as an office manger. They have no children. They have all the money they need. But because they have devoted so much time to work, they have developed almost no leisure activities. The only thing Malcolm has done consistently is play some tennis, swim occasionally, and watch television. Jean has been a consistent reader since childhood and has developed no other activities. She has little interest in sports.

Their Plan A, carefully worked out, is to explore and, if necessary, eliminate one leisure activity after another until they come up with a satisfactory, long-term mix. They plan to travel to see how appealing that is. They expect to join a country club to see if they like that lifestyle. They plan to take bridge and dance lessons and so on until they have found the leisure activities that fit their needs. They have given themselves two years in which to do this.

What kind of success do you predict for the Paynes? See the author's comments in Appendix C.

SELF-QUIZ

True	False	
_____	_____	1. The vast majority of retirees have an easy time learning not to work.
_____	_____	2. Pure leisure (Plan A) means total inactivity.
_____	_____	3. If you do volunteer work, you are not following Plan A.
_____	_____	4. Of all three plans, Plan A is the most difficult to achieve satisfactorily.
_____	_____	5. Retirees who stretch out domestic tasks to occupy time have more success making Plan A work than those who do not.

(Answers in Appendix C.)

7

Plan B: Leisure Plus a Money Job

I go on working for the same reason a hen goes on laying eggs.
H. L. Mencken

If you are ever in Honolulu on a working day, you might find three interesting male retirees having lunch at Arthur's. All three tried pure leisure (Plan A) in Hawaii, where it should work like a charm, and all failed. Their solution? Working part time (not more than 20 hours per week). The result? All claim to enjoy paradise more. One says: "We have the best of both worlds."

Work, to many retirees, is a good four-letter word. To some, work is the most meaningful part of retirement. To others, work is more satisfying than recreational activities. Because of these factors, many individuals work far into their retirement years.

Mr. Jensen Mr. Jensen is over 80 years of age, but he still spends a few hours each day working in the business he founded. "I've worked all my life. It is part of me. It brings me joy. Maybe it is because I've been

59

goal-oriented since I was a kid that I need to do something useful to make my leisure more interesting. Anyway, working adds to my other enjoyments in life—golf, church, travel, and Kiwanis Club. It's the perfect combination for me."

Achieving a Suitable Blend

Plan B, when successful, is a special balance of leisure and work that fits the style of an individual. It is a compromise between working full time and leisure. For most retirees, it means working 15 to 20 hours per week. Individuals must design their own plan. When the proper balance is found, both work and leisure may be enhanced.

What is your situation? Would retirement be better for you under Plan B? Can you design a balance that will improve your leisure hours? Is it important that you supplement your income to achieve the best possible retirement?

If you gave working a high rating (above 20) in the IRA profile (Appendix A), you have a strong signal that Plan B might be the direction to take. You will know even more about yourself and Plan B if you complete the following Work-Leisure Preference Scale.

If you scored above 70, it may be an indication that a blend of part-time work and leisure is for you. If so, this chapter can help. If you scored below 60, you should explore Plans A and C more carefully.

Work Rewards

Why do so many retirees work part time? What are the rewards that cause them to give up much of the leisure time they worked so hard to get in the first place? Below are ten rewards. Check the box if you want that reward. The more boxes you check, the more satisfaction you would receive from Plan B.

Reward 1   *Additional money.* Earning more money is often necessary to maintain or improve your standard of living.
☐

Reward 2   *Insurance benefits.* Having an employer pay for medical benefits and contribute to the pension plan and other insurance benefits can be a compelling reason to stay on a payroll after retirement.
☐

Reward 3   *Ego satisfaction.* Having a job, even though less important than the preretirement position, can help your self-image.
☐

Reward 4   *Scheduled activity.* A job helps structure your day. You don't have to plan how to spend all of your time.
☐

Reward 5   *Leisure hours appreciated more.* Working helps make leisure hours more important, fun, and exciting.
☐

WORK-LEISURE PREFERENCE SCALE

This scale is designed to help you discover if you would be happier after retirement with a part-time money job. You should gain additional insights by comparing the score of this scale with that of the Pure Leisure Preference Scale (Chapter 6). Circle the number that best describes your situation and total your score in the space provided.

The work ethic is in my bones and I admit it. I hope a part-time job will satisfy this need.	10 9 8 7 6 5 4 3 2 1	I've squeezed the work ethic out of my system.
I need to have a feeling of accomplishment each day; only a money job will do.	10 9 8 7 6 5 4 3 2 1	I can get a better feeling of accomplishment through a hobby, craft, or other activity.
Working for money is necessary to my ego. I need the recognition.	10 9 8 7 6 5 4 3 2 1	I can satisfy my ego in other ways.
I've got to have a money job to wake up to; I can't fill my days on my own.	10 9 8 7 6 5 4 3 2 1	I love to sleep late and then enjoy leisure activities.
Work keeps me in the mainstream and in contact with younger people.	10 9 8 7 6 5 4 3 2 1	I can keep in touch with others without a money job.
Work will keep my mind active. I can't do it on my own.	10 9 8 7 6 5 4 3 2 1	There are many things other than work that will keep my mind active.
I need the money or I need the good feeling that earning money gives me.	10 9 8 7 6 5 4 3 2 1	I'm tired of working for money. I don't even want to think about it.
Working part time will help me enjoy my leisure far more. It's the combination I like.	10 9 8 7 6 5 4 3 2 1	Having to work for money would spoil my leisure time.
Work is pleasure for me—as long as I get paid for it.	10 9 8 7 6 5 4 3 2 1	I would get more pleasure out of leisure activities or a volunteer job.
Work is therapeutic; it will keep me alive longer.	10 9 8 7 6 5 4 3 2 1	Work tears me down, makes me a nervous wreck. I can't handle it.

Total Score _____

Reward 6
☐

Eliminates down periods. Too much leisure can cause depression. A job helps you keep better control of your positive attitude.

Reward 7
☐

Better home life. You appreciate home more when you are not there so much. Those who are married provide more freedom for their spouses.

Reward 8
☐

People contacts. A job helps you communicate with others, both at work and after work.

Reward 9
☐

Feeling of purpose. Working is an excellent way to make a contribution to society. You feel you are paying your own way.

Reward 10
☐

Therapeutic. A job involving activity keeps you in better shape mentally and physically.

Working should not be something to simply fill time. It should provide both tangible and psychological rewards.

Finding the Right Part-Time Involvement

Retirees have experience, knowledge, and skills that society needs. They constitute a giant reservoir of ability and talent. But finding the right part-time retirement job is not always easy. It is estimated that for every two retirees who work part time, at least one more person would like to work. With Plan B, you have some choices. For example, you can continue to use skills you already possess or learn to do something fresh and different.

Completing the Retirement Job Tree exercise may help you focus on a possible retirement career. Select the career limb that is most appealing to you; then see if there is a specific job (leaf) you want to investigate.

The service limb contains part-time jobs that help others. These are often available to retirees. Today, more than 60 percent of all jobs fall into this general area. If other limbs do not appeal, why not give service careful consideration? You might enjoy the people-contact aspect, and your hours could fit into your free-time schedule.

The independent-service limb is for those who want to work for themselves. Here again, the opportunities are many. You can start a business or do "fix-it" work, babysitting, gardening, or many other jobs on your own terms. Not only do you protect your freedom, but the contact with people is also excellent. If you like this limb best, you should explore additional job possibilities.

Some retirees desire to work only in creative pursuits. They hope to turn hobbies into money-producing activities. Often these

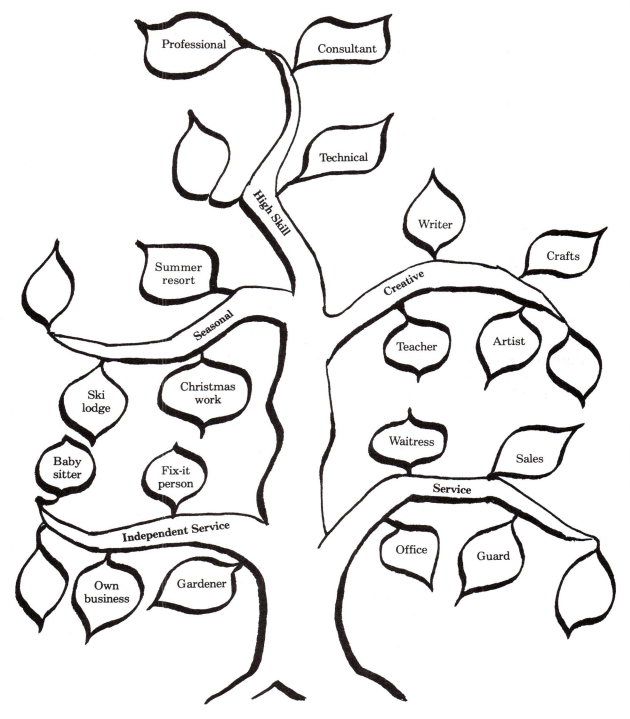

individuals refuse to consider other opportunities. It is creative work or nothing at all.

The seasonal limb often makes sense for two reasons. First, seasonal jobs are easier to get. Second, it is possible to work full time for a few months and then pursue leisure activities with more freedom. For example, many retirees work in department stores around Christmas or at resorts during the summer.

The high-skill limb is reserved primarily for those who want to stay with their profession. They are happy with their work before retirement and want to continue on a less-demanding basis. They mix work with leisure at their own design.

As you explore the Retirement Job Tree, keep your self-satisfaction in mind. Examples of people I know who have selected Plan B include a corporate president who grows and sells flowers, a wealthy farmer who leases his land so he can raise exotic birds, and a retired RIA who charters his boat for fishing expeditions. If you plan carefully, you should be able to find the type of job that best fits your situation.

The Winning Combination

It is not always easy to make Plan B work at a quality level. Some retirees, especially those who need additional income, can place so much emphasis on their job that leisure hours are neglected. Instead of using the extra dollars to create some excitement in their lives, they sit at home. They expect too much from their jobs. They say:

* "I'd be happier if I could work more hours."
* "My job is the only thing I look forward to."
* "By the time I work 20 hours a week and take care of my daily chores, there isn't time left for fun."

These individuals are not working to improve their leisure hours; they are working to use up time. They apparently don't realize that if they take charge of both work and leisure, retirement can be more exciting. Neither work nor leisure will do the trick; it is the combination. Here are a few profiles of retirees who feel they have the proper balance between work and leisure. See if you agree.

Jane and Steve

Jane and Steve Adams decided they could enhance their retirement years if each could find the right part-time job. The extra money would permit them to travel more. Also, work would help keep them mentally and physically involved, and they would not have too much time together to get on each other's nerves.

Jane, a retired teacher, landed her job first. She is a research assistant in the local public library from 9 a.m. to 1 p.m. five days a week. The library is within walking distance, and Jane receives the minimum wage.

Her husband, Steve (a retired supervisor for a food-processing firm), had more trouble finding a position. One afternoon their minister mentioned that the church was looking for a new gardener. Steve said nothing at the time, but the following day called and said he would like to apply. He always enjoyed his own garden and considered himself well qualified to trim trees, grow flowers, and fertilize. Steve got the job and agreed to accept minimum wage for 18 hours a week. His work hours were up to him.

Several months after both started working again, Steve said: "Working a little is just right for us. Jane loves her involvement at the library, and I take pride in my work too. We have afternoons free for other activities. We make the most of our leisure time and have put some of our earnings aside for a trip to visit our grandchildren next spring."

Herb's Solution

Herb was the best-liked letter carrier in town. He took the job soon after World War II. Although he could have moved into supervisory work, he elected to stay on his mail route. Last year his retirement at age 65 was accepted sadly by those he served. In addition to a formal party at the post office, he received many gifts from people on his route.

Herb did very little for the first six months—some work around the house, a little golf—but not enough to keep him occupied. One day he stopped at the service station he had patronized over the years to get gas. The owner asked how things were going. When Herb said he was bored, the owner asked if he would like to work part time collecting money from customers using the self-service pumps.

That was six months ago. Today Herb is delighted. He loves the interaction with people, and he enjoys the extra money. He told me: "There is no way I could be happy without a little work. Mind you, 20 hours is enough; but my golf game has improved, relations with my wife are better, and my outlook is 100 percent ahead of last year at this time."

Doris Dayton

Doris Dayton was primarily a homemaker before she retired. The only time she was on someone's payroll was when family finances required it. None of her temporary positions amounted to much. Last year, as a widow of 63, she faced up to her problems. First, her income was barely enough to get by; and second, she had too much time on her hands. She decided the solution was to find a part-time job. This way she could solve her two problems and still have enough leisure to enjoy life.

Some months ago she accompanied a friend to the local college where her friend was taking a course in word processing. Later, Doris asked herself some questions. Why couldn't she do the same? She had excellent English skills and good dexterity. But who would hire a 63-year-old widow?

After talking to a college counselor, Mrs. Dayton enrolled in the same course as her neighbor but made faster progress. Her confidence grew and she later had an interview with a local insurance company that needed a part-time information processor.

After getting the job, Doris said: "I can't tell you how great I feel. Knowing I am acceptable in the work world is a great booster. Also, I'm making better use of my leisure hours, including social activities with new friends. It's a whole new life for me."

Getting the Right Job

In a way, doctors, lawyers, dentists, and other professionals are fortunate when it comes to Plan B. They can reduce their work hours and expand their leisure hours. No career change is necessary.

Some retirees, including professionals, can convert a lifelong hobby into a Plan B that makes money. Others study themselves, look around their communities, and establish low-overhead businesses that provide both involvement and money but do not interfere with their leisure hours. The possibilities are endless, but most retirees are not in a position to create their own jobs. To get a job, they must sell themselves to an employer. They must find a firm that will see the value of having them on the payroll. If you are in this category but fear the interviewing process, you should complete the Confidence-Building Exercise.

Summary

If not overdone, working for money can enhance retirement for some.

Like Plans A and C, Plan B provides certain psychological rewards that deserve careful consideration.

Despite experience, skill, and maturity, not all retirees find it easy to secure a suitable part-time job.

PROBLEM TO SOLVE | **Plan A or Plan B?**

Miss Ritter intends to retire in two years when she is 65. An English teacher, she will have taught only 20 years, and her retirement

CONFIDENCE-BUILDING EXERCISE

This exercise is designed to help retirees who want part-time employment but may not have the confidence to take the first step. On the left are possible disadvantages to the employment of those over 65 (many are myths). On the right are the advantages. Check both your disadvantages and advantages. Your advantages should build personal confidence and help you communicate why an employer would be smart to hire you.

Possible Disadvantages (check only if you agree)	*Advantages* (check only if you agree)
☐ Slightly less strength for heavy physical work.	☐ More dependable, thus a better absentee record.
☐ Slightly slower in physical movements.	☐ More responsible than younger employees.
☐ Slightly slower in learning new skills.	☐ Better at following directions and rules.
☐ More difficult to fit into pension and benefit plans.	☐ Will appreciate job more, thus stay longer.
☐ Older image projected to co-workers and customers	☐ Less socialization on the job.
☐ Too late in life to be a long-term career employee.	☐ Higher productivity.
☐ Not interested in full-time employment.	☐ Less supervision required.
☐ Under certain situations might be less flexible.	☐ Less distraction by outside interests.
☐ Older value differences might create conflicts with younger workers.	☐ Better with human relations and customers.
☐ More accident prone, thus more of a risk.	☐ More accurate.
Total _____	Total _____

When seeking employment follow these rules: (1) stay close to home; (2) make an interview appointment by telephone; (3) communicate your confidence; (4) mention your advantages during interview.

cheque will be skimpy. She has not worked sufficiently to qualify for the full Canada Pension.

Miss Ritter has dreamed of retiring into leisure, where she could attend theatre festivals in Stratford and Niagara-on-the-Lake, Ontario. She also wants to be an active member of the local art association and spend time with her friends. Retirement, she reasoned, could be the best part of her life.

However, Miss Ritter has a fear that will not go away. She worries that her income will be insufficient. She believes life may become increasingly restrictive because of inflation. As a result, she has decided to take courses in typing and word processing. Because her English skills are outstanding, she expects to earn top grades in her classes. "My plan," she explained, "is to work for about five years to increase my Canada Pension payments on top of my teacher's retirement. Also, I should earn about $8,000 a year working part time. Although I would prefer not working, I think I can still enjoy some leisure. In five years I should be able to take a full retirement. It may prove difficult to enter the labor market at my age, but I feel I can make it because I have the skills."

Do you think Miss Ritter is wise to develop a Plan B? Can she make it work? Would you hire her on a part-time basis? Compare your thoughts with those of the author in Appendix C.

SELF-QUIZ

True   *False*

1. Plan B is for those who can't handle pure leisure and like money too much to volunteer their services.

2. The big danger of Plan B is that retirees will permit work to squeeze out their valuable leisure hours.

3. Earning money is not a reward for wealthy retirees.

4. Working to use up time is the secret to retirement.

5. To make the most of Plan B, a retiree should not work more than 20 hours a week.

(Answer in Appendix C.)

8

Plan C: Leisure Plus
Volunteer Activities

Wherever a man turns, he can find someone who needs him. Even if it is a little thing, do something for which you get not pay but the privilege of doing it. For remember, you don't live in a world all your own. Your brothers are here, too.
Albert Schweitzer

When you volunteer your services, you give more of yourself and you usually get more back. You interact with other dedicated people and involve yourself in worthwhile causes. Fellowship can add new dimension to your life, and your leisure hours can be enhanced.

Volunteerism is a big thing in Canada. It is estimated that more than one-third of all retired people do volunteer work, ranging from one hour per week up to a full-time commitment. It is possible to provide your services free to several organizations. It is also possible to hold down a paying job and a volunteer position at the same time.

71

VOLUNTEERISM

True   *False*

_____   _____   1. Middle-aged women are volunteering less because they have joined the work force. Retirees are picking up the slack.

_____   _____   2. It is estimated that there are more than 100,000 organized volunteer groups in North America.

_____   _____   3. Generally speaking, society underestimates and undervalues the services of volunteers.

_____   _____   4. A Harris Survey in 1974 found that 4.5 million people over 65 were serving as volunteers.

_____   _____   5. Some small business organizations benefit from volunteer programs where retirees offer guidance. One such program is CASE (Counselling Assistance to Small Enterprise), sponsored by the federal government.

_____   _____   6. The Foster Grandparent Program is a local rather than a national organization.

_____   _____   7. CESO, the Canadian Executive Service Overseas, is sponsored by the Canadian International Development Agency to get talented retirees to contribute their expertise to developing nations.

_____   _____   8. It is easy to find the right volunteer program.

_____   _____   9. The New Horizons program was established in 1972 by Health and Welfare Canada to promote the social participation of older adults.

_____   _____   10. There is less need for volunteers today than in the past.

Number correct _____

Answers: (1) T; (2) T; (3) T; (4) T; (5) T; (6) F; (7) T; (8) F; (9) T; (10) F (the need is far greater).

But volunteerism is not for everybody. Only certain people gain the true rewards it offers. Those most rewarded are usually people with a humanitarian attitude. They feel inadequate if they only satisfy their own desires. Pure leisure or working only for money is not satisfactory. They want to contribute something they feel is significant. They seek different retirement rewards.

Have you given volunteerism careful consideration? As an introduction to the possibility, please take the accompanying true-false test on volunteerism.

The more you learn about those who donate their services, the more enthusiastic you will become. You hear a variety of positive comments.

* "My retirement didn't have meaning until I gave time and energy to a cause where I was committed."

* "Once you have led a full, beautiful life, you feel good about contributing to those less fortunate."

* "It's the time of life to deal with your special passions. Mine happens to be animals, so I donate my time to a pet shelter."

* "I'm putting good deeds instead of money into my bank."

* "All I gave my church before retirement was money; now I give some of myself."

You need to know yourself well to determine if volunteerism is right for you. If you rated yourself high in volunteer work (category 16 in the IRA exercise), Plan C is a possibility for you. Know your personal values well if you seriously consider this choice. The following Volunteer-Leisure Preference Scale may help you in this respect.

If you scored over 70, volunteer work may be part of your answer. To help verify this, compare your scores on all three of the scales.

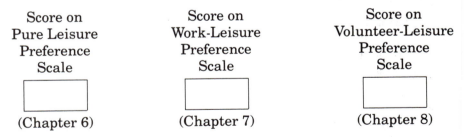

Score on Pure Leisure Preference Scale	Score on Work-Leisure Preference Scale	Score on Volunteer-Leisure Preference Scale
(Chapter 6)	(Chapter 7)	(Chapter 8)

If you scored higher on the volunteer scale, you should give volunteerism a chance. A certain activity in your church, for example, might satisfy your needs better than pure leisure or a work-leisure combination.

Reward Checklist   Below are ten rewards that people receive from doing volunteer work. The more squares you check, the more satisfaction you would receive.

VOLUNTEER-LEISURE PREFERENCE SCALE

Many retirees find happiness through the right combination of volunteer work and leisure. This scale is designed to help you discover if you fall in this category. Circle the appropriate number and total your score.

I recognize I can't handle leisure, but I don't want the pressure of working for money.	10 9 8 7 6 5 4 3 2 1	Volunteer work would provide as much pressure as real work to me—and no benefits.
I need a consuming mission in life; only volunteer work will provide this.	10 9 8 7 6 5 4 3 2 1	I do not need or want a big mission in life—just leave me alone.
I don't need money—just group involvement and personal contacts for my mental health.	10 9 8 7 6 5 4 3 2 1	If I have to deal with group politics, I want to be paid for it.
I'm not the bridge-playing, country-club type; I've got to have a purpose to my life.	10 9 8 7 6 5 4 3 2 1	I want leisure, fun, and games, even if I have to make money to achieve it.
Volunteer work appeals to me—involvement without structure or daily responsibility.	10 9 8 7 6 5 4 3 2 1	I'm just not the volunteer type, and I know it.
I can't work for money, but if I don't do some volunteer work, I will climb the walls.	10 9 8 7 6 5 4 3 2 1	Volunteer work would cause me to climb the walls.
Organizational politics would not bother me.	10 9 8 7 6 5 4 3 2 1	I've had all the organizational politics I can handle.
Volunteer work is the only thing that will get me out of the house regularly.	10 9 8 7 6 5 4 3 2 1	My leisure activities will get me out of the house with ease.
My observations tell me that volunteer workers are the happiest of all.	10 9 8 7 6 5 4 3 2 1	Nothing I've seen convinces me volunteers are happy.
I know myself. I'm not a leisure person or a money-making person. Volunteer work is my cup of tea.	10 9 8 7 6 5 4 3 2 1	I'm happy we have volunteer workers; I'm just not one of them and I know it.

Total Score _____

Reward 1 ☐ *Comradeship.* Fellowship becomes increasingly important after retirement. When this need is combined with a worthy purpose shared by others, the rewards are multiplied.

Reward 2 ☐ *Recognition.* When you are on a payroll, money itself can be the main form of recognition. In a volunteer position, recognition and ego satisfaction come from many directions. Certain groups, like a hospital auxiliary, carry considerable prestige.

Reward 3 ☐ *Freedom to withdraw.* You are not tied to a volunteer role in the same way you are to a money job. You can come and go more easily.

Reward 4 ☐ *Sense of mission.* Retirees who have a sense of mission are often the happiest of all. Giving time to something you believe in can be rewarding beyond expectations.

Reward 5 ☐ *Keeps mind active.* A good volunteer activity is like a mental-health insurance policy. It will keep you alert and ready for other facets of your life.

Reward 6 ☐ *Beautiful substitute for work.* In a sense volunteerism is work; but, if handled properly, pressures can be eliminated and enjoyment can be at a higher level. In short, you can get the values of paid work, including physical activity, but you don't have the pressure of satisfying an employer.

Reward 7 ☐ *Compatible people.* In a money job you work with employees or co-workers. In a volunteer activity you work with colleagues. The difference is significant.

Reward 8 ☐ *Chance to develop new skills.* Volunteer work often provides opportunities to learn new things. This can strengthen personal confidence.

Reward 9 ☐ *Enhance leisure hours.* The enthusiasm of meaningful volunteer work can spill into leisure hours.

Reward 10 ☐ *The give-back idea.* Some retirees feel they have taken from society during their lives. They feel good when they are able to give something back.

You can get special rewards from Plan A and Plan B; but the rewards from Plan C often overshadow those received from the other plans.

Mr. and Mrs. Alvin

It is a pleasure to be around Mr. and Mrs. Alvin. Their enthusiasm for life is catching. Mr. Alvin is a volunteer counselor at a senior center. He has also been trained by

Revenue Canada and helps retirees with their income-tax returns. Mrs. Alvin volunteers her services three mornings each week to a day-care center. Mr. Alvin says: "Retirement, to us, is a balance between leisure and making a contribution. One reinforces the other. It's the perfect blend."

Mrs. Jetty

Mrs. Jetty spends two hours each day feeding guests at a nursing home three blocks from where she lives. The regular staff recently gave a special appreciation party for her. The director of the home said this about Mrs. Jetty: "She is so gentle with our guests. They obviously love her. When she doesn't show up, which is rare, we call to see if she is all right."

Mrs. Dastrop

Mrs. Dastrop spends 15 hours each week at the senior desk of her local library. Not only does she help retirees find what they ask for, but also she makes suggestions about what they might enjoy reading. The head librarian has said: "Mrs. Dastrop has a fan club. They come to the library when they know she is working. We are presenting her with a special award at our annual dinner."

Volunteer Activities Should Be Selected with Care

To make money we sometimes select jobs that fall short of what we enjoy. A paycheque helps compensate for the effort. With no pay, a person should be careful. The key to the right volunteer activity is to know yourself and to be honest with yourself. This means matching that which provides the most rewards for you with what is available in your community. If your rewards are right, you will probably stick with it. If the rewards are not right, you should leave. Your volunteer role should do something for the organization, but it also should do something for you. The Mutual Reward Theory must work so everyone will come out ahead.

The Volunteer Activity Tree is designed to help you. Study it carefully. If you are a religious person, you may want to contribute your services totally to your church. If you like to help people who are ill, and you would be comfortable in the atmosphere of a hospital or nursing home, look carefully at the opportunities on the health-care limb. If you love children and work well with them, you may want to make your contribution on the educational limb. The cultural limb appeals to many, especially those who like activities with prestigious organizations. The opportunities are many.

At the top of the tree are a few of the many national organizations that accept volunteers. There are advantages to affiliation with these fine groups. Fellowship and prestige are usually present, and often there are some leadership opportunities. It is possible to start

VOLUNTEER ACTIVITY TREE

as a local volunteer and, in time, achieve a position on a national committee. Organizational membership and volunteer activities go together. If you join the right group, the organization will fill all the volunteer hours you want to give.

In selecting a volunteer position, consider all your interests, aptitudes, and desires.

This activity tree represents only a small portion of the many organizations that need volunteer workers. To discover new groups and learn more about those on the tree, contact New Horizons or your local library.

Volunteer Your Services with Confidence

It is estimated that for every two retirees who volunteer their services, an additional person has the desire but not the confidence to take the first step. If you are in this category, visit the organization directly after making a telephone appointment to learn more about opportunities to do volunteer work.

Advocacy and Volunteerism

If your feelings are strong enough to support a cause, then Plan C may be for you. Look over the accompanying advocacy wheel to see if you identify strongly with any of the causes listed.

Are you disturbed about the way senior citizens are being treated? Do you want to devote some of your time to advancing religion? Are you a committed environmentalist?

Most volunteers need strong feelings about what they do. Those who commit themselves to a worthy cause often find that they are sustained and able to stay involved.

Volunteerism and the Human-Relations Triangle

The triangle shown here provides insight into the human relations involved in being a volunteer.

As the volunteer you have been placed at the top of the triangle. This signifies that you have a special relationship with people who are paid for their services. You are entitled to this status, but you should not take advantage of it. The better you cooperate with others, the more rewards you will receive. The last thing you need in a volunteer job is a problem in human relations.

Your sponsor or director, paid or not, is the key. This person is responsible for your contribution and should be the person you consult if problems arise.

You have a responsibility to get along well with paid employees. Always try to meet them at least halfway. Make an effort to know them and help them understand why you are a volunteer. If you make their job easier instead of more difficult, you will probably build a warm relationship. There are a few things, however, that you should not tolerate.

* If you are under the direction of an individual who devalues free work, take your services elsewhere. Volunteer work is not paid status and the difference must be clear. The fact that you work for free should bring sensitive treatment from others. Volunteerism should have dignity.

* If you are consistently assigned demeaning work that others avoid, you should talk to your sponsor. Because psychological rewards are the only pay you receive, they should not be withheld.

Volunteer

Paid employee   Sponsor/Director

* Watch out for overloads. If you discover too much work is coming your way and pressures are mounting, discuss the situation with your sponsor. You did not volunteer for stress.

* If you discover, perhaps because your talents are exceptional, that you are resented by an employee, address the problem directly. Under no circumstances should you permit human-relations problems to build.

Take charge and protect your volunteer status at the top of the tri-angle. The moment you do not look forward to your volunteer activity is the moment to consider action. Your involvement should contribute to a better retirement, not detract from it.

Decision Time Before moving to the next section, think about which of the three plans would enrich your retirement years the most. It is a decision you can always change or modify later. The sooner you feel committed to one plan, the sooner you will feel comfortable with retirement. Walter found a way to combine parts of Plans A, B, and C.

Walter's Combination

Walter's close friends can't believe his energy at age 69. They suspect he secretly collapses each night. Working in a 16-hour weekend job as a waiter in a nice restaurant adds to his income. He volunteers at the local YMCA 15 hours each week doing errands. This has rewards because he can use the exercise equipment and pool at no cost. His leisure hours are filled with social activities, including seeing several lady friends. On top of all this he takes care of his own apartment, does his laundry, and so on. When asked about his activities, he said: "It is the best schedule for me. I love being a waiter. The YMCA was great to me as a kid, and I want to pay them back. And I still have time for fun activities. I'm happy when I am busy."

Summary Volunteerism offers special rewards not found in paid jobs. When these rewards are not forthcoming, the retiree should look elsewhere.

Finding the right volunteer activity is as difficult as finding a good job.

The right volunteer activity can and should contribute to a more enriching retirement.

PROBLEM TO SOLVE **A Case of Resentment**

Mrs. Greer is a wealthy woman with religious convictions and humanitarian motives. During her younger years, she was president of the local art association. Last month, at the urging of her church moderator, she agreed to greet new members in their homes and collect information for the weekly newsletter.

After two months, it is obvious that Mrs. Greer enjoys her new responsibility. Her friends say she looks younger. The church officials have been most complimentary. Mrs. Greer feels her role is mutually rewarding with one exception. The paid church secretary, Mrs. Adamson, seems increasingly resentful of Mrs. Greer. She is critical of the handwritten profiles and often rude on the telephone when Mrs. Greer calls. She is openly hostile when Mrs. Greer visits the church office each week.

Experience helps Mrs. Greer recognize that the resentment is deep and probably will not disappear. She feels she has some choices. First, she can take Mrs. Adamson to lunch and try to dissipate the hostility. Second, she can approach the minister with the problem and offer to withdraw her services in the best interest of the church. Third, she can confront Mrs. Adamson at an appropriate time in the church office, making clear the difference between a paid and a volunteer worker.

Which step would you recommend? What other solution is possible? Compare your answer with the author's in Appendix C.

SELF-QUIZ

True	False	
_____	_____	1. Human-relations problems are less frequent in volunteer jobs.
_____	_____	2. If any organization or sponsor devalues free work, you should withdraw your services.
_____	_____	3. Volunteers should be able to get more rewards from their activities that those who get paid.
_____	_____	4. Generally speaking, those who like to make money do not make good volunteers.
_____	_____	5. Volunteerism is on the decline.

(Answers in Appendix C.)

III

WELLNESS

The number one concern of retirees is health — physical and mental. When you complete this section, you'll be able to: design and execute an exercise program to fit your retirement needs; adjust your diet to achieve better health; reduce your down periods.

9

Physical Exercise—A Must

Wellness is a word that everyone should take with them on their journey into retirement. It suggests a good physical, mental, social, and spiritual condition in one package. It is a holistic concept, saying that the sum (wellness) can be greater than all the contributing parts. If you can put all these elements together, you can achieve a good feeling that should be the essence of retirement living.

The intriguing thing about wellness is that you know when you have it and when you don't. When you are well, there is a feeling of vitality and personal confidence. You feel in tune with your environment. When unwell, you feel tired, draggy, and down. Nothing seems right.

The diagram shown above illustrates three major contributing factors to wellness. We will deal with all three in the chapters ahead.

Those who are involved in physical fitness know the benefits it brings. But whatever your exercise patterns may have been, after retirement you must work to maintain the wellness feeling. It is essential to pay more attention to physical exercise, diet, and mental outlook to get the same results as when you were younger. Once you achieve wellness, you enjoy it more. Like the feeling after a refreshing swim, there is nothing else quite like it.

Wellness is not something you should expect less of when you retire. Rather, it is something you can control providing you follow a few basic rules.

Physical exercise is a major source of wellness, but how well informed are you on the value of exercising? You can find out by answering the accompanying true-false questions about exercise.

Regardless of how you scored, you now have some valid information on why exercise is so good for you. Answers are on page 88.

Our Bodies Can Renew Themselves

We sometimes compare our bodies to machines. We say we are "run down" or that we "wear out." It is an unfortunate analogy, because a machine is an inorganic contraption that is incapable of renewing itself. Our bodies, on the other hand, are growing, reproducing, renewing organisms.

Like lubricating and fine-tuning an expensive machine, good body maintenance includes having a rubdown, manicure, or pedicure; but to be effective, it is crucial to go beyond cosmetics. Through regular

PHYSICAL EXERCISE PRETEST

True	False	
_____	_____	1. Chronological age is how long you have lived; functional age is how old your body is.
_____	_____	2. Inactivity ages us.
_____	_____	3. Physical exercise improves muscle strength but does nothing for heart and lung functions or blood pressure.
_____	_____	4. It is possible, through exercise, to set the clock back a few years.
_____	_____	5. After 80 years of age, it is impossible to improve one's longevity through exercise.
_____	_____	6. So far, exercise is the closest thing we have to a successful antiaging prescription.
_____	_____	7. As a stress reliever, exercise is ineffective.
_____	_____	8. Exercise is the best possible tranquilizer.
_____	_____	9. Because exercise releases endorphins, it is useless as an antidepressant.
_____	_____	10. By relaxing the neuromuscular systems through exercise, we respond less to any given stress-producing event.
_____	_____	11. The heart's ability to pump blood declines by about 8 percent each decade in adulthood.
_____	_____	12. It is estimated that roughly 90 percent of seniors do not engage in regular exercise.
_____	_____	13. Fitness cannot be stored.
_____	_____	14. Lung capacity increases as you grow older.
_____	_____	15. Tests show that 3–5 percent of muscle tissue is lost every decade.
_____	_____	16. To keep the same proportion of fat to lean body mass (not the way you look outside but internally), you have to weigh less and less as you grow older.
_____	_____	17. Organic fitness refers to vital organs and limbs; dynamic fitness refers to the efficiency of your heart and lungs.
_____	_____	18. Tiredness increases with greater activity.
_____	_____	19. Age destroys your capacity to exercise.
_____	_____	20. Among seniors, walking is the most popular form of exercise.

Total Correct _____

exercise, we must constantly renew and rejuvenate our bodies. The more our bodies stay active, the longer they will last and the better they will perform.

Physical activity is part of being alive. Without activity, a body will deteriorate. Exercise is not merely a way to control an overweight condition; it also helps digestion, circulation, muscular control, balance, and flexibility. The best news of all is that those who have had the least amount of exercise in the past can benefit the most if they begin a sensible exercise program.

Take Your Choice   Why are more people devoting additional time and attention to exercising? There are many excellent reasons, some of which will be more important to you than others, but all are convincing. Read each of the twelve reasons listed here carefully, and then rank them according to their importance to you. Place the number 1 in the box opposite the reason that is most important to you, the number 2 for the second most important, and so on.

As you make your decisions, keep in mind the credibility of each reason. If you believe a statement is partially true or exaggerated, then give it a lower priority. There is no correct pattern. Your priorities will be uniquely your own.

1. A good physical exercise program will help you transmit a better image to others. You will project a more trim silhouette because exercising helps you stand straighter. You will have what military people call *bearing*. This will enhance your

personal pride and give you more confidence to take charge of your life.

2. Most medical specialists agree that exercise in the right amount and intensity will strengthen your largest and most important muscle—your heart. Consistent, regular exercise—without overdoing it—is the key. Someone who has had a heart attack should rest until the heart has had time to repair itself, and then begin slowly exercising until a stronger heart can be rebuilt. If you have a strong heart, exercising the right way in the right amount will keep it strong.

3. It is generally agreed that exercising contributes quickly to a feeling of wellness. For example, if you do calisthenics, take a brisk walk, jog, or swim for 30 minutes before breakfast, you will enjoy your breakfast more and feel better all day. You will have a better attitude and be more sensitive in your dealings with others. You will achieve more and encounter fewer frustrations. Your day will go better because you have prepared your body to handle it.

4. Many experts claim that consistent exercising of the right kind helps to prevent backaches. If you have suffered the excruciating pain of a back problem, you will probably give this one high priority. Exercise of the right kind will help your back muscles stay stronger and take strain better. Avoid unnecessary awkward or heavy lifting. To protect your back, the more preventive steps you take, including exercise, the better.

5. Exercising contributes to a more healthy-looking image. Those who do not exercise often have a pasty look. Those who exercise have a more vigorous appearance, with more color, better skin tone, and a younger look overall.

6. Some people believe exercising on a regular basis helps them stay mentally alert. They are convinced that a relationship exists between physical well-being and mental capacity. This is consistent with the concept of holistic wellness mentioned earlier. These individuals claim they make better decisions, are more creative, and stay self-motivated because of regular exercise. They say time spent exercising (30 to 60 minutes per day) is more than offset through better performance. Most runners and joggers will give this one high priority.

7. Researchers use the terms *elasticity* and *joint lubrication* to communicate the possibility that exercising can help prevent arthritis or, at least, control its effects. The premise is that the more you use the various parts of your body, the more you will

be able to use them in the future (as long as it is not overdone). There are some exceptions; for example, deep knee bends or holding your hands above your head too long can do more harm than good. The older you are, the higher priority you may give to this one.

8. A reasonable premise is that the more you exercise, the more you will maintain your strength. Muscle provides more strength to the body than fat, and exercising builds muscles. This means you will be able to do more things (playing golf, dancing, walking, driving) longer. People who want to remain active understand the importance of exercise.

9. You may not give this one top priority, but many believe the stronger you remain physically and the more alert you remain mentally, the fewer accidents you will have. Home accidents, like falling in a shower or bathtub, are too common among retirees. Those who exercise regularly, even in modest amounts, are in better shape to avoid such accidents.

10. Combined with the proper diet, exercising can help you lose weight. Exercising replaces fat with muscle. A better balance can be achieved between the two. Excessive weight places additional strain on the heart and joints and has a negative impact on blood pressure. Almost everyone acknowledges that keeping slim has long-term health benefits.

11. Many doctors recommend exercise for patients who complain that they can't sleep. Insomnia can be a major problem. A brisk walk after dinner can help you relax, which in turn will help induce sleep. You can't buy exercise in a bottle, but it is an excellent antidote for insomnia.

12. Retirement does not guarantee a pressure-free existence. There is no way to isolate yourself from financial, health, or other worries. Here again, regular exercise can help. Exercise helps relieve tension and thus promotes serenity, insulating you from the negative effects of pressure. The more stress in your life, the higher priority this reason should receive.

Weaving Exercise into Your Retirement Lifestyle

If you have not been exercising regularly but are convinced you should, you have taken a giant step toward a better retirement. You have made a sound decision.

The first thing to determine is when to exercise (that is, finding the time slot that fits best into your personal lifestyle). Before breakfast? Midmorning? Midafternoon? Just before dinner? Or should you have two daily exercise periods? Study your circumstances and daily routine. Find your best time and stick with it.

If you elect to exercise on your own (without the help of a television or group program), the amount of time is also important. Most experts say exercise should not be less than 30 minutes. If you are starting from scratch, it may take a week or more to build up to 30 minutes. Once you get on track, 30 minutes should be a minimum period.

You might favor a group activity. You could join an organized exercise class, walk with friends, or buy a membership in a commercial club or gym where you have access to special equipment (perhaps even a pool or spa). This may help you define your visits and also provide supervision and group reinforcement to get you started.

These decisions are minor. Whatever fits your lifestyle best is the way to go. Whatever is least painful and most satisfying is the program you will probably stick with the longest.

As you decide how to become more fit, keep these suggestions in mind:

* *Start out slowly.* Give yourself time to reach the performance level (amount of exercise) you desire. You will know when you are there, because you will feel better physically (wellness) and will feel proud for having reached your initial goal. If you decide on a pure exercise regimen, such as calisthenics, work into them (arm exercises, situps, toe touches, etc.) gradually. If you elect to walk or swim, increase by a block or a lap at a time. Give yourself time to achieve results. If you attempt too much too soon, the result can be discouraging. If you have special health problems, be sure to check with your doctor. It is also a good idea to have a complete physical before you begin a fitness program.

* *To help, it must hurt a little.* Although almost any exercise is helpful, some retirees are satisfied with so little that the benefits are insignificant. They never really reach a feeling of wellness and thus are not motivated to continue. Often they underestimate their capacity. Token exercising is not enough. It must tire you a little or you are deluding yourself. When you puff and strain in moderation, the trade-off is the minor temporary discomfort for a great feeling that can stay with you for hours.

* *Do it your way.* It is not the purpose of this chapter to provide a formal pattern of exercise or recommend one routine over another. There are many fine books and articles that can help you. What is important is that you design a workable pattern that will give you personal satisfaction.

Failure to develop a program you are proud to discuss with others means you probably will not stick with it. When we let others know what we are doing, we commit ourselves more because we do not want to admit failure.

* Herman is proud that he walks his 18 holes of golf three times a week. If you give him a chance, he will tell you about it.
* Most of Mrs. Draper's friends are aware that she purchased a bicycle exerciser that she uses regularly while watching her favorite soap opera on television.
* Everyone in Maggie's bridge group knows she enjoys a 40-minute, fast-pace walk each evening with Trudy.
* Bob's family, even the grandchildren, are proud of the fact that he swims 30 laps twice a day in his pool—weather permitting.
* It's no secret that Mrs. Q belongs to a jazzy exercise salon and is proud to be one of the oldest members.

Once you get into a pattern and feel the results, stay in charge. Give this part of your day top priority. To avoid getting out of your routine on trips, develop substitute exercises. If you do, exercise will soon become as much a part of your lifestyle as eating. When this happens, you will probably acknowledge that nothing contributes more to a feeling of wellness that regular exercise.

Summary

Regular physical exercise is a primary contributor to the holistic concept of wellness.

The health benefits that come from sufficient and consistent exercise are impressive.

Each individual must determine the most suitable, effective program to weave into his or her lifestyle.

PROBLEM TO SOLVE   **A Decision for Mrs. Carroll**

Mrs. Carroll is distressed. For almost a year she and two other women have been taking 60-minute walks in their neighborhood. These walks have been special times for her. Not only have they been enjoyable socially, but she has felt better physically since she started. She has lost weight and looks better.

Yesterday, she discovered that her two walking companions, both in their fifties, have joined a new morning exercise class sponsored by the park. A young physical therapist is conducting the class as part of a program scheduled by a local college, and no fee is involved. Both of her friends reluctantly announced that they would not be walking anymore because the class takes too much out of them. They urged Mrs. Carroll to join the class with them.

Mrs. Carroll is hesitant, because everyone wears tight-fitting exercise clothing; she is both modest and embarrassed by her figure. Also, she fears that she can't keep up with the others. Finally, she has heard that walking is ideal for people her age, whereas more strenuous exercise can be dangerous. Since she has never been a physical person, she believes walking is ideal for her and fits her style; group exercising does not.

Her distress comes because she cannot find replacements for her companions, and she feels unsafe walking alone. She has become, however, a strong believer in physical activity and does not want to give up walking.

What solution would you suggest for Mrs. Carroll? Compare your thoughts with those of the author in Appedix C.

SELF-QUIZ

True	False	
_____	_____	1. Retirees benefit less from physical exercise.
_____	_____	2. Exercise is the closest thing to an antiaging prescription available.
_____	_____	3. Benefits from regular physical exercise are both short and long term.
_____	_____	4. Many retirees settle for a form of "token" exercise.
_____	_____	5. You can lead new retirees to a suitable exercise program, but most won't accept it.

(Answers in Appendix C.)

10

Playing the Nutrition Game

What contemptible scoundrel stole the cork from my lunch?
W. C. Fields

As we approach retirement, our dietary needs change. We need less food and we need different foods. Some foods we should eliminate altogether—easy to say, hard to do.

Is a new, streamlined diet, like a new exercise program, essential to a better retirement? The answer is yes. Regardless of your dietary habits in the past, the challenge to attain a balanced diet takes on a new dimension as you age.

This chapter will not make you an expert on nutrition. To accomplish that, you would need to read highly technical books or attend classes taught by professionals. Instead, this chapter provides a game that will help you discover how good or poor your current eating habits are.

The game is self-scoring. It will help you learn dietary changes that are good for you. You can compare your score with friends or spouse.

This game may lead you to a better diet, but it will not provide or advocate one. If you want a prescribed diet, you should look elsewhere.

Before you start, it is important to find out how much you already know about some of the recognized facts concerning nutrition. Answer the following questions and score yourself. The answers appear at the end of the test. Once you complete these questions, you will be in a better position to play the game.

Whatever your score on the pretest (you were not expected to know most of the answers), it is important to remember that the study of nutrition is complex. New things are discovered each day. Some individuals seem to go overboard on nutrition and pick up all the latest diet fads. Others refuse to deal with the subject at all. You must decide what priority you intend to give dietary matters. There is no argument that diet is a major contributor to wellness.

NUTRITION PRETEST

True	False	
_____	_____	1. Water constitutes about one-third of body weight.
_____	_____	2. Fats are digested faster than other nutrients.
_____	_____	3. Nutritionists suggest that between the ages of 55 and 65, calories should be reduced by 5 percent; between the ages of 65 and 75, 5 percent; and age 75 and older, another 7 percent.
_____	_____	4. A calorie is a unit used to measure the energy factor in different foods; vitamins are organic substances; minerals are substances that are neither vegetable nor animal.
_____	_____	5. Excessive use of sugar is a major cause of obesity.
_____	_____	6. Osteoporosis is a thinning of the bones due to a loss of calcium.
_____	_____	7. The nutritive process (digestion) works better at night when you are asleep.
_____	_____	8. Very large meals can be stressful on the heart.

True	False	
_____	_____	9. Water is not one of the six major nutrients.
_____	_____	10. Fiber is a form of carbohydrate that in itself is not digestible by humans and is therefore useless.
_____	_____	11. There is currently a rebirth of nutrition education in Canada.
_____	_____	12. Yogurt, apricots, and wheat germ are scientifically classified as "youth elixers."
_____	_____	13. Long-lived people around the world generally have a lower caloric intake.
_____	_____	14. Fortunately, diet has nothing to do with the fact that 60 percent of older persons have dentures.
_____	_____	15. There is no evidence that nutritional deficiencies lead to decreased learning, performance, depression, disorientation, fatigue, general malaise, apathy, and headaches.
_____	_____	16. RDA stands for Recommended Daily Allowance.
_____	_____	17. A potassium deficiency can easily be corrected by eating a banana every day.
_____	_____	18. In 1970 it was estimated that 10% of seniors were malnourished.
_____	_____	19. The calories provided by sugar are loaded with vital vitamins and minerals.
_____	_____	20. When it comes to nutrition, more is not always better.

Total Correct _____

Answers: (1) F (water constitutes about two-thirds of body weight); (2) F (fats are digested more slowly and, as a result, keep us from getting hungry again so quickly); (3) T; (4) T; (5) T; (6) T; (7) F (it works better when we are active); (8) T; (9) F (water is essential for digestion, circulation, and other vital processes; we should drink more of it); (10) F (fiber is not digestible by humans, but it is vital to the elimination process); (11) T; (12) F (no single food or combination of foods can truly be called "youth elixers"); (13) T (there is ample research on this); (14) F (there is a direct relationship between diet and the condition of one's teeth); (15) F (there is at least limited evidence); (16) T; (17) T; (18) F (the estimate was 40%); (19) F (they are empty); (20) T.

The Nutrition Game's objective is to get the highest possible score. The maximum of 100 is theoretically possible but highly unlikely since you are competing only with yourself, and complete honesty is the only way to measure the adequacy of your present program. It is a fact, however, that if you have been paying attention to your diet, you are already something of an expert on nutrition.

The game is based on the premise that it is best for the body to receive all nutrients through food intake rather than supplements. This is not a criticism of vitamin supplements; it simply places emphasis on the selection of the right foods.

It's time to play!

First, read each of the statements carefully. Next, decide which of the three boxes to check. If you currently meet the highest standard stated, check the top box. If you are closer to the second standard, check the middle box. If you do not meet either standard, check the lowest box and assign your own score. Figure your total score after completing the game.

NUTRITION GAME[*]

1. It is generally accepted that sodium (salt) should be restricted in our diets. Doctors normally limit salt consumption in cases of heart disease, kidney disease, hypertension (high blood pressure), and edema. An average person gets 15 to 20 milligrams of sodium per day—or almost 10 times more than required. We do need sodium in limited amounts because it helps maintain water balance, but there is usually enough in the food we eat. One possibility of deficiency could come from excessive perspiration in extremely hot weather. Under such conditions, moderate replacement may be necessary. You can learn to enjoy unsalted flavors and eliminate the need for a salt shaker.

I'm eliminating salt.

My only sodium intake comes from that naturally occurring in foods. I never use salt in cooking. I never use a salt shaker at the table. I read food labels and refuse to buy food with excessive sodium content.

Check one

☐

7 points

---

[*]This game has been constructed on the basis of material found in current nutrition books and pamphlets. All statements are general in nature and no attempt has been made to fully verify or document them or to make the inventory a quasi-scientific instrument. It is nothing more than an accumulation of some broadly acceptable nutritional ideas in a form that readers should find challenging.

I have my salt intake under partial control. If I add salt when cooking or eating, I do it lightly. I also limit my consumption of high-sodium snacks.

4 points

I love salt. I have not restricted my use of it in any way.

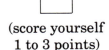

(score yourself 1 to 3 points)

2. Calcium is critical to our diet as we grow older. It may be too late for it to do much for our teeth, but we should do what we can to maintain strong bones. If you don't get enough calcium, the body secretes a hormone that causes the needed calcium to be taken from your bones. This process, called *demineralization,* causes bones to become porous. The medical word for this is *osteoporosis.*

I'm getting my calcium.

The best sources of calcium are milk products. Most other foods contribute only small amounts. If you want to meet recommended daily calcium needs (800 milligrams), you need the equivalent of 2½ cups of milk (whole, skimmed, or buttermilk) per day. One cup of yogurt or cottage cheese is the equivalent of one cup of milk. If, for other reasons, you are trying to stay away from dairy products, you can eat large amounts of green, leafy vegetables, dried beans, and peas or use calcium-supplemented soybean milk. Sardines provide calcium if the bones are eaten.

Check one

I am extremely aware that I need calcium, and I weave it into my diet one way or another every day.

6 points

I am aware of my calcium needs, and I am making a limited attempt to get enough into my diet.

4 points

I have, as yet, made no concerted effort to include calcium in my diet nor do I use a supplement.

(score yourself 1 to 3 points)

Pass the sugar please.

3. Sugar, like salt, is more a habit than a necessity. The only contribution made by sugar is taste and calories. Certain foods, like ice cream, would not be tasty without sugar. Pancakes, without syrup, would probably not be worth the effort. Sugar is basically a dietary luxury.

Much of the sugar we consume is added to processed food products. So to really cut back, it's best to avoid processed foods and get natural sugar from fruits and vegetables. The best way to avoid sugar is to resist candy, ice cream, cakes, cookies, and regular soft drinks. Also, you should be careful and select canned fruits and boxed cereals without sugar.

Check one

My entire sugar intake comes from natural products and, on a limited basis, from processed foods.

☐

6 points

I get my sugar calories (energy) mostly from natural foods, processed foods, and an occasional sweet treat.

☐

4 points

I do nothing special to keep my sugar intake under control.

☐

(score yourself 1 to 3 points)

I'm happy the way I am.

4. One of the best reasons for taking this game seriously is to help control your weight. Watching your food intake will help you avoid crash programs that provide a short-term weight loss but can have serious side effects. As we get older, we need all the energy we can get, but we should not pay an exorbitant price for it. Energy can be derived from fats, carbohydrates, and proteins. Although fat provides more than twice as much energy as carbohydrates or proteins, adding one pound to your weight means it takes 3,500 fewer calories to get it off.

The problem comes down to balanced fat intake. The greater your ingestion of fat, the more you need exercise to maintain your weight.

To get where you should be may require action in both directions. The choice is yours.

Check one

I have achieved an ideal balance between my calorie intake and exercise. My current weight is at the proper level.

8 points

I'm doing better, but I fluctuate. I eat too much, and then I cut back to try to get rid of the excess through more exercise. I'm within reach of a good balance, but I'm not sure I'll ever get there.

5 points

I'm seriously out of balance, and I doubt if I can do much about it. I'm totally discouraged.

(score yourself 1 to 4 points)

5. You are aware when you shop that you have a choice of buying white bread or a variety of whole-grain breads that have rich, brown colors and a rougher texture. Wheat, rice, corn, rye, and barley are seeds of grasses. Each seed has a hull, bran layer, starchy layer, and germ. A whole-grain cereal or bread contains everything but the hull. This is what you want. In white bread, the nutritious, health-giving parts (bran layer, starchy layer, and germ) are refined out.

Of course, some bakeries put some of these goodies back through enrichment. Most experts feel, however, that it's better to have all these vitamins and minerals naturally rather than through enrichment. What is put back, they say, is not always what is taken out.

Only the whole grain for me.

Check one

I insist on the whole grain (less hull) being present in all bread, cereal, and other flour products I purchase. If the whole grain is not present, I don't buy it.

6 points

I've heard this before.

I purchase and use products with the whole grain when it is convenient. I violate the principle now and then, especially with bakery products.

4 points

I prefer refined, white bread and regular bakery items and make no effort to get the whole grain in such products. I don't bother checking whether or not baked goods have been enriched.

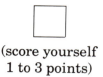

(score yourself 1 to 3 points)

6. Some say that four or five small, nutritional meals per day are better than two or three larger ones—especially if one is a big meal at the end of the day. The reasoning is that the digestive and assimilation process works better with more frequent but smaller amounts. The smaller meals, however, should not be junk food. Instead, good snacks should include fresh fruit, raisins, raw carrots, celery sticks, and so forth.

The idea is to discipline yourself away from bad snacks. The best solution is not to buy them in the first place, but it also means refusing them politely when they are offered at parties or other social events.

If you have occasional snacks, make sure they are coordinated with your other meals so you don't consume excess calories.

Check one

The only snacks I eat are highly nutritional and carefully integrated into my planned diet.

10 points

I generally avoid snacks except under certain situations like parties and an occasional treat at home.

6 points

Snacking is part of my lifestyle.

(score yourself 1 to 5 points)

Two quarts every day?

7. When the weather is hot or when we exert ourselves, we become aware of our need for water. Thirst tells us we need more. Sometimes this process continues even though we may not be aware of it. That is a danger called *dehydration*. To prevent dehydration, we must ensure that our bodies receive enough water each day—not just when we feel thirsty. We need about two quarts of fluids each day to replace the water we lose. We get this fluid from liquids we drink, foods we eat, and recycled water in our bodies.

If insufficient fluid is taken in, thirst will trigger a hormonal action causing the kidneys to save water by making our urine more concentrated. If we drink more fluid that we need, the opposite happens—kidneys produce a less-concentrated urine.

Water is good for our bodies. It is a lubricant for our joints as well as a regulator of body temperature. Maintaining the right balance of water within our system is critically important. This means getting enough fluids into our bodies every day through what we eat and drink (two quarts) whether or not we think we need it.

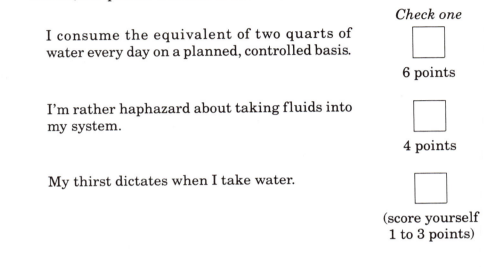

Check one

I consume the equivalent of two quarts of water every day on a planned, controlled basis. ☐

6 points

I'm rather haphazard about taking fluids into my system. ☐

4 points

My thirst dictates when I take water. ☐

(score yourself 1 to 3 points)

I'm never constipated.

8. If you read nutritional literature, you know that experts tend to agree that every diet should have sufficient fiber for good health. Because fiber can absorb many times its own weight in water, its major benefit is that it creates large, soft stools that stimulate the colon naturally, thus eliminating constipation. Some researchers maintain there is good evidence that a fiber-depleted diet will increase the incidence of certain diseases.

The best way to ensure that you are getting sufficient fiber in your diet is to eat plenty of plant fibers. This means constantly having a variety of vegetables—consuming many of them raw—and fresh fruits, which seasonally come on the market at a reasonable price. This takes planning.

Perhaps the best substitute, if fruits and vegetables are not readily available, is to consume bran on a regular, deliberate basis. Bran, the outside husk of wheat, can be purchased at most supermarkets and consumed as a cereal.

Check one

I keep myself regular (free of constipation) through daily consumption of a variety of vegetables and fruits. Natural fibers are the best.

5 points

I find it necessary to supplement fresh fruits and vegetables with bran.

3 points

I use other methods to relieve my problems with constipation.

(score yourself
1 or 2 points)

9. There is limited evidence that moderate use of alcohol might have some advantages. For example, it may promote relaxation and lessen symptoms of stress. But the disadvantages greatly outweigh any advantages, especially when alcohol is used in excess. These disadvantages include:

* Consumed before a meal, even a moderate amount of alcohol tends to stimulate the appetite and cause overeating.

* Alcoholic beverages are high in calories and low in nutrients; thus drinking can rob one of needed nutrients.

* Excessive, chronic drinking promotes undereating, because it acts as an appetite depressant and throws a diet out of balance.

* Alcohol is toxic to the liver, stomach, pancreas, and intestines, causing them to act less efficiently in digesting, absorbing, and metabolizing nutrients.

* Taken in combination with certain other drugs, alcohol can cause life-threatening reactions.

Check one

I abstain completely or limit myself to one drink on social occasions.

7 points

Except when I go to parties, I limit my consumption to no more than two drinks per day.

5 points

I enjoy drinking. It is part of my lifestyle, and I do not normally limit myself to a specific number of drinks per day.

(score yourself
1 to 4 points)

*Life must have some
pleasures.*

10. It is always a temptation to discard a diet when eating out. After all, there should be exceptions to everything, especially diets. Eating out is fun, especially if it doesn't happen often. But some folks overdo it to the point where they seriously cripple their diets and damage themselves needlessly. Some can overdo it at potluck dinners. Others lose all resistance in cafeterias. Those who eat out often may be unable to diet because it takes more self-discipline than they can muster.

Other factors add to the problem. Starchy foods on menus are often less expensive. "Specials" are often tempting, but may not fit the diet. And a cocktail ahead of time can cause one to make food choices with wild abandon.

Cafeterias have the advantage of offering a wide selection that permits a person to adhere to his or her diet. But it is essential to have self-discipline as an appetizer while standing in line.

I'm eating out tonight.

Check one

When I eat out, I choose my food carefully and, as far as possible, stick with my diet. I still have fun, however.

☐ 5 points

I don't go totally overboard, but I frequently violate my diet when I eat out.

☐ 2 points

I relax and don't worry about diet at all when I eat away from home.

☐ 1 point

11. Although all diets are debated, most agree that a balance between the four basic food groups is important. A typical recommendation might be:

I'm in a nutrition rut.

Milk group: Equivalent of two glasses per day, preferably nonfat milk.

Meat group: Two 4-ounce servings per day. Fish and poultry highly recommended. No more than three eggs per week. Avoid fatty meats.

Fruit-vegetable group: Equivalent of four ½-cup servings per day. Dark green or deep yellow vegetables every other day. Citrus—½ cup three times per week. Fruit often.

Bread-cereal group: Three to four servings per day. A serving is one slice of bread or 1/2 cup of cereal—whole grain preferred.

It requires dedication and planning to have a balanced diet day after day.

Check one

I plan and control a balanced diet for myself (and spouse) using all four basic food groups as suggested.

8 points

My diet is somewhat planned and balanced but not carefully controlled.

4 points

I have some awareness but no actual planning. I just let it happen.

☐

(score yourself 1 to 3 points)

12. Here are two factors to consider if you want the best possible diet:

* The way food is cooked is a part of the nutrition game. Depending on the cooking method, a percentage of any nutrient will be lost. When vegetables are boiled in water, vitamins disappear quickly. Much of their mineral content is also lost unless the water in which they were boiled is consumed.

* A portion of fruits and vegetables should be consumed raw. Research in this area indicates that pectin and bioflavonoids, natural parts of most fruits, will lower blood levels of cholesterol more effectively than drugs. Both of these elements are found abundantly in unpeeled apples. There are many other positive reasons for eating some fruits and vegetables raw.

To ensure good nutrition, don't overcook vegetables, and eat plenty of raw fruit and vegetables. You may also consider steaming vegetables, which saves most of the nutrients.

Check one

I adjust my diet carefully by eating some raw fruits and vegetables. When I do cook them, I don't overcook. I try to preserve as many of the natural nutrients as possible.

☐

8 points

I know about overcooking and the need to eat certain fruits and vegetables raw, but I often don't bother.

4 points

I'm not going to change my traditional cooking habits. I'm not interested in controlling how much raw fruit and vegetables I eat. If it happens, it happens.

score yourself
1 to 3 points

13. Most individuals who are serious about improving their diet recognize the enemies of good nutrition—those subtle forces that get you off the nutrition track. A few of these factors include:

Inflation: The high cost of foods can push people into poor diets. With planning, it is possible to have good diets on a tight budget.

Affluence: At the other end of the spectrum are those who have money to eat out a lot and lose control of a good diet because of the availability of rich food.

Impluse buying: Supermarkets are clever in the way they make food appealing. Also, they sometimes offer price incentives to get us off our diets.

Advertising: Retirees watch more television and have time to read newspapers more thoroughly, As a result, advertising can suggest products to them which can upset their diets.

Labels: Labeling can be confusing and misleading.

A good diet on my income?

Check one

I am aware of the many forces at work to prevent me from having the best possible diet. I concentrate on sticking with my diet plan.

8 points

I often permit forces, including my own apathy, to keep me from having the diet I really want.

4 points

Dieting is not for me. Forget it!

score yourself
1 to 3 points

I supplement everything!

14. The best way to get all nutrients in proper balance is to eat the right foods in the right amounts—without supplements. Still, getting the nutrients you need through supplements is better than not getting them at all. Many people use supplements, sometimes under the direction of their doctor, but usually just using their judgement. It can be a complex undertaking to get the right amounts of vitamins and minerals, which is why many people feel protected by taking an all-purpose vitamin whether necessary or not.

There are two way to gain maximum points in the last segment of this game.

Check one

First, if you honestly feel you are in such good control of your diet—careful selection, wide variety, suitable amounts—that it is not necessary to take any food supplements, check this box. This means you really work at the nutrition game.

The second way to check this box is to do an excellent job with your diet and follow a program. You exercise control with natural foods and back that effort with an intelligent supplement program.

10 points

If you do an average or fair job with your natural diet (only partially planned) but protect yourself with a well-planned supplement program, check this box.

7 points

If you are currently doing a below-average job with your natural diet and do not have a supplement program, check this box.

score yourself
1 to 6 points

Total Score _____

How did you do in the Nutrition Game? If you achieved a score of 80 or above, you are a winner. You have put together some of the basic elements of good nutrition and really have your diet under control. If you scored between 50 and 80, you still win because you are

---

TARGET EXERCISE

Write the score you would like to achieve when playing the Nutrition Game again in 30 days: _____.

List specific areas—from the 14 possibilities—where you intend to make improvements. For example, you might improve your score by cutting down or eliminating salt.

1.

2.

3.

4.

5.

6.

TAPE THIS EXERCISE TO YOUR REFRIGERATOR DOOR

---

measurably above average. You can feel good about your program, but you can still improve. If you scored below 50, you should take a closer look at your diet, read some additional literature, and complete the above exercise.

Summary

Our nutritional needs change as we grow older.

Nutrition is a major, integral part of any health program.

The Nutrition Game is a nonscientific exercise designed to help players focus on areas of needed improvement.

PROBLEM TO SOLVE **Less Is Better**

The "arrangement" between Opal and Ronald began two years ago. They fell in love soon after Opal moved into her mobile-home park, but they have not married. Ronald has proposed marriage, but Opal insists it is not necessary and they should keep separate homes even though both are restricted financially.

Ronald eats most of his meals at Opal's. Part of their arrangement is that he pays for the food. It was his idea, and he is happy to do it, but a problem has surfaced. Opal overbuys and overcooks. Ronald hates to complain because she is an excellent cook. He often eats more than he should. The cost of food is straining his budget, and he has had to adjust his spending in other areas. There is no money to do extra things for Opal. He is even thinking about selling his car. The ideal solution, in Ronald's mind, would be to marry, live in one home, spend less on food, and do more together.

A few months ago he tried to show her how they could eat well for less, but they wound up having one of their few arguments. Ronald is afraid to risk another confrontation because he does not want to lose her.

Ronald feels that Opal demonstrates her love for him through her meals. He also knows her buying and cooking habits came from her mother. She seldom bothers to check prices when she shops, and she always buys top-quality food in larger amounts than are necessary. Shopping is fun for Opal, and the evening meal is the highlight of her day.

Recently Ronald received an unexpected bill that upset him. After lying awake worrying, he decided he must again talk to Opal and somehow convince her that "less is better."

What approach would you suggest for Ronald? Keep in mind that the last thing Ronald wants to do is to upset the "arrangement." Compare your thoughts with those of the author in Appendix C.

SELF-QUIZ

True   *False*

_____   _____   1. To improve one's diet, it is necessary to become a nutrition expert.

_____   _____   2. Retirees rate substantially above other age groups when it comes to nutritional control.

_____   _____   3. Those with reduced incomes (near or below poverty levels) are automatically prevented from having good diets.

_____   _____   4. Water and alcohol consumption are not factors in a good diet.

_____   _____   5. Physical exercise is more important than a good diet.

(Answers in Appendix C.)

11

Mental Health and Down Periods

At a certain age some people's minds close up; they live on their intellectual fat.
William Lyon Phelps

A retired friend of mine believes mental exercise is as important as physical exercise. Not long ago, following a game of golf, we were philosophizing in the lounge when he pointed to his temple and said: "I'm as concerned about keeping things active up here as keeping the rest of my body active. I can't afford to put my body in a rocking chair or my mind on a shelf."

Bravo!

My friend is saying that we must give mental health the same emphasis that we give physical exercise and diet. It is also a major part of the wellness concept.

There are many misunderstandings about mental capacity and aging. Claims are often made that we will experience a substantial decline as we age. This is not true and need not happen. We may

111

become a little slower, but we can learn as well as ever, and the more we use our mental faculties the longer we will keep them.

One secret is to keep our minds in gear by keeping them tuned to special interests.

Mrs. Holcomb   Mrs. Holcomb has an inquisitive, volatile mind. Learning anything new excites her. She was the first in her bridge group to see *Star Wars* and to read Alvin Toffler's *Third Wave,* and she was the only one to attend a local forum entitled "The Age of Computers." She explains her attitude this way: "Maybe it's simply curiosity, but I like to stretch my mind the same way I exercise my body. For example, I had a mental block against learning the metric system. I even resented that it was being pushed on us by others. Then I realized I was setting up barriers to protect my mind instead of using it."

Mr. Andrews   Mr. Andrews uses his mind in a different way. Rather than direct it into abstract areas, he studies do-it-yourself trade and mechanical magazines and applies what he learns. Mr. Andrews worked for more than 30 years as an accountant for a manufacturing concern. He never had sufficient time to do "fix-it" work. Now, following his retirement, he has a real campaign going. He says: "I've never come close to being an intellectual, but I've always enjoyed doing things with my hands. Once I got involved, I discovered I could accomplish more than I believed possible. The first thing I built was a cabinet from a kit. It turned out fine and gave me confidence to attempt more complex projects. Now I'm developing a range of skills, including tuning my own car."

I'm up.

I'm down.

Mr. and Mrs. Jay

Mr. and Mrs. Jay refer to retirement as "culture catch-up time." Mr. Jay was always intrigued with photography. His new equipment (a retirement gift to himself) and a darkroom he built, along with time, are allowing him to master his new art. Mrs. Jay's childhood dream was to be a ballet dancer. She now has time to pursue other areas of art as the newly elected president of the local art association.

The Jays attend plays, belong to the philharmonic association, and plan their travel around artistic and cultural events.

Mr. Jay proclaims: "What a great time of life to be able to fulfill creative needs that we had to forgo earlier. Not only are we getting satisfaction from our adventures, we are also keeping our minds active."

Down Periods Can Increase After Retirement

Down periods are usually short in duration. They often occur when problems accumulate to the point where we are pulled into a negative mood. We do not always know why this happens. Suddenly we sense something is wrong. We begin to feel tired, and nothing we do is easy. Our focus is more negative than positive. We are out of tune with our environment, and we have temporarily lost control.

It is not a new feeling. Most people have had bouts with down periods throughout life. The better these periods have been handled in the past, the better they will probably be handled during retirement. But despite any success in the past, it is essential to take charge of down periods once you retire. Otherwise they have the potential of becoming more frequent, deeper, and longer lasting.

There are reasons for this. After retirement you travel a more uncharted road. The way you deal with down periods is a key to a better retirement. You need to work at forestalling down times as much as possible. If this fails, you must actively work at climbing out of the rut. You want as few down periods as possible, because you didn't spend all that time working hard to be in the "pits."

The more you keep your mind occupied with special interests and intellectual pursuits the better, but everyone has occasional down periods that must be dealt with to maintain good mental health.

A Practical Approach to Down Periods

Molly and Ethel are having their daily telephone conversation. They have finished breakfast and are trying to adjust to the new day. After a few minutes, Molly says: "Ethel, I can tell I'm going to be out of sorts today. Let's take the bus to the shopping center and have lunch." Ethel replies: "Good idea! I'm feeling a little low myself. I'll meet you at the bus stop in 20 minutes."

Molly and Ethel are anticipating a down period. By altering their normal daily routine, they are trying to forestall it. Good move!

A few days later Molly talks to Ethel again and tells her: "I've been in a blue mood for days. I haven't mentioned it because I thought I could make it back on my own. Nothing is working, though. If I fix lunch, will you come by and help get me out of this mood?"

This time Molly was unable to forestall a down period, but at least she is not reluctant to ask for help.

Several months later, after trying to get Molly out of a long down period, Ethel counsels her: "Molly, our old techniques are not working. I'm discouraged and so are you. Maybe we need help from another source. I've talked to our priest, and he has offered to see us this afternoon. He thinks he can help. I think it's time to take this step. A short down period is one thing, but a long-term depression is serious. We've got to do something to protect your mental health."

Another smart move!

Both Molly and Ethel are to be congratulated, especially Ethel for recognizing that Molly's problem was sufficiently serious to get professional help. All of us should have such loyal, concerned, perceptive friends.

Down periods are common for people of all ages. Sometimes these escalate into serious mental-health problems. Clues to this escalation include: decreased appetite, insomnia, loss of interest in things normally pleasurable, chronic tiredness, and feeling inadequate. These indicators could be a sign that professional help is needed. Most of the time, with the help of a good friend, we can pull ourselves out. This should be our goal.

The Price Can Be Higher After Retirement

The biggest danger is that a succession of down periods will lead to serious depression. Professional help will then be required to pull you back. But there are other dangers. You are not as effective during such periods. You may do things you regret later. You tend to make more mistakes because your behavioral characteristics match your mood. Your behavior can tax the understanding of your friends and relatives, who make efforts to cheer you up because they care. But if you fail to respond, they may feel they have let you down. What might eventually happen is that they may look for excuses not to see you. Your down periods can chase away the people you care about the most, just when you need them more than ever. Molly was fortunate to have Ethel. You or I might not be so lucky.

Some People Prolong Their Down Periods

Just as there are ways to control down periods, there are also ways to deepen them. If you give in to a depressed mood instead of fighting it, the descent becomes steeper. Begin feeling sorry for yourself, and your self-pity will grease the slide. Another way to make the hole deeper is to engage in long periods of self-reflection and introspection. Many call this brooding. Finally, you can extend the period further by convincing yourself there is a certain pleasure to being down. This masochistic tendency can keep you depressed long after you should be. The longer you stay down, the more likely you will need professional help to get out.

Down Periods Versus Serious Depressions

A down period is psychological in nature. To a large extent you can learn to handle it yourself. Your moods may be a little like a roller coaster, except you are in charge. You have control. You know it, and so do your friends.

A depression is a deeper psychological problem. Often mental illness occurs when you lose control. You can see the light, but you feel powerless to reach it. You know something is wrong, and so do your friends and family. The symptoms of a serious depression are often recognizable even to a lay person.

Most of us can deal with down periods. Depressions, however, often require the help of a psychologist, psychiatrist, counselor, or related professional. We nonprofessionals must learn to seek and accept help when we cannot pull ourselves out. We must also help relatives and friends locate such professionals when necessary.

When to Seek Professional Help

There are many people—ministers, doctors, social workers, senior-center advisers, counselors, perceptive friends, relatives—who can either help you themselves or refer you to help. You can also find assistance by calling your local hospital or mental-health center. Simply ask for help.

How do you know when to do this?

The following checklist will help you measure the depth of a down period. If you place a mark in more than three squares, you probably need to take action.

- ☐ My down periods are more frequent, deeper, and longer lasting.
- ☐ Things I used to do to pull myself out of down periods no longer work.
- ☐ My last down period was the most severe that I have ever had.
- ☐ I feel tired much of the time.
- ☐ I'm not sleeping as well as I used to.
- ☐ I spend less and less time making myself presentable.
- ☐ Nothing gives me much pleasure any more.
- ☐ It's increasingly difficult to leave home.

☐ I have lost control over keeping my home or room neat and orderly.

☐ I am resorting more and more to alcohol.

Forestalling Down Periods Through a Change of Tempo

The best way to forestall a down period is to prevent it in the first place. It means anticipating what might happen and taking action to ensure that it doesn't. This usually means changing your tempo. Think of a pilot approaching a storm. That pilot needs to have a radar scanning for approaching storms. Like the pilot, sometimes we can sense a stormy period on the horizon. When this happens, we should take diversionary action.

Ginny's Danger Signals

Ginny seems to have her own radar for anticipating and avoiding down periods. Here is how she expresses it: "I get these little signals that a mood change is coming—like a danger sign on a mountain road. Sometimes I ignore them, and suddenly I'm in a down period that takes a major effort to escape. When I do react to the signals, however, I try to do something silly. I call on my sense of humor. It doesn't always work; but if I can eliminate any down period, it is worthwhile."

Dan's Diversion

Dan has learned to keep his negative moods to a minimum. He does this through physical exercise when he senses one coming. His explanation? "I've learned that my moods follow peaks of high concentration. For example, if I am on a special project for three or four days, I'm in a danger zone. I seem to run out of steam or patience or something, and down I go. When this happens, I do something to relieve the tension. A walk or swim or round of golf will usually do the trick. If I don't take this action, however, I wind up in a down period every time."

The Replacement Theory

Although keeping busy with special interests can be an excellent way to forestall or eliminate negative moods, sometimes these activities can also trigger slumps. When this happens, something called the "Replacement Theory" can work. This theory advises the replacement of one activity with another.

Without knowing it, you may be doing something on a regular basis that pulls you down instead of building you up. Examples could be visiting a negative friend or relative regularly (sense of duty), belonging to the wrong group, or even engaging in a pleasurable activity for too long without a break.

Mrs. N's Visits

Mrs. N visits her Aunt Hazel, 89, on a weekly basis. After each visit, she has a down period because Aunt Hazel demeans and criticizes her. Solution: Visit Aunt Hazel once a month instead of once a week and tell her why.

Helen's Ups

Helen, an accomplished artist, discovered that she does extremely well on Monday and Tuesday, but her concentration starts to ebb on Wednesday. Apparently her creativity is high after a weekend of relaxation, but after two days it reaches a point of diminishing returns. Solution: Anticipate the down period by doing something else on Wednesday.

Felipe's Downs

Felipe has been a member of a fraternal organization for more than 20 years, but now meetings put him into a dark mood. Solution: Replace this activity with another.

Sylvia's Rut

Sylvia has belonged to a bridge group for 10 years. Recently, she has had to force herself to attend. A non-bridge-playing friend has been asking her to learn to play golf, and it sounds like fun. Solution: Replace bridge with golf.

Down Times You Can Anticipate

Many people discover that certain times during the year bring on difficult moods. Christmas, a joyous time for most, may have the opposite effect on others. One way to combat such periods is to come up with a replacement. For example, if holidays at home depress you, plan a vacation or visit. Replace the environment that pulls you down. This way you take action before it takes you.

Eloise's Solution

Eloise lost her husband seven years ago. Her friends have been complimentary about the way she has adjusted. What these friends don't know is that Eloise has worked out a system to protect herself. During the first year, she discovered that she got down during weekends. Also, Easter hit her hard (it was near this holiday that she lost her husband). Christmas was traumatic because she was alone. To eliminate these periods, she deliberately planned activities during the weekend such as church, shopping, visiting friends, entertaining in her home, and so on. At Easter, she took a bus to see her sister. At Christmas, Eloise volunteered time to a local charity that repaired toys. She called her plan "my mood elimination system." Instead of permitting traumatic periods to pull her down, she took charge.

Other Considerations

As you deal with down periods in the future, keep the following considerations in mind:

* Physical exercise may be an excellent antidote.
* The more you learn to anticipate down periods (and know their causes), the more successful you will be at preventing them.

* To protect your mental health, you must sometimes insulate yourself against negative factors over which you have no control.

* You should avoid environments or groups that drag you into negative moods.

* Sometimes staying with a single activity too long can initiate a down period.

* A diversification of activities may be your best insurance against down periods.

* Having a special friend or confidant is extremely important.

ACTION EXERCISE You have control over most of your moods. If something triggers a feeling of depression, there is probably a counteraction you can take to eliminate or neutralize it in the future. This exercise is designed to help you pinpoint factors and then help you decide what action you can take. Keep in mind that any improvement is worthwhile. If you eliminate a single down period, you have accomplished a great deal.

To complete the exercise, follow these four steps:

(1) Place a sheet of paper over the author's suggested action steps in the column on the right. Do this now.

(2) Go down the list (column on left) and check those causes you feel may trigger a down period.

(3) Write the action you feel will eliminate or reduce it on your paper. Confine yourself to a single action response that can be expressed in one sentence.

(4) Remove the paper and compare your answer with that of the author.

As you complete the exercise, remember the suggestions already made in this chapter. The suggested answer may match your response, or it may offer another direction for you to take. The important thing, of course, is for you to recognize the causes of your personal down periods and take action.

Twenty-two factors are listed. The more you check, the more down periods you are susceptible to, and the more important the exercise may be.

Check those that apply to you	Causes of Down Periods	Action I can take in the future (Cover author's suggestions)
☐	1. I often get the holiday blues; Christmas is worst of all.	Plan a different activity before the holiday arrives.
☐	2. My physical condition causes me to occasionally feel sorry for myself.	Visit someone worse off physically than yourself.
☐	3. Rather than looking forward to weekends, I dread them.	Increase your activity schedule.
☐	4. I feel guilty over something in the past.	Reduce the impact of guilt by talking with a confidant.
☐	5. I have an unhappy relationship with someone close to me.	Initiate an open, two-way communication session with the person in an honest attempt to solve the problem.
☐	6. I am depressed when I spend too much time alone.	Force yourself to make contact with others.
☐	7. I fear the future and the changes it may bring.	Start living one day at a time.
☐	8. Winter depresses me.	Change your winter lifestyle through a new activity schedule.
☐	9. Not having a plan when I wake up creates lethargy.	Write out a daily schedule before you go to bed each night.
☐	10. I have a negative friend who makes me negative.	Protect yourself by seeing this individual less frequently.
☐	11. I can't get over the loss of a significant person in my life.	Increase activities to shorten your bereavement period.
☐	12. I can't put my finger on the causes of my down days.	Keep busy until you can; discuss your feelings with a friend.
☐	13. My financial situation causes undue worry.	See a financial adviser.
☐	14. I live in fear of being robbed or harmed physically.	If you live alone, invite the police to inspect your home and make suggestions about security.
☐	15. The world is in such a mess it puts me into negative moods.	Restrict the time you watch television news and read newspapers.

☐ 16. I'm okay during the day, but being alone at night is a problem.

Consider a pet to keep you company.

☐ 17. I frequently feel nobody loves me any more.

Make a greater effort to openly express your love to others.

☐ 18. My neighborhood has deteriorated to such a point that I get discouraged.

Do something nice for your neighbors to gain their support or change locations.

☐ 19. I feel like a failure when I don't reach my goals.

Have fewer goals or make them more realistic.

☐ 20. When I feel lethargic, I don't cope well.

Get more physical exercise.

☐ 21. I'm discouraged about my image.

Do something dramatic like getting a new hair style, losing weight, wearing your best clothes.

☐ 22. I've lost control over my ability to stay out of down periods; I am almost always depressed.

Seek professional help.

Some people, even after reading this chapter, will close their eyes to their mood swings. By refusing to take positive action, these individuals suffer needlessly. Others—those who try to control their down periods—put more quality and style into their retirement years.

Summary   The more your body and mind are exercised, the fewer down days you will have.

A down period need not lead into a more serious depression.

There are many actions we can take to eliminate or minimize periods of depression.

Getting out of a blue mood is primarily a do-it-yourself project.

When individuals are unable to pull themselves out of extended down periods, they should seek professional help.

PROBLEM TO SOLVE   **The Possible Connection**

Frank and John met last month when they enrolled in a "Quality of Life" seminar at a local university. They have become good friends and regularly meet for coffee after their evening seminar. Frank is the more intellectual of the two. John is more pragmatic and direct.

Last night the class had a speaker who discussed "Mental Activity and Physical Well-being." He offered the proposition that there may be a direct relationship between staying mentally alert and maintaining good physical health.

After the meeting, Frank praised the speaker, saying: "It seems logical that there is a tie between mental and physical health. Perhaps the connection is through our nervous system. I believe one of the reasons we are both in good physical shape is because we have mental discipline. I've noticed that people who succumb to pressures wind up with physical problems. There's got to be a connection."

John replied: "Sorry, I don't see how there could be any significant relationship. Our minds and our bodies are either healthy or not as a result of diet and exercise. I agree that the best way to push back senility is to keep learning, but I don't buy that it will help my physical life."

Compare your ideas with those of the author in Appendix C.

SELF-QUIZ

True	*False*	
_____	_____	1. Moody periods are more common among retirees than other age groups.
_____	_____	2. Those who fill their days with activities have fewer down periods.
_____	_____	3. Regular physical exercise can help prevent negative moods.
_____	_____	4. Prolonged personal introspection is the best way to escape depression.
_____	_____	5. There is little individuals can do to control their moods.

(Answers in Appendix C.)

IV

HUMAN SUPPORT SYSTEMS

This section deals with personal relationships during retirement. When you complete it, you should be able to: build better relationships; create a strong inner-circle support system; do a better job of dealing with family demands; explain the difference between the two languages of love and decide which best fits your comfort zone.

12

Retirement Relationships

You can always tell a real friend; when you've made a fool of yourself, he doesn't feel you've done a permanent job.
Laurence J. Peter

You generally get back the kind of behavior you send out. If you want better service at a restaurant, you're more likely to get it by being patient, pleasant, and positive. If you want help from a telephone operator, you'll have better luck if you put a smile in your voice as you make the request. Good relationships with others start with you, not with the other party.

If you want better treatment from others and want to set the stage for new friendships, learn to send out positive signals first. You must earn, through your actions, the kind of behavior you seek from others. You should do this even when you are tempted to respond differently.

125

Three Positive Signals

In a crowded bus a young man stumbled and fell on a man with a cane. Did the man reply with hostility? Not at all. Laughingly, he said, "You are the first person to sit on my lap in a long time." Later the young man helped him off the bus.

A woman in her fifties was bumped by an exuberant young girl while waiting in a crowded cafeteria. How did the lady respond? She smiled and engaged the teenager in a conversation. Before they reached the food counter, the two were having a good time.

A retired couple, on vacation, found themselves in a rented condo next to an old house where young people played their music so loud it was bothersome. In a friendly voice, the man asked the young people if they could play some Laurence Welk music. Everyone had a laugh and the volume was reduced willingly.

Such friendly gestures don't always work, but grouchy behavior will almost always bring back negative responses. When you respond out of frustration, you often upset yourself and make life less beautiful. You also eliminate the possibility of making new friends.

Sometimes, through your positive actions, it's possible to turn the negative behavior of others around so that both parties benefit.

Mr. Johnson

Mr. Johnson is dependent on the only garage in town that can repair his car. During his last few visits, he has received insensitive and undependable service. The more he complained, the worse it got. Then he did an unusual thing. One sweltering afternoon, he took some ice-cold soft drinks to the owner and his crew. From that point on, service improved.

Some Upsetting Behavior

A pleasant widow constantly became upset with the inconsiderate behavior of the receptionist in her doctor's office. She complained to her doctor, but he simply shrugged his shoulders. The next time she had an appointment, she brought a small gift to the receptionist. Things improved so much that eventually the receptionist offered to fill out her insurance forms for her.

As you move into retirement, there is a danger you may expect automatic, sensitive treatment from others, especially those you think care about you the most. Be careful. They may be so involved solving their problems that they forget you have some of your own. You are often left with two choices: either become resentful and chase people away or turn situations around so that you come out ahead.

Retirement is a time when you will need more human companionship, not less. The reinforcement you receive from others will mean more and more to you. Often retirees leave some of their best relationships behind in the workplace. Others reduce relationships further by moving.

What does this mean? It means that when you retire you have a new human-relations challenge. It means you should work harder to keep current friends and make new ones. How good you become at this can make a difference during your retirement years.

HUMAN-RELATIONS ATTITUDE SCALE

This scale is designed to help you measure your attitude toward improving your human-relations skills and friendship-building techniques. *Circle the number where you feel you belong between the two opposite statements.* After you have finished, total your score in the space provided.

Upon retirement, I will need to renew my efforts to build better relationships.	10 9 8 7 6 5 4 3 2 1	I have no intention of making any changes in this direction.
I intend to send more positive signals to strangers.	10 9 8 7 6 5 4 3 2 1	I don't intend to send out more signals; I may not respond to those I receive.
I'm going to work at being a nicer person.	10 9 8 7 6 5 4 3 2 1	People can take me as I am or leave me alone.
I will remain positive and friendly even when those around me may not be.	10 9 8 7 6 5 4 3 2 1	Why should I make special efforts?
I'm going to triple my efforts to meet new people—especially some that are younger.	10 9 8 7 6 5 4 3 2 1	I'm going to let people come to me.
I'm going to be more sensitive to the needs of others.	10 9 8 7 6 5 4 3 2 1	I think it is time for others to be more sensitive to me.
I'm enthusiastic about building new and better relationships.	10 9 8 7 6 5 4 3 2 1	I'm tired of building relationships with others.
If I damage a relationship, I will make every effort to restore it.	10 9 8 7 6 5 4 3 2 1	You win a few and lose a few.
I want to be a better listener.	10 9 8 7 6 5 4 3 2 1	I'm good enough already.
I'm willing to learn how to be a better conversationalist.	10 9 8 7 6 5 4 3 2 1	I've got all the skills I need.

Total _____

The Human-Relations Attitude Scale will help measure your attitude toward this challenge. If you scored 80 or above, there should be no trouble expanding your relationships after retirement. In fact your retirement years should be filled with exciting, new friendships. If you scored between 50 and 80, more effort on your part may be necessary. Your attitude may cause you to miss some potentially beautiful relationships. If you scored below 50, you apparently are willing to settle for a retirement with fewer human contacts.

The Mutual-Reward Theory

If you accept the challenge of building better relationships, you should consider using the Mutual-Reward Theory. The Mutual-Reward Theory (MRT) says that in a relationship both you and the other party must benefit somewhat equally. There must be a balanced reward system. You should get something you need from the other individual, and that person should get something he or she needs from you. In this way both parties come out ahead.

Olive's Realization

Everyone was kind to Olive after she lost her husband. Even two months later she had three or four callers each week. In time, however, Olive only got an occasional call. How quickly people forget!

Was it because she was negative, complaining about her problems? On the contrary, Olive was pleasant and positive. Then why did people back away? Without knowing it, Olive was not practicing the Mutual-Reward Theory. She was in a habit of accepting more than she was giving. Her friends were initiating all the contacts.

One day, while she was thinking about her friends, Olive realized she was not doing her share. She vowed to initiate more, and soon her friends and family were calling regularly.

You have heard that it's better to give than to receive. Giving should be its own reward. This may be all that is needed by some people. Ultimately, however, the person who constantly gives without receiving starts to back away. Everyone needs something out of a relationship. MRT is a human-relations fundamental. Those who ignore it usually spend a lot of time alone.

MRT and the Art of Conversation

Communication is the lifeblood of any relationship. Relationships prosper almost entirely through your ability to communicate. No matter how good your other human-relations skills may be, without good communication skills, your life will be lacking.

People need affirmation that they are all right—that they are in tune with life. A good conversation is highly rewarding. Like good wine, the older we become the more pleasure we should find in our conversations.

Yet, at the very time when communication becomes more important, some people seem to lose their communication skills. Have you experienced being in a perfect environment for a meaningful conversation—such as a restaurant setting with a private table, good food, and ambiance—and then wasting the evening because your partner is insensitive? Maybe you did all the listening. Or perhaps your dinner partner introduced all the topics for conversation. What was your feeling when you realized you were not being heard? After such an experience, one cannot help but wonder how many potentially good relationships never develop because one party failed to understand the importance of a dialogue.

How can we develop and improve the art of our conversation? First, when someone listens to you, they are providing the highest reward of all. They are receiving your signals so they can send a reinforcing message or, at the right moment, make a contribution. The more, longer, and better they listen, the more valuable your reward. The reward should be returned. You, too, should listen at the same high level, or the communications system will break down.

The accompanying illustration shows an ideal reward-exhange system for a hypothetical conversation.

Everything is working. Both people listen and talk about the same amount. Each introduces relevant, positive material and responds at an appropriate time in a sensitive manner. As a result, the conversation is symbiotic; both parties come out ahead.

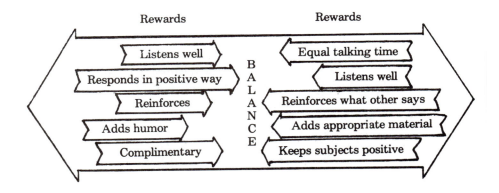

These same principles apply even more to telephone conversations:

* Do you have a friend who dominates the conversation even though your need to talk may be great?

* Do you often wish an individual had not called?

* When your telephone rings, do you sometimes leave it unanswered because you don't want to talk to a certain insensitive party?

These instances suggest you are dealing with someone who does not understand the value of MRT. Unbalanced telephone conversations can quickly destroy relationships. The individual who is repeatedly on the short end of the reward system will find ways to avoid contact with the other party.

How can you improve your art of conversation? How can you improve your present relationships and build new ones? Here are some suggestions:

* *Give out more rewards.* It starts with your behavior. Be an outstanding listener. Make your comments fit into the fabric of the conversation. Listen with your eyes as well as your mind. Work hard to implement the process.

* *Be sure that you receive rewards in return.* Be an involved rather than passive conversationalist. If you are doing most of the listening, take action. Intervene in a sensitive manner. With a smile on your face and a twinkle in your eye, say:
—"That's interesting—I once had something similar happen."
—"To add to what you just said. . ."
—"Would you like a reaction to that?"
If you are consistently on the short end of a conversation with a reasonable person, you have only yourself to blame.

* *View conversation as an art.* Refuse to take conversations casually. Set the stage for each opportunity by eliminating interference. Give each exchange your best effort, and take pride in your skills as a conversationalist.

* *Intervene when others start to repeat themselves.* You do your friends a disservice when you pretend to listen to their jokes, problems, or stories a second, third, or fourth time. Stop them with the admission that you often do the same thing. Say with a smile:
—"I remember that—you covered it the last time we met, remember?"

—"I've heard that somewhere before."

Then quickly get the conversation on a different track, making certain it has a positive effect. If you are guilty of repetition yourself, ask your friends to help you get out of the habit. Make a game of it. They should be happy to play because they are the primary beneficiaries.

* *Redirect negative conversations.* Positive conversations are rewarding; negative ones are debilitating. If you sense a conversation is becoming negative, don't hesitate to ask a question or make a point that will get the conversation on a more positive track, such as:

—"I understand you had a great time in San Francisco. Tell me about it."

* *Rehearse difficult conversations ahead of time.* If someone you care about has been negative during recent conversations, say at the beginning that you have something exciting to share. This should help guarantee some equal time. The idea is to make sure at the beginning that there will be a balanced exchange before the meeting is over. You are not getting out a stopwatch, but you are saying that you are placing some conditions on your conversations.

* *Send a special reward when you have been guilty of overtalking.* No matter how hard you practice MRT, there are times when you need to dump problems on another person. When this happens, send a small reward—a thank-you card, flowers, or whatever will express gratitude for being a caring listener. This way you can start the next conversation without feelings of guilt.

* *Avoid too much alcohol.* A glass of wine can often make a positive contribution to the art of conversation. In moderation, it is not unusual for both parties to relax more and communicate better. Too much alcohol, however, can cause a person to talk too much, too loudly, and too incoherently. Everyone loses.

* *Feed your mind fresh, positive conversational material.* You cannot be a good conversationalist unless you have a reservoir of thoughts from which to draw. If you like jokes, make certain you have new, appropriate jokes for those you frequently see. If you are a storyteller, keep in mind that it is fun to hear a well-practiced story the first time but not the second. If you enjoy intellectual conversations, avoid talking about the same theme too often. Also, be sensitive in expressing opinions on controversial subjects. Those who constantly get on the soap box

risk adding an emotional dimension that will distort a relationship.

We can all improve our conversational talents and increase our circle of friends, but it takes work.

Summary

Retirees need to replace work relationships by meeting new people.

Generally speaking, you get back the kind of messages you send out. The more positive signals you send out, the more opportunities you create to make new friends.

Application of the Mutual-Reward Theory is an excellent way to strengthen present relationships and build new ones.

Communication is the lifeblood of any relationship. Improving your conversational skills is critical.

PROBLEM TO SOLVE　**Gloomy Gertrude**

The Castellinis and the Simpsons moved to the Retirement Cove about the same time. They have become good friends, playing cards together three or four nights a week. Recently, Gertrude Simpson has become so negative in her conversations that the Castellinis have discussed pulling away. Even Gus, Gertrude's husband, is becoming irritable.

Gertrude seems to take every illness or death she learns about so personally that it depresses her. She introduces negative news into conversations and then does most of the talking. An information magnet, she knows everything that goes on but deals only with the negative news. She seems to enjoy being gloomy.

Gus visited the Castellinis alone one afternoon and asked for help. He mentioned he had tried to retrack Gertrude's conversations into positive channels with little success.

Mrs. Castellini made this suggestion: "Gus, perhaps you could convince Gertrude to turn her preoccupation with bad news into a positive experience. That's what I try to do, by saying to myself that I am fortunate to feel so well. Could you convince her to try this approach?"

Mr. Castellini suggested: "Every time I hear that someone is seriously ill or has died, I become more determined to improve my own health program. Somehow I gain more courage, not less. We hope you can convince Gertrude to change her views. Unless she can be more positive, we will spend less time with you."

If you were Gus, how would you approach Gertrude? Would you recommend the strategy of either Mrs. Castellini or Mr. Castellini? Do you have your suggestions for helping Gertrude?

Views of the author appear in Appendix C.

SELF-QUIZ

True	False	
_____	_____	1. The nice thing about retirement is that you don't need to work so hard at human relations.
_____	_____	2. You know when MRT is working because both parties come out ahead.
_____	_____	3. Conversation should be viewed as an art.
_____	_____	4. You do people a disservice when you pretend to listen to their problems, jokes, or stories a second time.
_____	_____	5. MRT does not apply to telephone conversations.

(Answers in Appendix C.)

13

Developing a Stronger
Inner-Circle Support System

We are in great measure architects of our added years. It may not be in our power to arrange for ourselves good living quarters, a decent wage, but it is within our power to enrich our later years by maintaining wholesome personal contacts with our fellows and by using our leisure in some useful activity.
Ethel Percy Andrus

If you were asked to name your all-time favorite teacher, you would probably have little trouble doing so. If asked to explain why you selected that person over all others, the reason might be that the person encouraged you to accomplish something special.

My favorite teacher was Jean Wilson. She challenged me and inspired me to attempt college. Thirty years after being her student, I learned that she had passed away. Only nine of her former students attended her funeral. I wondered how this could happen after all she had done for students over the years. I learned the answer. Miss Wilson, after retirement, had become a recluse. She failed to

135

maintain or build a human support system. When the police found Miss Wilson, she was surrounded by several hungry cats. Perhaps, for her own reasons, she preferred cats to people. But, it was sad to realize that at the time of her death no one was keeping in close touch with her.

Build a Support System Early

Without planning, it is possible, especially for those without family members close by, to wind up almost alone. By taking charge, you can create a human support system.

A human support system consists of those who provide frequent spiritual, emotional, psychological, and, occasionally, financial support. This group constitutes your inner circle. They are the people with whom you have built the best reward systems.

The word *support* simply means that, when you need help these people will see you through your problem. You would probably not have to ask them, because they would voluntarily come to your aid in one way or another. They keep in touch and do things for you.

When it comes to human response, there are no guarantees, which is why any inner-circle system should include several people.

It goes without saying that you must help earn any support you may require *before* you need it. This means you should start working now to build sustaining, mutually beneficial relationships. Often you will be on the support end more than the receiving end. Love and compassion must be the bedrock of your support system.

The accompanying illustration demonstrates Mrs. Reynolds' inner-circle support system. Although recently retired, she began building a support system years ago. She is proud of her efforts. It gives her a feeling of security to know there are people who care about her. The system is uniquely hers, but it serves as an example, especially if you are working on one of you own.

The squares indicate family relationships, and circles signify friends. A double line around a square or circle indicates the relationship has been neglected, but Mrs. Reynolds has decided to change this. Not all family members qualify as inner-circle members. Distance often makes it impossible to include a relative, and sometimes an irreconcilable conflict is present. Even in ideal situations, a balance between relatives and friends is a good idea.

The closer a relative or friend is to the center of the circle, the more important the relationship. In the diagram, both Grace and Joan are friends of Mrs. Reynolds, but there is a stronger bond with Grace. As a result, Grace plays a more significant role in Mrs. Reynolds' life.

MRS. REYNOLDS' INNER-CIRCLE SUPPORT SYSTEM

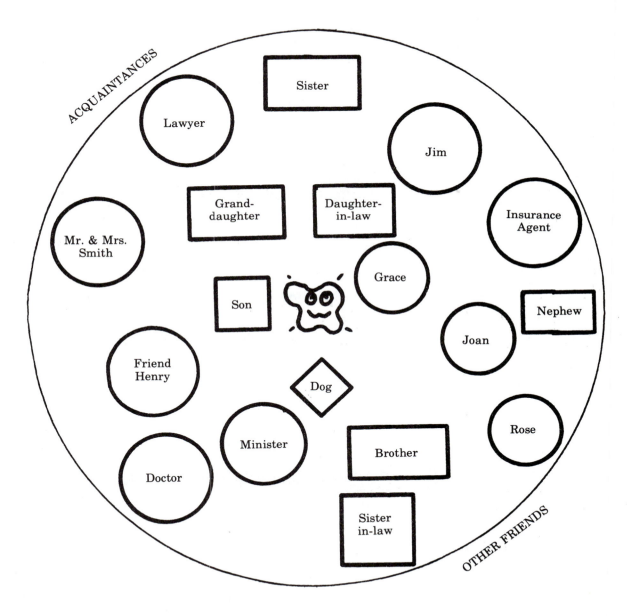

There are 18 people in Mrs. Reynold's support system. This is a large number. Generally, a system should have between 5 and 20 people.

Mrs. Reynolds understands that her contemporaries may not outlive her, so she maintains some relationships with younger people. In addition to family members, she has developed strong relationships with her young lawyer and a neighbor named Jim. She is proud of these relationships.

Her closest relationship is with her son. This is understandable and, in her case, fortunate, because the relationship is mutually rewarding and loving. They enjoy being together. If help is required, her son would be called first and Grace next. Notice that her daughter-in-law and her only granddaughter are also close to the center. Mrs. Reynolds works hard to keep an excellent relationship with both.

Others in her circle are there for various reasons. Her minister plays a spiritual role in her life. Jim keeps an eye on her and helps with things needing to be done around her home. She pays him through her friendship and excellent baking skills. Her brother lives far away, so their relationship is maintained primarily by telephone. Mrs. Reynolds knows, however, that he would come to her rescue if needed. Her other friends are special in their own way. They are all concerned about her, and she knows they can never be fully replaced.

You will notice that her lawyer, her doctor, and her insurance agent are included. Although these are purely professional relationships, they provide necessary skills and contribute to her life. She feels more secure by having them in her inner circle and makes a special effort to keep close communication with all three. They receive monetary rewards for their support, but they are also considered friends.

Her dog, Shady, is also in her support system. Pets can be very important.

Mrs. Reynolds is fortunate to have such a good support system at this stage in her life, but it did not happen automatically. She practiced MRT in her relationships for many years. She worked at being an unselfish person. Also, she does not take her inner circle for granted. She knows that as she becomes older, the more important her system will be and the more difficult to maintain.

If you like the concept of the inner-circle support system, you should evaluate what it will take to develop one or to improve one that you already possess. These considerations will be significant.

Each Inner Circle Is Totally Different

Mrs. Reynolds' system can be a guide, but your inner circle will be uniquely your own. It will have its own composition and design.

Start from the middle and work to the outside. If you are married, you and your spouse should consider doing one together. If you are alone and have only a few relatives to put into your circle, it will be necessary to build it primarily with friends and professional people. Whatever you eventually design should provide a new perspective on relationships and help you focus on the human side of your life.

Adding People to Your Inner Circle

After you choose those you want to include in your inner circle, you will occasionally add a person who has become special in your life. Don't, however, bring someone into your circle simply because you suddenly like him or her. A mature, durable, two-way relationship takes time to develop. In fact, when a new member is added, you should be proud because you helped it to occur by building a relationship.

With new members, you must ensure that you maintain each relationship. Ask yourself these three questions:

* Can you spend adequate time to keep the relationship alive and active?
* Can you take care of new members without neglecting older ones?
* Are you willing to provide, if necessary, the same kind of support you would anticipate receiving if you needed it?

Remember, it's usually better to have a small, well-kept garden than a larger one that you are forced to neglect.

An Inner Circle Is a Private, Highly Personal Matter

Once you have completed your circle, it isn't necessary to broadcast the results. You might share the information with those closest to you, but generally it's best to keep it contained.

Building an inner circle may appear to be self-serving, but it isn't. It is nothing more than a way to help you focus on your most significant relationships. It is not meant to encourage an exclusive club that would cause you to ignore other friends. In fact, inner circles often motivate people to work toward building new quality relationships.

Building a New System from Scratch

Sometimes circumstances make it necessary for an individual to rebuild an inner circle almost from scratch. When this is required, all of your human-relations skills must be employed.

Mrs. Hemingway

In preparation for retirement, Mrs. Hemingway sold her home and moved near the seashore—many miles from her old neighborhood. She was determined to keep her special friends (she didn't have any close relatives). She also was aware that she needed to add new members to her circle. Mrs. Hemingway took the initiative and within six months had made outstanding progress. Using MRT as a guide, she built a few new, exciting relationships with others living nearby. Within two years, she had a new inner circle. These were people willing to give her the kind of human support she was willing to give them.

Strengthening Your Inner Circle Is a Good Way to Prepare for Retirement

Retirement should give you time to strengthen present relationships, restore those that have been neglected, and add new friends. Those who have already established such a group have a jump on retirement, because once an individual leaves the workplace, friends take on increased importance.

Knowing those you want to spend more time with after retirement constitutes a human-relations plan. When new members are added, excitement is added. The nice thing about working on your circle is that you don't have to wait years for it to pay off. The rewards are immediate.

You Cannot Hoard Relationships

One nice thing about a paid-up, financial endowment is that you can depend on it. A cheque will come every month. Wouldn't it be nice if we could depend on relatives and friends to provide human support in the same manner?

Unfortunately, it doesn't work that way. Relationships are often capricious. For example, even when you have developed an outstanding relationship, that individual might move away. You could have a highly supportive child living nearby one day and across the country the next. People also have changes in their lives that can cause them to pull away. This is why you must work constantly on your inner circle. Thus, if you lose members, for whatever reason, you will not be alone.

The Immediate-Replacement Theory

Some mental-health specialists subscribe to the idea that the best step to take when there is the loss of a pet or friend is to find a replacement. They feel a substitute is better than a vacuum. Replacement is not the best word, because it isn't possible to replace someone special, but it may help to partially fill the void.

Retirees with a highly developed circle have less of a problem when it comes to replacing friends. Others are there to help.

Consider Doing a Circle of Your Own

The process of developing a support system should produce many benefits. Here are a few:

* It should cause you to place more emphasis on the human side of your life.

* You will pragmatically study it as an insurance program against future situations.

* You may find you have neglected a few special people and do something about it.

* You may find you want more people in your life.

* You may discover you are spending too much time on one relationship at the expense of others.

* It should motivate you to work harder at building relationships outside your circle as potential future replacements.

* It may convince you to cultivate relationships with a few younger people now.

Other advantages and insights can occur. Best of all it is an intriguing exercise, and you should enjoy the process. (See page 142.)

Keep Your Inner Circle Alive and Well   Once you have completed the exercise, you will want to maintain it. Here are some tips you may want to consider:

* Think about the kind of rewards you want to provide to those important to you (both inside and outside your circle).

* Work to improve your communication. Make a special effort to upgrade conversations with those you care about.

* If you lose a member, find a new member.

* If appropriate, tell people that they are part of your inner circle. It is the greatest compliment you can pay them.

* Keep working to locate new friends so people will be available to move into your support system if necessary.

* Accept rewards (love) from others gracefully.

* Keep in mind that if someone is in your circle, you are probably in theirs. Make sure you deserve to be there.

Summary   The Mutual-Reward Theory is the key to building an inner-circle support system.

Loneliness is usually not planned. Retirees who wind up lonely often ignore building relationships until it is too late.

DIAGRAM YOUR OWN INNER-CIRCLE SUPPORT SYSTEM

You now have the rationale with which to build a diagram of your own, an inner-circle support system. You may want to try it here.

ACQUAINTANCES

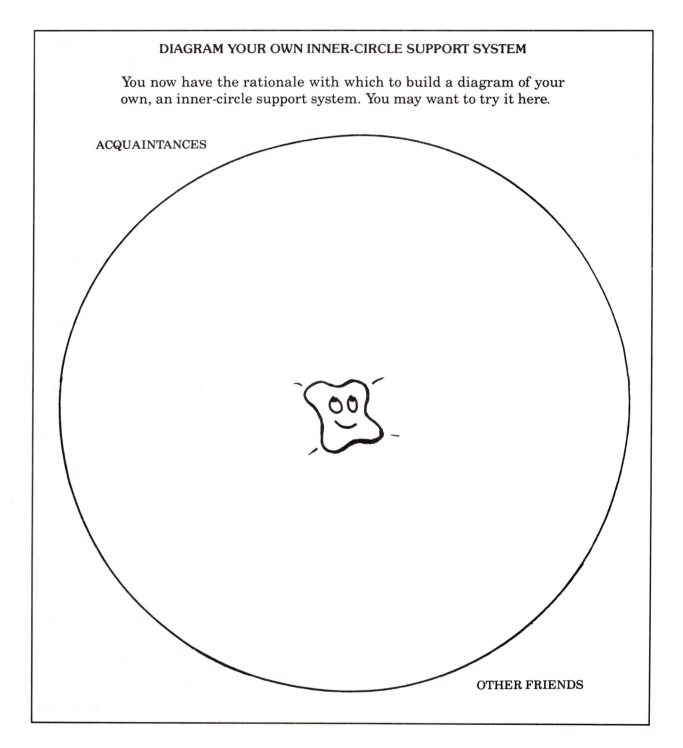

OTHER FRIENDS

No matter what kind of a support system you have, it can be improved. Now is the time to take action. No one can do it for you.

Properly implemented, an inner circle will enhance the quality of your life and the lives of those you love.

PROBLEM TO SOLVE   **Preretirement Emphasis**

Mr. and Mrs. Eberhardt have done an outstanding job of financial planning for their retirement years. They started early, used the services of a professional financial planner, and now feel secure about their future. They have not, however, given similar attention to the human side of planning their retirement.

Mr. Eberhardt comments: "We have devoted our energy almost completely to the financial side. I feel the rest will take care of itself." In defending their position, Mrs. Eberhardt says: "We have always been self-sufficient—almost loners. We enjoy each other's company more than that of others. I anticipate we will be so busy traveling after retirement that our circle of friends will get even smaller. No matter. We can always handle our human needs as they surface."

Do you agree or disagree with the attitudes of Mr. and Mrs. Eberhardt? You may want to compare your thoughts with those of the author in Appendix C.

SELF-QUIZ

True	*False*	
_____	_____	1. The only reason to develop a support system now is to have it available in later years.
_____	_____	2. In building an inner circle, a balance between relatives and friends is a good idea.
_____	_____	3. The more people you include in an inner circle the better.
_____	_____	4. Pets should not be included in support systems.
_____	_____	5. MRT should play a major role in the building and maintenance of any human support system.

(Answers in Appendix C.)

14

Dealing with Family Demands

If you have children, they usually occupy key roles in your life. Most of the time they are pillars of your support system. Sometimes, however, they have problems of their own; so, instead of receiving support, you provide it. This can be a shock if you believed you would be free of responsibility after retirement. Changing values, economic conditions, and other factors that may not have been present a generation ago often dictate otherwise.

Mrs. Troutline   Although Mrs. Troutline's husband left her with a nice home, a reasonable income, and a few investments, she must deal with a multigenerational problem she never anticipated and does not want. Mrs. Troutline is 67. Her mother is 87 and lives in a long-term health-care facility. Her mother is not a financial drain, but she is an emotional strain because Mrs. Troutline feels compelled to visit her mother twice each week. Another unexpected demand on her is her middle daughter, Mary, whose marriage fell apart three years ago. Because of economic conditions, Mary and her two young children moved in. Although Mary has some income, Mrs. Troutline finds her home expenses higher than ever. To complete the frustration, her oldest granddaughter is pregnant and refuses to marry the man responsible.

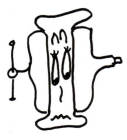

Mrs. Troutline's attitude? "I have never felt so much pressure—and all of it from my own family. I seem to be the primary responsible person for three generations. Everyone comes to me when they have a problem. I am caught in the middle with nowhere to go. I'm trying to be a good daughter to my mother, a good mother to my daughters, and a good grandmother. It bothers me that my husband worked hard to prepare for retirement, and then he didn't live long enough to enjoy it. Now, I'm stuck, but very determined not to let my family engulf me. I'm in charge and intend to remain so. One thing I insist upon is to keep my own friends. They are available to listen to my problems and make sure I get out now and then. Without friends I would be in real trouble. When my family problems finally clear up, I'm determined to live for myself."

Mrs. Troutline's predicament may seem unusually difficult. Multigenerational problems similar to hers, however, are common. The freedom movement of the seventies may have provided its generation with more opportunities, but sometimes the older generation pays the price. Family configurations have changed. Many retirees find themselves caught in family problems they never anticipated and can't escape.

Mrs. Troutline is to be respected for her compassion, strength, and flexibility. More than anything, though, she should be commended for staying in charge. She could easily let her mother drain her. She could let her daughters take over. She could devote all of her time to family and pull away from friends. She is doing none of this. Despite the demands, she keeps a few nonfamily people in her support circle. They are her safety valve. When the family problems clear up, she will still have her friends.

Improving Relationships with Adult Children

You cannot be happy in retirement if you walk away from your children or grandchildren. Rather, you should take a positive view and build better relationships with your adult children while simultaneously protecting your own freedom. Provide your family with the required support (financial or otherwise), but don't neglect other members of your support circle. Your adult children may require more from you than they are currently in a position to give. Things may change later and, when you need it, their support will be there.

In reviewing relationships with adult children, we need to dispel three myths.

First is the idea that the generation gap is wider today than ever. Evidence suggests the opposite. The gap has been closing for the past several years. Families are getting together more, not less. Communication is improving.

The second myth is that conflict within families is always bad and should be avoided. Some conflict and negotiation is present in all relationships and should be anticipated. Too often parents avoid problems that need to be discussed because they fear conflict. The same is true, perhaps more so, with their adult children. Confronting problems can be healthy; otherwise they may remain unsolved for years.

The third myth is the belief that love will solve all problems. As a parent, all you need do is love your children enough, and eventually everything will turn out all right. The truth is that love can sometimes be a barrier to good communication. Love is the most beautiful emotion, but it can make both parties so sensitive that both sides will bury problems that should be confronted and solved.

Anything you can initiate to improve relationships with your children will strengthen your support system. No matter how good you think the relationships are, some improvement usually can be made. If a relationship is bad, it can usually be turned around with effort. Here are four commitments you can make to help with your family relationships. Check those you feel to be important:

☐ Nothing positive will happen unless I become a good listener. I must endeavor to understand how my children feel and what their problems may be.

☐ I should forget old misunderstandings and start with a clean slate. I understand we can't discuss new problems if we continue to allow old wounds to be opened. Even if time has proven me right, old problems need to be buried.

☐ More communication on serious matters needs to be initiated with my children. When such sessions are necessary, I will not be talked out of them.

☐ I intend to discuss the inner-circle concept with my family and explain why a balance is necessary between family and friends. In this way I can explain why my freedom is important.

How to Handle Your Child's Divorce

Divorces occur at all ages, but they're most common among younger people. You may face an unexpected or unwanted divorce with your children. If grandchildren are involved, things can be traumatic.

Comparatively little attention has been paid to the impact of divorce on grandparents. Yet, aside from losing a spouse, discovering you have a serious health problem, or getting a divorce yourself, it can be devastating. The shock could cause you to behave in a way you could regret later.

* "We were planning to take our son, daughter-in-law, and three grandchildren to Hawaii next year. When they split, we were so upset we called it all off and made some selfish, unkind comments."

* "What happens when you have shared family treasures with a daughter and son-in-law and they separate? You do some reevaluating, that's what."

* "When my son got his divorce, I immediately changed my will to express my sentiments."

Reactions such as these are understandable, but they also have the potential to permanently injure one of your most important relationships. You could alienate those you love the most.

How might you accept their trauma and disappointment without damaging your own happiness? Here are some tips:

* No matter how upset you are, don't close the door. Keep communication open. Remember that your children have their own lifestyle and, as adults, are responsible for their actions. You don't have to like it, but you must respect that it is their life—not yours.

* Protect your freedom. Don't rush to open your home or bank account until you are sure what you want to do. It's easy to overreact and regret it later.

* Accept the premise that they are paying enough of a price without your making them pay more.

* Make every effort to maintain good relationships with both parties. Avoid, when possible, taking sides.

* Keep in mind a daughter-in-law or son-in-law can be very special.

* When grandchildren are involved, think about family continuity. Decide what role you want to play with your grandchildren. A new alignment of relationships may be required.

* Try not to cut off access to your grandchildren.

* Keep an open mind on any new partners that develop on either side.

This advice does not mean a passive role on your part is best. You are not required to simply sit back and take it. You have a need to talk about the problems with others and also to express your feelings with those immediately involved. It is essential that you deal with the problem openly. You should remain determined to stay in charge.

Retirement Creates a New Kind of Parent

When making the transition to retirement, you will need to reconsider your role as a parent. You should not remain the totally giving, protective parent you may have been earlier. Does this come as a surprise? If so, consider the matter from an objective perspective.

The parent-child "giving process" can become a real problem. Giving usually means more than money. It can include love and emotional support, taking care of the grandchildren, as well as other responsibilities. To make the most of retirement, some factors probably should change. In other words, the reward system between you and your children should be evaluated. You may need to withdraw certain rewards and add others. Your adult children should also make adjustments. Over the years, you have helped them become adults. It is now your time to enjoy the freedom of retirement, to kick up your heels with as few strings as possible.

The accompanying diagram shows the various stages between childhood and mature adulthood. Also shown is the typical role of the parent. As you move from left to right—into retirement—a two-way emancipation process should begin taking place.

When the child reaches mature adulthood (often rather late in our society compared to others), a change usually takes place. Both parties start to give different rewards. The child should view parents as individuals who have finished their mission of parenting. Old demands should not be present. Instead, adult children should protect the retirement years of the parent by taking responsibility for their own lives.

But what often happens? Instead of the parents becoming less and less involved in their children's lives, they cling to old roles and slow their own growth as well as that of their children.

CHILD-PARENT CONTINUUM

Birth to 12	13 to 18	19 to 30	30 to Retirement
Childhood	*Adolescence*	*Young Adulthood*	*Mature Adulthood*
Period of heavy protection. Total giving by parent.	Explosive period with role of parent diminishing. Giving continues but with provisions.	Role of parent is to back away but be around in emergencies. Limited giving.	Child totally on own. Reversal of giving process starts to take place.

Why? The reasons are complex. Some parents cannot separate the giving process from love. They never reach the point where they can say: "It is time to step back from parenting. It does not mean I love my children less; we are simply at a new stage in our relationship."

Some parents are not very successful at building new friendships and therefore fill their time with children and grandchildren. They drag their families into their lives whether it is desired or not. Some use selfish, divisive techniques to accomplish this. When this happens, freedom is surrendered by all parties.

It also works the other way around. Some adult children never reverse the giving process. They continue to receive more than they should. A few seem to deliberately encourage their parents to continue being givers. They protect their own freedom but don't offer their parents the same courtesy.

Adult children often want their parents to stand still while they change lifestyles. They fail to realize that their parents deserve a new lifestyle, too—especially after retirement.

Sitting on Your Money Some retirees feel guilty about holding their money. Often the more they have, the more guilty they feel. They see themselves with an excellent financial position while their children are still in the process of building. Often these folks accelerate the giving process when it would be best for both parties not to do so. They shell out to soften guilt feelings that should not be there in the first place. This causes both parties to keep roles that should be left behind. Retirees often fail to give their children space to build their own lives. Adult children often fail to understand the new roles their parents want and need.

How can you get the most out of retirement and still be the kind of parent you should be? How can you make the transition and maintain excellent relationships with your children? Here are some thoughts that may or may not apply (or appeal) to you. Check those that do.

☐ Do not subordinate yourself to the needs of your children. Consider yourself first. It is your turn now.

☐ Generate activities away from your adult children. Demonstrate that you are in charge and want to live your own life. Be with your children when you want to be with them.

☐ Give your children the freedom to live their own lives. Refrain from intervention. If you give too much, it can be awkward for them, especially if there are strings attached, real or implied. Give them the privilege of handling their own problems.

☐ If your children ask for more help than they should, learn to say no in a loving but firm way. The reward-reversal process will not start until this happens.

☐ Keep in mind that you have had enough worries in previous stages of your life. If your children do not ask you to assume their worries for them, why do it?

☐ Work to see your children as adults—not the way they used to be. Recognize that they are capable of handling their own problems. Provide support only when necessary.

☐ Discuss how reward systems can change over the years. Anything you can do to help them understand your new role will help.

☐ Discuss why, as a retiree, you need to stay in charge, why you need to protect your nest egg, and why you may develop a new lifestyle.

☐ Don't use your children or grandchildren as time fillers. Enjoy them and have fun, but maintain your own leisure activities.

☐ Don't bypass your children just to enjoy your grandchildren.

It is not easy to build an ideal relationship with your adult children. You want them as pillars in your inner-circle support system, but you don't want to lean on them too soon, nor do you want them to lean on you. It is a delicate balance. Tell them you love them and respect their need to be free. Make sure they respect yours.

Summary   As children mature, you need to become a different kind of parent.

New family configurations sometimes make it difficult for retirees to protect their lifestyles.

A good support system requires that better relationships should be built with adult children.

Problems with adult children need to be dealt with openly, especially those relating to divorce.

Everyone needs to recognize the changing roles on both sides.

PROBLEM TO SOLVE   **Upset Plan**

Mr. and Mrs. Brant developed retirement plans when they were almost 60. Both worked until age 65 to get their home paid for and their income to a good level. They are proud of their efforts and excited about the years ahead. They feel they have developed a solid Plan A that will provide their retirement years the richness they desire and deserve.

There is one problem. Cindy, their 36-year-old daughter, is in an emotional and financial bind. The story is typical. While in college, Cindy found herself more involved in causes than preparation for a career. As a result, she married early, had three children, and did not graduate. Three years ago, Mr. and Mrs. Brant learned that Cindy was getting divorced. It threw them for a loop, but they adjusted by telling Cindy to work it out in her own way. They offered no financial help.

Cindy, who is capable and attractive, quickly found a good job. She was able to make enough money (with child-support payments) to take care of things herself.

A year later Cindy showed up for Christmas with her children and a new husband. Mr. and Mrs. Brant believed Cindy had found a good husband, who cared for her children along with those of his own, and they were relieved.

The year they retired, however, Cindy was divorced again and also lost her job. After she ran out of unemployment insurance, Cindy was forced to go on welfare. Today things are even worse. Cindy is behind on her house payments, and her children are living on bare necessities. Cindy has lost her assertiveness and self-confidence. The matter so disturbs Mr. and Mrs. Brant that they argue about what to do to help. Their retirement dream is in jeopardy. They decided there are three viable alternatives.

Alternative 1: Draw heavily on their retirement income to help Cindy through her situation. This would mean making Cindy's house payments and providing extra cash until she can get back on her feet. Because Cindy lives 300 kilometers away, help under this alternative would be essentially financial.

Alternative 2: Invite Cindy and the three grandchildren to live with them. They adore the grandchildren (ages 7, 9, and 12), and their home is large enough to accommodate this. This alternative would simply delay their leisure plans until a later date.

Alternative 3: Let Cindy work out her own problems, except for some minimal, short-term help, and proceed with their retirement plan.

Which of the three alternatives do you favor? Why? What other suggestions would you make? Compare your suggestions with those of the author in Appendix C.

SELF-QUIZ

True	*False*	
_____	_____	1. Love should be the only constant in a changing relationship between adult children and their retired parents.
_____	_____	2. The giving process between parents and children should never change.
_____	_____	3. The generation gap is getting wider.
_____	_____	4. When love is involved, problems are easier to solve.
_____	_____	5. After retirement, it is easier to be a good parent.

(Answers in Appendix C.)

15

The Two Languages of Love

To grow old is to pass from passion to compassion.
Albert Camus

Norma, 68, and Sidney, 72, met while swimming in the retirement center pool. Each was attracted to the other and, following their marriage, have no trouble satisfying each other's sexual desires. The quality of life has improved for both individuals.

Sylvia, 64, and Brian, 60, met at a fund-raising event for a local charity. Each is attracted to the other romantically, but they have not been intimate. They see each other frequently, and the quality of life for both has improved.

There are two dimensions to sex. Both are exciting and have their own special rewards. Each can be a beautiful manifestation of affection and love between two people.

Physical sex starts out with touching, kissing, teasing, massaging, and culminates with the exciting climax of sexual intercourse. It is

155

an experience people of all ages can achieve. It is the primary language of love. It adds to the quality of life.

But love is also enjoying the company of another, with little or no physical contact. It is intimate conversation and the sharing of private thoughts. It is a candlelight dinner with romantic overtones. It's doing fun things together. Mature people have a way of making the most of this so-called second language of love. Some enjoy it as much as the first language.

We will deal with both levels, but first, let's dispel some of the myths and misunderstandings about sex and age. Social scientists have begun serious research in this vital area and only recently has the subject been dealt with openly. To measure your knowledge in this area, review the questions in the Pretest. Correct answers follow the questions.

Although research and education are eliminating some of the misunderstandings surrounding sex, others remain. For example, a few would like to perpetuate the myth that sexual activity will extend life. This is hard to substantiate and probably has no basis in fact. That romance can add spice to life is a different matter. Many individuals who have existed in a chronically depressed state change

---

PRETEST ON SEX AND AGE

True   *False*

_____   _____   1. Female sexual activity knows no age limit.

_____   _____   2. A new partner will keep a male's sex activity at a higher level indefinitely regardless of his age.

_____   _____   3. The sharp decline in sex interest for women after menopause has a sound physical foundation.

_____   _____   4. Biology has established a mandatory age for sexual retirement among men.

_____   _____   5. There is a greater loss of sexual ability in men than among women who are past retirement age.

_____   _____   6. Sexual intercourse without affection becomes more meaningful with age.

_____   _____   7. Fifty percent of men over 70 function sexually.

_____   _____   8. Few changes are more threatening to the male ego than loss of ability to function sexually.

PRETEST (*continued*)

True	False	
_____	_____	9. Cardiac energy expenditure during a sexual climax is approximately equal to climbing two flights of stairs.
_____	_____	10. The decline in sexual activities is steeper than other physical levels such as endurance, mobility, or general health.
_____	_____	11. A Duke University study found that approximately 15 percent of the subjects over 60 years of age grew sexually over the 10-year time span of the study.
_____	_____	12. Much impotency diagnosed as organic, attributable to aging, is actually attributable to psychological factors.
_____	_____	13. Primary opposition to sexual freedom among seniors comes from adult children who have already accepted greater freedom for themselves.
_____	_____	14. Some retirees foolishly abstain from sex to avoid painful feelings of frustration, anxiety, or depression over their declining sexual performance.
_____	_____	15. Sexual problems experienced by aging males are often reversible.
_____	_____	16. It is not important to your identity to feel good about yourself sexually.
_____	_____	17. Sex is totally a physical thing.
_____	_____	18. The sexual activity of females is directly related to their partners.
_____	_____	19. Lack of interest is the main cause of declining sexual activity.
_____	_____	20. Some retirees, who have negative attitudes and want to forget about sex, use age as an excuse not to participate.

Total Correct _____

Answers: (1) T (there is some decline in late, late years only); (2) F (may be responsible for higher level on a temporary basis only); (3) F (the reverse is true in many women, because there is no longer a fear of pregnancy); (4) F (a few men over 90 years of age are still potent); (5) T; (6) F (less meaningful); (7) T; (8) T; (9) T; (10) T; (11) T; (12) T; (13) T; (14) T; (15) T; (16) F; (17) F; (18) T; (19) F; (20) T.

dramatically when they are suddenly attracted to another. Result? A resurgence of life with some amazing behavioral changes. Hope is restored. This romantic involvement may not extend lives, but it increases a desire to live.

The Psychological Values of Romantic Relationships

Not everyone needs romantic involvement to be happy and fulfilled. Many do, however, and those who let the opportunity pass may be making a mistake by foolishly avoiding relationships that could enrich their lives. To discover some of the hidden psychological benefits of romantic relationships, review the reasons in the following Checklist that have value and meaning to you.

How many times did you answer "yes"? If five or more, it would appear a romantic relationship at either level would add to the

---

VALUE CHECKLIST FOR ROMANTIC RELATIONSHIPS

Yes   *No*

☐ ☐ 1. It is or would be important to me to express my romantic feelings in intimate ways with another person.

☐ ☐ 2. I value affirmation from another that I am still attractive.

☐ ☐ 3. It would improve my sense of self-worth to know that someone enjoys being seen in public with me.

☐ ☐ 4. Knowing another person intimately is like a "port in a storm." I would be protected from certain anxieties.

☐ ☐ 5. A sex-oriented relationship is a kind of defiance against stereotyping as an aging person.

☐ ☐ 6. It would help me be more self-assertive. I could express myself more openly on subjects important to me and know the other person would listen.

☐ ☐ 7. I take pleasure from being touched.

☐ ☐ 8. A sense of romance would give my life a lift.

☐ ☐ 9. I would have a feeling of sensual growth.

☐ ☐ 10. Having a close, sex-oriented relationship would be an affirmation of life. I would feel more alive.

Totals: *Yes* _____   *No* _____

quality of your life. If you do not now have such a relationship, perhaps you should do something about it.

Keeping Your Sexual Identity

Most gerontologists recommend that we do everything possible to maintain a strong sexual identity as we move into retirement. This means the opportunity to be the same romantic person as in younger years, but with additional style. This means keeping sexual feelings alive and nourished. It means being proud of these feelings, not sublimating them.

Two Cases

Mrs. A lost her husband three years ago. Because of her personal convictions about marriage and sex, she does not seek a physical relationship with another man. She does, however, have a strong sex identity. She enjoys being an attractive woman. She enjoys the company of men. She likes social activities and is proud of the attention she receives from men. She is sensitive to the reactions of other women and makes certain that she never favors one particular man. One luxury that she permits is to fantasize about what could happen. Mrs. A knows that her contacts with men help her keep a sexual identity. They contribute to the quality of her life.

Mr. K has been a widower for six years. He enjoys being around women. He dresses well and is a good conversationalist. He teases and loves to dance. All this helps him know he is still attractive to women. These contacts help him to stay motivated, exercise, and keep mentally alert.

The Art of Being Available for Contact

Many mature people who are alone reject the idea that they should take any initiative to make themselves available for romantic involvement. Some of this reluctance is based on the way things were in the past. Some fear that a relationship with another might destroy a valued memory. Often it is nothing more than a lack of confidence.

Any person who honestly believes a better life would be possible with a romantic involvement should not hesitate to make themselves available. This normally means looking as attractive as possible, mixing in groups, sending friendly signals to prospects at the right time, and receiving signals from others in a friendly and welcoming manner.

Elizabeth's Initiative

Elizabeth moved into a retirement center after her husband died. A religious person, she joined the local church. Nervous about being accepted in her new environment, she dressed in her best clothing and paid a visit to the hairdresser. At church, she took the initiative and introduced herself to others. Soon people were sending back signals of friendship. One day she noticed a man about her age watching her. It happened several more times. Although difficult, she sent back a friendly signal. They met that day at the coffee following service. Before long, they were having dinner weekly. Both people seem fully satisfied and adequately rewarded with the second level of love. Their needs appear to be communication and companionship rather than physical sex. The important thing is that this new relationship has benefited both individuals.

Some retirees who acknowledge that they would enjoy a romantic involvement do not have the self-confidence to do anything about it. They envy others, yet hesitate to take the first step. They feel awkward about sending out signals and use the excuse that it wouldn't be proper. In some ways it is unfortunate that we don't mirror certain cultures where women wear a flower over one ear if they are interested and over the other if they are not. Such signals could eliminate frustration. It's hard to believe, but even after six decades of living, some people are too shy to receive friendly signals from others, even though they would like to.

Another excuse you hear is "I might get involved in something I can't handle." These people seem to fear that any relationship that starts out innocently will automatically escalate to a sexual relationship. These people do not consider that the other person may fear such an escalation as much as they do. Once friendly signals have been exchanged, a timely follow-up is desirable if a new relationship is to blossom. The initial psychological barrier must be overcome to allow a relationship to develop. What happens after a relationship develops should not be anticipated in advance. Retirees should be able to develop rewarding second-level relationships without needless anxiety about what might happen later.

To throw away the beauty of close companionship because you fear physical activities is foolish at any stage of life. For mature people it is ridiculous.

What Mature Men Like in Mature Women

Why one individual is romantically attracted to another has always been a mystery, sometimes explained by the phrase "in the eye of the beholder." If you talk openly with men, they will tell you what they appreciate most in women. Following are some of the comments you will likely hear:

* "I like a woman with style—one I can be proud to take out socially."
* "I appreciate a woman who is satisfied to be her own age."
* "It is great to talk about common interests, not about children or problems all the time."
* "At our age it is an opportunity to have fun together."
* "I love a woman who looks like she has spent time getting ready for me and then doesn't keep me waiting."

What Mature Women Like in Older Men

Women like in men most of the same characteristics that men like in women. If you talk to women, you will get statements such as:

* "I like a sensitive man who listens well and is interested in me."
* "A man should look healthy and strong."
* "I like a man who takes me to nice places I wouldn't feel comfortable going to alone."
* "I like a man who takes charge."
* "Give me a man who is polite and considerate."
* "I like to be flattered."

Romantic Relationships and the Mutual-Reward Theory

The Mutual-Reward Theory says that for any human relationship to exist at a high level for an extended period of time, both parties must come out ahead. For this to happen, there must be an exchange of rewards. There may be a few exceptions, but in the vast majority of cases, each party needs to provide rewards important to the other person. Rewards that fall within the second language of love may be all that is required for some parties to come out ahead. In other relationships, some physical rewards may be required. At an appropriate stage in a relationship, this will need to be discussed openly.

Mr. and Mrs. Drake

Although Mr. and Mrs. Drake know nothing about the Mutual-Reward Theory, they have practiced it all their married life. It has been primarily responsible for the success of their marriage. Mr. Drake has been a romantic, attentive lover and excellent father. Although he never really enjoyed it, he has regularly taken his wife out socially—a reward she has appreciated. On the other hand, she has been a willing, romantic lover and an excellent homemaker and mother. Although she doesn't enjoy it, she has gone on countless camping trips to please her husband. There have been many other give-and-take examples in their reward system, but the balance has been fair. As a result, Mr. and Mrs. Drake have come out ahead in their marriage, and have both been winners.

Mr. G and Mrs. B

Mr. G and Mrs. B have an outstanding relationship made easy because both seem fully satisfied with the second language of love. He takes her to nice restaurants, art shows, and dances, and is always the ideal escort. She, in turn, cooks for him frequently and always makes him feel important. Both are sensitive to the needs of the other. Their friends envy their relationship because it is obvious they appreciate each other.

Understanding and applying the Mutual-Reward Theory can help everyone sustain a romantic relationship.

Are the Romance Cards Stacked Against Mature Women?

There is a country and western song titled "Older Women Make Beautiful Lovers." If you feel younger women hold all the aces when it comes to attracting and holding a man, I suggest you listen to this ballad. It says that older women also have some excellent cards—if they play them properly.

Some mature women think that there is an unwritten law preventing them from competing with younger women. Those who believe this are saying their experience and capacity to love is lost simply because they have aged. They are quitting without understanding what most men want. These comments tell the story:

* "It bothers me when mature women let younger ones establish the rules. It often happens for two reasons. First, older women downgrade their charms. Second, they feel it is inevitable they will lose out so don't even try."

* "I have a better time socially and sexually with mature women. I don't have to prove myself with them."

* "Mature women can give you the best time in the world, if they allow it to happen."

* "Some women needlessly tie themselves up with old-fashioned ideas that younger women have discarded. If they learn to accept some of the 'new freedom,' they can better compete with the younger women."

When it comes to love, mature women have their own aces to play. Many men have learned that a young woman may enhance their sexual performance temporarily, but in a long-term relationship they often lose more than they gain. Of course, some men will not discover this unless they are fortunate enough to meet women their age with confidence and finesse.

Summary

Both languages of love contribute to the quality of life.

The second language of love is enough for some individuals.

There should be no guilt feeling attached to enjoying either language.

The better one learns to engage in a given language of love, the more happiness will occur.

PROBLEM TO SOLVE   **Sid and Sarah**

Before his wife died, Sid, a successful lawyer, promised he would not remarry. It was his idea, because he loved her deeply and their marriage had been ideal. He did not want to risk another relationship. There also were some practical reasons such as the excellent relationship he has with his children and grandchildren. A new marriage could jeopardize these. As a lawyer, he has seen family jealousies and wants no part of it. Finally, a second marriage would complicate things legally.

Sid, however, has a strong sexual identity. Recently he became acquainted with several interesting women and has always enjoyed their company. He was satisfied with the second language of love until he met Sarah. The physical attraction between the two was intense, and after a while the second language of love was not enough. At this point, he suggested they develop a mutually rewarding arrangement that would protect their separate identities. Sid suggested that he live with her for a few weeks, and then they would share his condo for a similar period of time. Each would make an effort to enjoy the children and grandchildren of the other party. Both estates would be kept separate and intact for inheritance purposes.

Sid and Sarah spent many hours discussing the matter. Sarah told Sid it would not be in her comfort zone to participate in an arrangement such as that suggested by Sid. They could become bedmates, but Sarah felt living together was extreme. She felt she would have problems with her children in a live-together arrangement. She told Sid life was better because of him and each was getting the rewards they wanted, except for living together.

Do you see a solution for Sid and Sarah? What other avenues should they explore? Author's suggestions can be found in Appendix C.

SELF-QUIZ

True   *False*

———   ——— 1. The second language of love is basically communication with romantic overtones.

———   ——— 2. Younger people who practice sexual freedom themselves are often reluctant to grant the same freedom to their parents.

———   ——— 3. Sexual problems experienced by aging males are usually not reversible.

———   ——— 4. Single mature women should accept the fact they cannot compete effectively with younger women for the affection of males their age.

———   ——— 5. The Mutual-Reward Theory does not apply to the second language of love.

(Answers in Appendix C.)

V

FINANCIAL MANAGEMENT

More than any single factor, money will determine when people retire. This major section will provide help to accomplish financial planning. After completing it, you'll be able to: prepare and interpret a Personal Financial Statement; design a workable, effective budget; do a better job of stretching your dollars; improve your investments; determine the best financial strategy for your personal situation; complete your estate planning; prepare the best possible insurance package for yourself.

16

Controlling Your Money

Money is what you'd get on beautifully without if other people weren't so crazy about it.
Margaret Case Harriman

Despite the fact that their income is both limited and fixed, few people get more out of retirement than Mr. and Mrs. Jay. Their lifestyle is filled with parties, travel, and new experiences. When they are not enjoying friends in their mobile home, they are traveling through the west in their small camper. How do they live with such style on so little?

They manage their money. There is little relationship between having fun and the amount of money one spends. Retirees who operate on a cash basis can enjoy life as much as those who use a pocketful of credit cards. Those who save money by shopping at J. C. Penney's can have as much zest in their lives as those who shop at more exclusive stores. People who eat cafeteria food can enjoy life as much as those who frequent expensive restaurants.

167

Style is an attitude. It's putting poetry and enthusiasm into life. It's having fun in situations without a price tag. It is making the most of life from where you are. Many wealthy individuals live without style and often get little enjoyment from their money even though they spend it lavishly. Others, with limited funds, have fun wherever they go. These people are not individuals who squander their money or treat it carelessly. They make the most of what they have in maintaining their lifestyles.

Financial planning is essential both before and after retirement. Several experts say that the only thing that should be put ahead of money is health. No argument from me. It may not take a lot of money to live in style, but it does take some.

Regardless of the level of financial planning you have done, it isn't too late to begin. To make the most out of retirement, however, the sooner you start the better.

Once retired, people generally fit into one of the following three financial categories.

Fixed Income Most who retire are in this classification. It means their income is set usually through a pension, Canada Pension Plan (CPP), Old Age Security (OAS), or a combination of these. What's more, often they can't work to increase their income. Finally, they do not normally have appreciable money to invest. They may own their own home and have some life insurance plus a few small investments and a modest "nest egg" in the bank, but that's it.

Mrs. Raymond Mrs. Raymond is locked in so far as income is concerned. She receives her CPP and OAS, has a small savings account that draws limited interest, and a modest home that is paid for. She knows she can always gain some income by selling her home, but she doesn't plan to do this if she can avoid it. Because of poor eyesight, she cannot work. Her income, therefore, is limited and predictable; and she must make every dollar count.

People with a fixed income must pretty much make do with what they receive. It's often too late for anything else.

Fixed Plus Work Income Those in this category have an advantage. Their income is fixed, but they can still augment it by working.

The Drakes' Income Mr. and Mrs. Drake both receive CPP and OAS, have a modest cash reserve, and own their own mobile home free and clear.

Fortunately, Mr. Drake enjoys and is good at fixing things, so he adds to their income. People around the park like Mr. Drake and usually keep him in mind when there's a small job to do.

Inflation has caused more retirees to find work to supplement their fixed income. For some, like Mr. Drake, this has been a blessing in disguise.

Fixed Income Plus Return on Investment Capital

This is an ideal situation. It is like the first category except these fortunate individuals have investments that produce additional income for them.

The Kelley's Income

Mr. and Mrs. Kelley not only draw Canada Pension benefits but also have sizable investments that provide a luxurious lifestyle. They own some income property and have a sizable stock portfolio, two money-market accounts, and a tax-sheltered annuity they have yet to draw upon. Although Mr. Kelley does not work in a formal sense, he spends considerable time managing their investments.

Nobody knows how many retirees fall into this category, but the number is impressive. Banks and savings and loan firms advertise all sorts of special offers for these "big money" retirees.

Knowing where you fall within the three classifications should help position you on the Income Projection Chart. Select your age along the bottom of the chart and then move up to where you feel you belong. The retirement line is flexible. You can move it in either direction depending on your planned retirement age. Write in your anticipated or actual annual income on the vertical income line to the left.

If you are still in the preretirement portion of the chart, you can still determine where you eventually will be on the retirement line. For example, if you are 50 and make regular investments in an RRSP, you would substantially increase your worth if you retire at 60 or 65. The more you invest, the higher you will be on the line. Once you retire, there is less flexibility. Those on a fixed income normally drop to a lower level and remain there. Those on a fixed income plus a postretirement job can maintain somewhat higher spending until they elect to stop working. Those with a fixed income plus investments can go either way depending how successful their investments are after retirement. If they make intelligent investments and do not overextend, they can be better off at 75 than they were at 65.

INCOME PROJECTION CHART

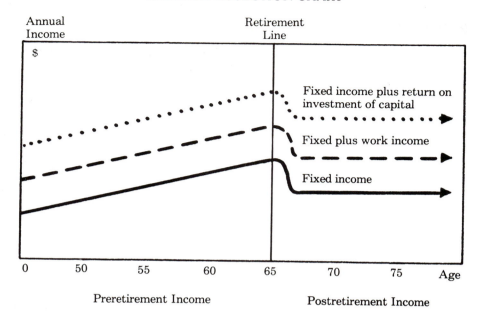

Inflation is the unknown factor in the chart. Although it hurts people in all categories, those on fixed income are hurt the most.

If you have already retired and find yourself on a lower line, does this mean financial planning is less important for you? Far from it! Most financial experts emphasize that the less money you have to work with, the more important financial planning becomes.

Mr. Taft Mr. Taft, a widower, was at the bottom of the financial totem pole. His income (primarily CPP/OAS and the guaranteed income supplement (GIS)) was meager and a physical condition prevented him from working. His attitude toward financial planning might have been: "Why bother? I have so little it wouldn't make much difference." His actual attitude was: "With so little I must plan carefully and squeeze out every possible dollar, so my life will be as good as possible."

Mr. Taft's attitude is to be admired. He is willing to help himself even though his income is both fixed and limited.

Regardless of where you placed yourself on the income chart, it is wise to prepare a Personal Financial Statement and a Monthly Budget. This chapter invites you to complete both.

PERSONAL FINANCIAL STATEMENT

Step 1 Take a few moments to look over the form on the following page. If you are not familiar with financial forms, it may appear complicated. It isn't. Accountants call this a *balance sheet* because it shows what you have on one side and what you owe on the other. It is a snapshot of your financial picture. Without preparing such a statement first, it is difficult to financially plan for the future. This form will help you see your financial situation more clearly. You may discover you are better off financially than you expect.

Step 2 On the left side of your Personal Financial Statement is a list of your assets. These are things you own or in which you have a partial equity. Equity is the value of any property above what is owed on it. For example, if you have a piano you could sell quickly for $2,000 and you still owe $600 on it, your equity is $1,400.

You have control over your assets, whether completely paid for or not.

The right side of the form lists your liabilities—that is, what you own. Retirees often owe less than younger people, because getting out of debt is a normal retirement goal. A liability is an obligation yet to be paid. When you subtract your liabilities from your assets, you wind up with your net worth.

This is a significant figure that is required for planning purposes. If you don't know what it is, it can be exciting to anticipate what it might be. You should know yours at the end of this exercise.

Step 3 You are now ready to fill in your monetary assets on the Personal Financial Statement. Do this with a pencil following these simple directions:

Cash   This is money you can get your hands on immediately. Total the cash you have in your pocket, cookie jar, chequing account (if you have one), or savings account. Often chequing accounts are also savings accounts these days, because you are paid interest on the balance.

Money Loaned to Others   If you have loaned money to others and are reasonably sure it will be repaid, enter the amount on this line. This could be a noninterest personal loan to one of your children, trust deeds on property, or an interest-paying loan secured by notes.

Investments   *Savings Bonds.* Write the face value of any Canada Savings Bonds you possess (we will assume you will hold them to maturity). If you have 50 $100 RS bonds, their value should be shown as $5,000.

PERSONAL FINANCIAL STATEMENT

NAME(S) _____ DATE _____

	Assets	Liabilities

MONETARY ASSETS

1. Cash
   - On hand _____
   - Checking account _____
   - Savings account _____
   - TOTAL CASH _____

2. Money loaned to others
   (repayment expected) _____

3. Investments
   - Savings bonds _____
   - Stocks and bonds _____
   - Mutual funds _____
   - Certificates of deposit _____
   - Money-market accounts _____
   - Tax-sheltered accounts _____
   - Cash value of
     life insurance _____
   - Cash value of annuities _____
   - Profit sharing _____
   - TOTAL INVESTMENTS _____

4. TOTAL MONETARY _____

FIXED ASSETS

5. Home and property _____

6. Other real estate
   investments _____

7. Automobiles _____

8. Ownership interests in
   small business _____

9. Personal property _____

10. TOTAL FIXED ASSETS _____

11. TOTAL ASSETS OF _____

12. Unpaid bills
   - Taxes _____
   - Insurance premiums _____
   - Rent _____
   - Utilities _____
   - Charge accounts _____
   - Other _____ _____
   - TOTAL UNPAID BILLS _____

13. Installment loans (balance due)
   - Automobile _____
   - Other _____
   - TOTAL _____

14. Loans (balance due)
   - Bank _____
   - Other _____ _____
   - TOTAL _____

15. Mortgage loans (balance due)
   - Home _____
   - Other _____ _____
   - TOTAL _____

16. TOTAL LIABILITIES _____

17. NET WORTH _____

Stocks and Bonds. Check with your stockbroker or consult a newspaper for the closing prices of stocks and/or bonds you own. Multiply the number of shares by the closing price of each stock or bond. Subtract brokerage fees and enter the total on this line.

Mutual Funds. Do the same as with stocks and bonds. Obtain closing price and multiply by the number of shares you own. Enter total.

Certificates of Deposit. If you own a certificate of deposit at a local financial institution, enter the amount due at maturity (again assuming you will hold it until then).

Money-Market Accounts. These accounts permit deposits and withdrawals at any time, and it is possible to write a few cheques on most accounts. Enter your current balance.

Tax-Sheltered Accounts. If you have a RRSP or RRIF, enter the amount in the account plus the interest that has accumulated.

Cash Value of Life Insurance. The easiest way to determine the cash value of your life-insurance policies is to ask your agent to calculate the worth for you.

Cash Value of Annuities. Determine the cash value of each non-sheltered annuity and enter the total of all annuities on this line.

Pension Plan. If you participate in a pension or profit-sharing program with your present or previous firm, enter the amount vested in your name.

You are now ready to total all of your money investments. Enter your total in the space provided.

Total Monetary Add your total cash, money loaned to others, and investments and enter this total. This important figure represents your liquid assets. It is money you should be able to get your hands on easily.

Step 4 We are now ready to complete the fixed-assets part of the statement. Fixed assets are as valuable as monetary assets, but it usually takes longer to convert them into cash. For example, if you hold out for a price above the market value of the asset, it may take longer to sell.

Home and Property To accurately determine the current selling price of your home (if you own one), ask a realtor for an approximation of its value or arrange for a written appraisal (which may cost you money). Enter your determination of the market price on line 5.

Other Real Estate Investments	Using the same method as above (your choice), list the market value of any other real property you may own.
Automobiles	You may obtain the approximate value of your car(s) from the *Blue Book* available at your library, bank, or automobile dealer. You should probably use the wholesale rather than the retail price, because it is probably closer to what you would get if you wanted to sell in a hurry. You may also check resale values on your car model and year in the classified section of your local newspaper.
Ownership Interests in Small Businesses	Enter here any equity you might have in a business. You may need to consult a C.A. for a realistic figure.
Personal Property	This requires a determination of the value of all other items you own beyond those previously listed. Personal property includes boats, planes, jewelry, furniture, antiques, clothing, and so on. To arrive at the value of each item, assume no more than what you feel someone would pay. In the case of precious stones, silver, china, glassware, and other such items, an appraisal might be in order. It is fun to go through your home or apartment with a calculator. The total can be a pleasant surprise.
Total Fixed Assets	Add all the figures entered in items 5 through 9 and enter the total at item 10.
Total Assets	Add lines 4 and 10 for the sum of your total assets.
Step 5	You are now ready to complete the right side of your statement. Keep in mind that a liability is an obligation you must pay now or in the future.
Unpaid Bills	*Taxes.* If you have yet to pay either the first or second installment on your property taxes, enter the amount on this line.
	Insurance Premiums. Enter only those currently due.
	Rent. Only if now due.
	Utilities. List only if they have yet to be paid.
	Charge Accounts. List what you have charged plus any previous unpaid balance, including charges not yet posted.
	Other. List anything else such as a television repair bill that has not been paid. List the total on the line provided.
Installment Loans	List the balance due on an installment loan for items such as furniture, automobiles, advance funeral arrangements, and so on. Then total them.

Loans | List the balance due on any bank or personal loan. Write in the total.

Mortgage Loans | List the balance of any mortgage you have on your home or on other properties. Total.

Total Liabilities | Total all liabilities and write it in the space provided.

Step 6 | With what you have done, it is easy to now figure your net worth. Simply subtract line 16 from line 11. The mathematical difference between assets and liabilities is net worth. It is the sum total of what you currently own. If it amounts to more than you expected, you should be pleased.

You now have a good idea of your resources. Whether your net worth is modest or considerable, the principle is the same. You know where you stand. You know what you have for emergencies. It is what you have to build a future lifestyle. It is what you may want to spend more freely as you grow older or, perhaps, leave to others.

RETIREMENT BUDGET

It is now time to prepare a retirement budget. If you have yet to retire, this is advance planning. If you have already retired, it is current planning. The smaller your net worth, the more important your budget is. A budget is what you plan to spend during a specific time period (for example, the month ahead). It is a control mechanism that helps you spend money wisely. It facilitates self-discipline. You can only spend the same dollar once. A budget helps make sure you spend it for the right thing.

Preparing Your Budget

The Monthly Retirement Budget form is easy to fill out, even if you have never done one previously. Once completed, you should adjust it from time to time until it is reasonably accurate. As you complete it, think about your current expenditures. You may discover an opportunity to eliminate or cut back on some unnecessary expenses that will provide more money for other things, including pleasure. Use the right-hand column entitled "Notes" to remind yourself about such opportunities. For example, if you plan to sell your car and use public transportation next year, make a note. If you find an expense you might be able to cut, write the word "investigate." Completing a budget will assist you to do some advance thinking and ultimately help you to make better financial decisions. Without a budget, this might not happen.

MONTHLY RETIREMENT BUDGET

NAME _____ DATE _____

	Monthly Cost	Notes
Mortgage Payments		
Rent		
Insurance—Life		
Homeowners		
Medical		
Automobile		
Other		
Taxes—Income		
Property		
Savings		
Investments		
Loan Payments		
Medical/Dental		
Medicine/Drugs		
Utilities—Gas		
Electric		
Telephone		
Water		
Heating		
Groceries		
Transportation		
Repairs—Auto		
Home		
Appliances		
Clothing		
Personal Care		
Entertainment and Vacations		
Household Supplies		
Home Furnishings		
Contributions		
Subscriptions		
Other		
TOTAL BUDGET		
CURRENT INCOME		LESS TOTAL BUDGET =
YOUR DISCRETIONARY INCOME		

Using a pencil, write the proper amount for items under Monthly Cost. The following suggestions may help, so read them before entering your numbers.

Mortgage Payments If you have a mortgage on your home or other properties, write in the amount you pay each month. Under "Notes," you might write the date it will be paid off.

Rent Write in the amount you are currently paying. Are you planning to move? Better location? Lower rent? If so, write in the word "investigate."

Insurance *Life.* If you have any policies on your life, write the amount of the monthly premium. Now that you have reached a "good age," you may want to revise your life-insurance program. You may want to keep a small policy for funeral expenses or one to pay taxes. You may also want to cash in policies to use the money for investments or perhaps to spend. Write the word "review" under "Notes" if this is the case.

Homeowners. Enter monthly insurance premium.

Medical. As you probably know, provincial health insurance plans do not cover all your medical expenses, so some supplementary coverage is usually advisable. Enter the amount of any supplementary insurance payments you make each month, or you may want to write "investigate" if you do not currently have a supplemental plan.

Automobile. Divide your annual insurance payments into 12 months and enter the amount. Under "Notes," you may write the date you expect to dispose of your car or change your coverage.

Other Insurance. Included in this category are special policies for jewelry, antiques, and so on. Enter monthly costs.

Taxes *Income.* If you have retired, enter what you paid last year (prorate for each month). If you have yet to retire, keep in mind that your taxes should be less when that time arrives.

Property. Prorate for each month if you own your home.

Savings If you have a savings program, enter the average amount you deposit each month. This, of course, is a variable expense that you can change at any time.

Investments
You may have entered an investment program where you make payments monthly. If so, enter the amount. If you are having second thoughts, write the word "review" under "Notes."

Loan Payments
If you are paying off a loan of any kind, enter the monthly payment. Under "Notes" write date when last payment will be made. Also, note if you expect to pay it off sooner. Do not include credit-card payments, because they show elsewhere in the budget.

Medical/Dental
This can vary greatly. You might be paying off a medical or dental bill or, depending on your medical history, allocating so much per month beyond your insurance payments.

Medicine/Drugs
Include vitamin pills and any other normal costs that are not compensated by insurance.

Utilities
Another big expense that can vary with the season.

Gas. Write in the average monthly amount of what you expect to pay based on history. Under "Notes," indicate whether an increase is anticipated and add thoughts about any way you feel you could reduce your use.

Electric. Same as for gas.

Telephone. Enter average monthly amount. Under "Notes," perhaps challenge your usage or consider buying the equipment.

Water. If applicable.

Heating. Other than gas and electricity bills. Use a monthly average cost for the year.

Groceries
Enter the monthly amount for yourself, spouse, or others (including animals). You may want to modify your expenses by building an improved diet that could cost you less.

Transportation
Include costs of your public transportation only.

Repairs
Auto. If you own one or more cars, be careful what you write down, because expenses vary greatly. Figure your average monthly costs for gas and oil. Also try to estimate total repair and other maintenance costs for the year and divide by 12. Under "Notes," write any ideas you may have to cut back on this cost.

Home. Estimate your average monthly costs based on what has taken place in the past. Include any anticipated big costs (new roof) and prorate this expense over a period of at least one year.

Appliances and Other. This is usually a small expense. Be sure to include payments on all appliances, especially the television set.

Clothing — You probably have a good idea on this, but a review may be necessary to ensure you reflect a monthly amount that is a good average.

Personal Care — Include trips to the beauty salon, barber shop, and an amount for cosmetics and toiletries.

Entertainment and Vacations — Let history be your guide. If you eat out regularly or visit relatives in a distant city each year, make sure you budget for it.

Household Supplies — Enter a reasonable figure. Often those items will be purchased at a supermarket. Try to keep them separate from food items, however.

Home Furnishings — Do you need new carpeting? Are you planning to have a chair recovered? Include a reasonable amount, prorated monthly.

Contributions — Include payments to a church, dues to a club, or contributions to charitable organizations. This can often be obtained from previous income tax returns.

Subscriptions — Newspapers, magazines, book clubs, and so on.

Other — Any additional expenses should be listed here. For example, you may have recurring veterinarian bills. A budget is useless unless you include all expenses.

Congratulations! You have completed your current budget. It is now vital to compare your budget with your income. So please total your present monthly income (include interest dividends, rents, etc.) and subtract your monthly retirement budget from it. If you find this impossible (that is, if your budget expenses are higher than your income), you must be living on your capital. There is nothing wrong with this, if it is planned.

Let's assume, however, that your budgeted expenses are less than your current income. What you have left is discretionary income. In other words, this is money left over that you can spend on entertainment, additional vacations, or luxury items not in your budget. The larger the discretionary income you can squeeze out of your income the better, especially if you do not have much of a nest egg set aside. A primary purpose of a budget is to help you spend the money you have intelligently so you will have more left over to satisfy your needs or other desires.

You should now have a better idea of your financial picture. If you have yet to retire, you should have a reasonable idea of what your assets will be when that date arrives. If you have retired, you should know how you stand and have a better idea of what it will take to provide the lifestyle you seek.

Idea department: If you have yet to retire, why not try to live on your proposed retirement budget for a few months before you take the step. This will allow you to test your estimate, and you may save some money in the process.

Summary A Personal Financial Statement (balance sheet) is necessary for sound financial planning.

A Monthly Retirement Budget is helpful in making good financial decisions.

For many, discretionary income (what one has left over) is the direct result of controlling expenses.

PROBLEM TO SOLVE **A Devastating Surprise**

Mrs. S, 68, is devastated trying to adjust to the announcement her spouse of 42 years made a few weeks ago. He said: "I have found another woman. I believe we both will be happier if I move in with her. If you want a divorce, you will have to file. I have divided our assets in the following manner. You can have the home, and I will take our other investments. As you know, they come out about even. You have your Canada Pension cheque and I have mine. We will split what is in the bank. I will leave the car with you. We have no liabilities."

If you were Mrs. S's best friend, what would you advise her to do? See a lawyer? Force her spouse to prepare a Personal Financial Statement before a division of property?

Author's comments are in Appendix C.

SELF-QUIZ

True   *False*

————   ————   1. You determine your net worth by deducting your liabilities from your assets.

————   ————   2. Discretionary income should be used to pay regular expenses.

————   ————   3. An accountant might call a Monthly Retirement Budget a balance sheet.

————   ————   4. Assets are either monetary or fixed.

————   ————   5. Budgets are less important to retirees.

(Answers in Appendix C.)

17

The Dollar Stretching Game

"Well," remarked Stella, "I've been good at stretching money all my life, because I remember how tight things were during the Depression. Although I was young, the penny-pinching habit got into my system, and it has stood me in good stead."

"Me, too," replied Gus. "I'm glad now because money management as a retiree is more of a challenge than I figured. With inflation and a fixed income, stretching a dollar is a whole new ball game."

Gus is right. When you retire, the way you spend money takes on a new significance. Inflation will probably shrink your dollars, but you'll have more opportunity to get better deals.

Goals of the Dollar-Stretching Game

To help you spend your money more wisely, consider the Dollar-Stretching Game. The general idea of the exercise is to make you a more professional buyer.

181

Before retirement you are often so busy making money you don't always find the best ways to spend it. After retirement, you have time to improve your consumer buying skills and save money.

The specific goals of the game are:

* To help you get more for your consumer dollar without sacrificing quality.

* To keep you from making needless mistakes.

* To challenge your current buying patterns.

Condition 1   The game applies to all consumer goods and services. This includes tangible items—everything you might buy in a supermarket, department store, specialty shop, drug store, health-food store, automobile agency or parts store, restaurant, swap meet, or garage sale. It also includes intangibles—services you buy at beauty salons, travel and rental-car agencies, as well as improvements or repairs you might do to your home. The techniques will also apply to the purchase of insurance programs, condominiums, and other major investments.

Condition 2   It is not a game that encourages you to be penny-wise and pound-foolish—just the opposite. Quality must never be sacrificed for price. The real purpose of the game is to increase your standard of living, not lower it.

Condition 3   You should benefit from the game regardless of your income or your previous buying habits. You win the game by future improvements you intend to make in your present buying practices.

Condition 4   To win, you agree to use your senior buying power in a professional, sensitive manner. As you know, after 60 you represent a large group respected by most retailers. Some recognize this age group's power by providing discounts. Others may be persuaded to give senior discounts or provide better services if they are approached in the right way.

The following comparison will illustrate your position as a senior buyer. When a professional buyer goes to the wholesale market to buy goods for a giant like Sears, that person has more clout than a buyer who represents a much smaller store. Companies pay more attention to such buyers and often give them better deals. After 60 you are in the position of a big-store buyer. There are millions of people behind you. This does not mean, however, that you should be high-handed with those from whom you purchase goods and services. It simply means you are in a good position to get the best possible price consistent with quality and good service.

A Hypothetical Situation

Assume that you want to save a minimum of $1,000 from the money you will spend on consumer goods and services during the next two years. Just how fast you do this should depend on how much you have to spend on consumer goods. Some will reach the goal in six months; others might take two years. Many are motivated to achieve this goal because they already have a special "something" to do with the money, such as a dream vacation or an extended visit with grandchildren. It could mean going on an Elderhostel vacation-study trip to England, saving for an investment, or doing something for your church. The choice is yours, but it should be something you couldn't or wouldn't do without the extra money.

As you play the game, certain professional buying techniques will be introduced. If you accept the technique as something you can apply in your own personal comfort zone (something that you would not feel uncomfortable using), follow the guidelines and award yourself a certain amount of money. This means that for each new technique, you decide how much money it can save you in the time you have allotted. There will, however, be limitations on your projected savings no matter how much you might save in actual practice. For example, if you honestly believe a technique will save you $200 but the limitation is $100, that is all you can take for the purpose of the game.

If, after finishing, your anticipated savings equal or exceed $1,000, you have won the game. You may, of course, save more than $1,000; you may also save less. Either way you should benefit from playing the Dollar-Stretching Game.

Buying Technique 1: Seeking Senior Discounts and Creating Your Own.

You might be able to save more from this single technique than from two or three that follow. And why not? This may be the first time in your life you have group power behind you when it comes to consumer purchases. Senior discounts are legal, and you should be able to build strong relationships with those who offer them.

It depends on your attitude. It would be unwise to start thinking of discounts as your right. On the other hand, if you are not sensitive to the possibility of discounts, you may miss several opportunities to save money.

Senior discounts are common practice in many industries, including:

Airlines	Retail stores
Rent-a-car agencies	Amusement parks
Public transportation	Insurance firms
Motels/hotels	Golf courses
Beauty/barber shops	Repair facilities

Although many discounts are well publicized, you can often use your power to get better deals. To accomplish this, the following skills are recommended:

* Get the best possible deal you can *before* you seek an additional discount. This will prevent retailers from saying they have already given a senior discount when, in effect, they would give the same price break to anyone

* The way you approach vendors is important. Always do it pleasantly. For example, you might show your Seniors card and ask: "Will this make a difference in the price you have quoted?"

* Your goal is to get the best possible discount and still maintain a good relationship. If you have a chip on your shoulder, it will show—and you may lose more than you gain. One exception, of course, is when you are being taken advantage of and are defending yourself.

* If you are told a senior discount is not provided, you have two choices. Accept the merchandise or service without it or back away in a nice manner and look elsewhere.

* If a discount is granted, always react with a "thank you" or other appropriate comment that will encourage the vendor to treat others as you have been treated.

How much additional money can you save from improving the way you use this technique? It depends on:

* How much time you spend finding those with discount policies for products and services you want.

* How you go about approaching those who may be willing to provide discounts but do so without a stated policy. It never hurts to ask, especially if you do it with a smile. Being turned down should not be interpreted as a sign of personal rejection. Think of yourself as a professional buyer who is trained to ask for discounts. If you think of it as a game, then you can play and win or stand on the sidelines and lose.

If you take advantage of senior discounts but feel that with additional effort you can double your savings, write the figure $150 in the box. If you have yet to explore such discounts and expect to become more assertive in getting them, give yourself up to a maximum of $300. If you are not eligible or prefer not to play the game at this stage, write a zero and move to other techniques that will fit better into your personal comfort zone. The choice is yours.

(limit $300)

Buying Technique 2:
Buy to a Retirement Diet

When professional retail-store buyers go to the marketplace they know what they want to buy before they leave. Often a computer has told them what their customers will likely buy by color, style, price, and so on. In other words, they go to market with a specific plan. Once there, they generally stick with their plan.

You should go to your market with similar preparations. As we learned earlier, less food is probably better as we grow older, and your diet should reflect this. If you buy a restricted, quality diet (plan), you should save dollars. This means a carefully prepared list, based on your diet, every time you visit the supermarket. Except for unusual conditions (a party perhaps), rarely should food be purchased beyond what appears on the diet list. Of course, everyone strays a little, because it is fun to reward ourselves now and then. The more you stray from your prepared list, however, the less you save—and the only thing you will gain is weight.

With this in mind, allocate those additional savings you believe you can achieve through this technique. Most can easily save up to $200.

(limit $200)

Buying Technique 3:
Buy Generic Items

Because of advertising and habit, most people buy name brands. They feel safe and comfortable in doing this. But inflationary pressures, competition, and new marketing techniques have caused changes. Now, for the first time, equivalent products are available at lower prices. The difference is often in the cost of the package itself. The unknown product is usually not in a fancy package, but the product inside is the same. These items are called *generic* because they are not identified with a well-advertised manufacturer or distributor.

For example, many drugstore chains provide generic (no name brand) food supplements and other pharmaceuticals under provisions that conform with legal requirements. The prices for these equivalent generic products are usually significantly lower than name brands.

Retail stores, especially large supermarkets, are also in the act. You can often find generic items on their shelves. Paper goods are frequent items, as increasingly are foods that fit into your diet. If you take time to read the labels to ensure you are getting a generic equivalent, you will save money without sacrificing quality. This is possible because packaging, advertising, and distribution expenses have been reduced or eliminated. Stores still make money selling generic items; they just pass some of their savings to you.

Finding and qualifying generic equivalents takes time, but the savings are real. If you want to get on the "generic bandwagon," write a reasonable figure in the square provided. If you only intend to take advantage of such opportunities when they conveniently present themselves to you, $50 might be a good figure. If you intend to dedicate yourself to finding and buying generic equivalents, a figure of $100 is more appropriate.

(limit $100)

| Buying Technique 4: Clip and Use Coupons | Nobody knows how long the "coupon craze" will continue. Name-brand manufacturers send a deluge of coupons into homes through newspapers, magazines, and mail. These companies hope you will select their merchandise over that of the competition. It is a good buying practice for you to use coupons under the following conditions: |

* If it is a food item and it fits into your diet plan.

* If it is a nonfood item, you actually need or would buy it anyway.

* If a food item, it's cheaper than an available generic equivalent after the value of the coupon has been deducted.

* If it does not cost you more than you would save by traveling to an out-of-the-way store to redeem the coupon.

Those who make the most of coupons are skillful and clever. For example, they are alert to "double coupons" with which they can double their savings.

If you believe coupons are more trouble than they're worth, write a zero in the box. If you have been doing a good job with coupons but think you can do better, enter $25 in the box. If you intend to make the most of coupons from now on, enter $50.

(limit $50)

Buying Technique 5: Take Advantage of Sales

Professional buyers look for or wait for deals. A good way for you to find deals on consumer goods is to watch for special sales. Supermarkets often advertise what they call "loss leaders." These are items featured in their ads, which they sell at a slight loss to attract customers. These are usually good buys providing you need the merchandise and don't drive too far to get it.

You may save even more when you are ready to purchase "big ticket" items. Furniture, appliances, tires, and some clothing fall into this category. Often, it is wise to wait for a sale to get the best price on these items. Stores have traditional sales a few times a year when they are willing to take substantial markdowns to clean up their inventories.

Caution: When buying anything on sale, make sure you follow these three rules:

* Make certain the merchandise on sale has previously been offered by the same store at a higher price. Some merchants buy special merchandise to offer as sale items, but it has never been sold at a higher price. Stay away from items that say "value $12.95, sale price $7.95." Buy merchandise that says regular price $12.95, sale price $7.95."

* Do not fall for the "bait and switch" technique. Some stores advertise an item at a very attractive price (the bait), but when you come in to buy they discourage the purchase and suggest something higher in price (the switch). This is illegal but it still happens.

* Do not buy anything on sale that you would not eventually buy anyway. We sometimes get caught up with sale items and purchase things we never use. When this occurs, our money is wasted.

If you intend to take better advantage of sales in the future, write what you think you can save in the box.

(limit $100)

Buying Technique 6:
Rule-of-Three Shopping
Practice

This means to compare the prices of identical or similar items of equal quality using three different sources.

Let's assume you need tires for your car. The rule says that you should check with three different outlets to get prices on the same quality tire. It is always a good policy to inform each store that you are shopping at other suppliers and will eventually take the best price consistent with quality. Once you narrow your choice, then ask if the tires you intend to buy will be on sale in the near future. This could turn out to be a double savings. Finally, you can ask if a senior discount might also apply

Keep in mind that certain items almost always are on sale by merchants. Tires and shock absorbers fall into this category. Also, household appliances, shoes, clothing, and many other items are regularly on sale. Apply the rule of three on any item selling above $50.

Here are three rules to remember:

* Compare a traditional retailer (department store) with a discount house (K-Mart, Bi-Way) to get a marketwide comparison. Discount houses frequently offer fewer services in a less posh setting but have lower prices on identical items.

* Don't neglect catalogs. One way to do this (say at a Sears store) is to find the exact merchandise you want on the floor; then check the catalog division to see if you can order it at a lower price.

* Make certain the item you eventually choose is the same as or better than those offered by others. It is a mistake to shop and then settle for something of less quality that will bring on buyer's remorse. The expression "quality is remembered long after the price is forgotten" is always applicable.

Retirees who follow the rule of three often enjoy doing it. Making the best possible deal is a game that's fun to play. If you do not enjoy comparison shopping or begrudge the time it takes, this technique will be used with less enthusiasm and you will save less. Enter up to $100 if you feel you can save more using this technique than you have saved in the past.

(limit $100)

Buying Technique 7:
Making a Favorable
Contract

Professional buyers sign purchase orders when they buy from vendors. These documents deal with specifics of the purchase and guarantee the rights of both parties. In a sense, you do the same whenever you agree to have repairs done on your automobile, home, or other possessions.

Assume you need to have your automobile tuned. In this case, you might shop (using the rule of three) by telephone before deciding on a certain garage. If the prices are close, you may feel most comfortable with your regular mechanic. You should, however, get a fixed estimate for the work to be done. Ask the necessary questions to ensure you are getting the service you desire. Sign a work order only after making sure it conforms to the conditions desired and agreed upon. At this point, the mechanic should be told that if any additional work is needed, you personally must authorize the work. Should you receive a call, for example, informing you that new brakes are required or you have a major problem with your clutch or transmission, feel free to return to the rule of three and get other opinions. If your mechanic resists, it could be a signal you are paying for unnecessary repairs.

Contracts require good communication, so don't let anyone rush you. The goal is for you to be satisfied and the contractor to make a reasonable profit. Try to make the agreements mutually rewarding. This is especially true when you work with painters, interior designers, and those who do home repairs. To accomplish this, you must stay in charge.

Both small contracting jobs (having your television repaired) or big jobs (installing a new roof) can present problems if the specifics were not discussed in advance. Questions should be asked before, not after. It is much better to get a good contract initially than to be forced to create one later to correct misunderstandings.

It is a good policy never to pay a bill until you are fully satisfied. If a painting job has been done in your home, carefully inspect the work before you pay the bill. This way someone will always return to make corrections and get their money.

How much do you believe you can save by making better contracts? Write in a suitable figure based on changes you intend to make in the future.

(limit $100)

Buying Technique 8: Avoiding Major Ripoffs

Everyone is vulnerable to con artists now and then. We must always stay alert, especially after retirement. Here's why. A few dishonest operators seem to prey on older people. They do this because they believe retirees are more vulnerable and can be confused into making a poor decision.

A friend agreed to talk to a salesperson about installing aluminum siding on her home. Not one but two men arrived and used a complicated sales presentation that caused her to become confused and sign a contract. Fortunately, after she thought about what she had done, she contacted her lawyer. He reminded her that she had rights under the three-day consumer-protection law allowing cancellation of any contract made in your home within a three-day period. This law is specifically designed for such cases, and it should be kept in mind. My friend canceled the agreement immediately.

What can you do to protect yourself?

* Stay aware that there are unethical individuals who will try to trick you into something you do not want or should buy from another source.

* Consult a second party before signing anything that is not routine. An example would be buying an insurance policy from a representative you have not dealt with previously.

* Do not sign until you have done some research and verification. Remember to use the rule of three.

Give yourself up to $50 if you will stay alert to the possibilities of a ripoff artist.

(limit $50)

Buying Technique 9:
Satisfaction Guaranteed

If you purchase a product in good faith and it does not live up to your expectations, return it no matter how much time has elapsed. This is true whether or not you have a warranty or guarantee. Most retailers stand behind what they sell—not all, but most. This is because they want you to be happy to protect their relationship with you and your friends.

Many retirees hesitate to return merchandise. Some undoubtedly are not familiar with their consumer rights. Others anticipate a hassle or embarrassment and are reluctant to inquire. They would rather keep inferior merchandise than make the effort to exchange it.

If you have been lax in returning merchandise but intend to return things you are not happy with in the future, give yourself up to $50.

(limit $50)

Buying Technique 10: Buy Only What You Need or Will Use

A fashion buyer for a retail store knows that if she selects dresses her customers won't buy because of fashion or price, she will have to reduce the price drastically to get rid of them. If you buy clothing and hang it in your closet without wearing it, you also have lost money.

The idea is to spend your discretionary funds to enrich your life. If you buy something you don't need, then you are denying yourself something you could enjoy. Like most people, you probably have too much tucked away in closets or drawers gathering dust.

How can you avoid unnecessary purchases? One way is to keep asking questions such as:

* Am I buying this for myself or my heirs?
* Do I really need it? Will I really use it?
* Would I rather add to my possessions or increase the fun I could have?
* Do I already have enough of what I am about to buy?

There should be a shift in buying habits after you retire. You should buy more for today and less for the future. This could mean spending less on material possessions and more for services such as eating out or travel.

By avoiding unnecessary purchases, you can add substantially to your savings and reach your special goal sooner. Write in a figure you can justify.

(limit $200)

Buying Technique 11: Shopping by Telephone

The expression "let your fingers do the walking" should be taken seriously. It is amazing how much time you can save (our most precious commodity) and how much money, too, by shopping and collecting information on the telephone. You can easily apply the rule of three by telephone. If you don't have time to visit three stores personally, you can always call and compare prices.

Other ways to use the telephone to save money:

* Verify that a store has the item you seek before you go there.

* Ask whether a sale is pending so you can decide to delay a purchase and save.

* Learn ahead of time if the store has a senior discount program or policy.

Some merchants seem to feel that retired people have more time to spend and should be patient while waiting for services. These people need to learn that retirees value time more, not less.

If you appreciate that shopping more by telephone can save you money, enter a figure in the box that represents what you might save by using the telephone.

(limit $25)

Buying Technique 12: Negotiate When Required

Most people in Canada do not like to bargain for a price. They accept prices or conditions to avoid a hassle. Professional buyers, on the other hand, learn to negotiate and enjoy it. Believe it or not, they earn more respect from customers and their bosses when they negotiate well. The same is true for you. Vendors will respect you more when you learn to negotiate properly.

Here are some conditions under which you should consider negotiating:

* When you sense the quoted price is flexible, and others may be getting a lower price than you.

* When the seller invites you to make an offer. This is sometimes stated openly; at other times it is implied.

* When it is a buyer's market. For example, when automobiles, homes, and similar products are not selling well and you know it.

A gentle way to discover if negotiation is possible is the simple question: "May I make an offer or are your prices firm?" If you get a "no" answer, you know where you stand. If negotiation is welcome, then you should make sure that your offer is realistically low so there is room for additional negotiation by both parties. Here's an example. Assume you want to buy a car from a private owner, and the price is listed at $3,000. You might offer $2,300, then negotiate back and forth before settling on a price of $2,600. This is called "low balling" and is an acceptable practice. If you fail to investigate whether negotiation is appropriate, you are probably paying too much.

One tip: If you feel uncomfortable negotiating, take someone along who enjoys it. This person will feel good about helping you get a better price on something, and probably will appreciate being asked.

If you agree you can sharpen you negotiating skills on future purchases, write your figure in the box. Don't be too conservative.

(limit $200)

Buying Technique 13: Work with Other People's Money

Purchasing agents learn to use the money of the seller rather than that of their own firm. For example, they delay payment of bills up to the contractual limit to keep their money earning interest. If you use credit cards (Mastercard, Visa, etc.) and delay making your payment until toward the due date of the statement, you are following this principle. You might take a trip and charge $2,000 on your credit card. The bill arrives after your return, and you pay it early the week it is due. Good! You have used their money on the trip. If you had borrowed $2,000 at 20% interest, it would have cost you $33.50 for one month.

How else can you work with the money of others?

* When making contracts to get work done, make it clear that payment is due only after the work is completed.

* Use the maximum time for noninterest payment permitted by sellers (usually shown on your statement).

* Don't pay a bill until a few days before it is due.

* Keep your money in a place that will draw interest for you.

If you feel that you can make additional efforts in this direction, write an appropriate figure in the box.

(limit $50)

Buying Technique 14: Take Advantage of Low-Season Opportunities

When it comes to vacations, retirees often have more choice than those who work. Not only is it less expensive to visit a resort area during their off-season, but also there are fewer people to contend with in restaurants and while sightseeing. This is especially true in Hawaii, Mexico, or Florida, where the climate is temperate year-round. Off-season savings usually apply to hotel and motel accommodations, air fares, and rental cars, as well as meals and services. Savings are often substantial.

If you believe you can save more money in the future by being sensitive to seasonal price fluctuations, write a suitable figure in the square.

(limit $100)

Now total the anticipated savings you put in all the boxes and enter that figure here.

Total

Did you reach or exceed $1,000? If so, you have won the game and are to be congratulated. You have demonstrated a willingness to improve your buying skills and become a better money manager. Now all you need do is to put the various buying techniques into practice. Good luck!

Summary   Retirees have certain advantages over other age groups when it comes to stretching dollars.

Retirees have sufficient clout to make buying techniques work more effectively.

With sensitivity, most buying techniques can be applied successfully.

PROBLEM TO SOLVE   **Retirement Conflict**

Before retirement, Mr. Parker was a respected purchasing agent for a large industrial company. He was considered a workaholic, leaving his wife responsible for their personal purchasing decisions. She had ample money to buy what she wanted with little consideration for price.

After retirement, Mr. Parker became interested in the way his wife made buying decisions. After observing her buying patterns for a while, he suggested the rule of three be used for any nonfood purchase over $50. He told her: "At work we always bought better-quality materials at lower prices when we checked with at least three leading suppliers. This process could help you make better purchases and stretch our dollars."

Mrs. Parker was irritated at the suggestion since he had never complained before. He reacted that he was not objecting to the past, only suggesting that things change in the future.

Is Mrs. Parker's irritation with her husband justified? Might he have approached her in a more sensitive way?

See views of the author in Appendix C.

SELF-QUIZ

True	False	
_____	_____	1. It is not possible to take full advantage of senior discounts and still have good relationships with retailers.
_____	_____	2. Few generic foods and drugs live up to the quality standards of national brands.
_____	_____	3. Sometimes stores lose money on advertised items to build customer traffic.
_____	_____	4. Most retailers stand behind their products with satisfaction-guaranteed policies.
_____	_____	5. Whenever possible, you should work with other people's money.

(Answers in Appendix C.)

18

Making Your Money Work for You

If you have never had much extra money, you may think investing is a high-risk gamble only for the wealthy. Not so. Making your money work for you is what money management is all about. The more your surplus money earns, the more discretionary income you will have to use as you desire.

Investing becomes more serious after retirement, because normally your future earning power is limited when you are no longer on a payroll. Investing may be the only way to expand income or increase your capital.

Only a few extra dollars can produce income for you. A $1,000 balance in a 5½ percent interest-bearing chequing account will produce $55 in a year's time. A $1,000 investment in a money-market account at 8½ percent interest will produce $85 in a year—more if compounded daily. Not much, you say, but it is money you would not otherwise have to enjoy.

Think of money as something like a fresh plum. Leave it in the refrigerator for a few days and it starts to shrink. The same shrinkage occurs with uninvested money because of inflation. With inflation your money buys less, because the cost of living increases. Prices go up for everyone, including business, and this increase is passed on to you. As a result, your purchasing power is reduced.

Assuming we will continue to have inflation, the only way to keep your money from shrinking in value is to keep it busy. Inflation has forced almost everyone to become an investor. Sometimes, even after a good investment, you may not keep pace with inflation. Other times, you will come out ahead. When this happens, you are a successful investor.

One thing is sure, money won't take care of itself. When it sits in a purse, a jar, or a safe-deposit box, it is idle. Invested money (loaned to others at a favorable return) is kept busy. The idea is to keep your money busy earning as much as possible.

Financial Comfort Zones The intrigue of having extra money to invest is that there is an element of risk to it. The Financial Comfort-Zone Scale is designed to help you decide your level of risk taking. You should select a zone where you are most comfortable.

FINANCIAL COMFORT-ZONE SCALE

Low-Low	Low	Middle	High	High-High

Low-Low Those in this category often have limited retirement income and investment capital. With less to invest, they risk losing more if their investment fails. A high-risk investment would cause them to lose sleep.

Low These folks may have more to invest, but they are very conservative about it. They want to know what their money will earn in advance. Fixed-rate certificates with government insurance appeals to them. If they make a stock purchase, it is usually a conservative company that has a long record of stable performance and dividend payments.

Middle Many retirees are in this category. As conservative investors, they diversify their stocks and bonds and maintain a strong cash position. If they take a high-risk investment, they limit its size.

High This group includes risk-takers who love to play the market. They lose little sleep when one of their investments backfires. They do, however, protect themselves with a reasonable balance of conservative investments.

High-High These are the high fliers. Some are willing to take high risks because they are experienced investors and know the odds. Others have plenty of money and decide to gamble with it. These risk-takers are constantly in and out of the market, often dealing in investments such as commodities and precious metals.

Other Investment Factors Next to risk, some other factors deserving careful consideration should be introduced into any investment decision.

Amount of Return on Your Investment Return is the amount your money will earn for you. It is usually expressed as a percentage of the amount invested over a one-year time period. If you invest $5,000 in a common stock and the four dividends you receive in a year equal $500, then the return on your investment is 10 percent that year. Later, if you are forced to sell the stock at a lower price, the loss would be deducted from the dividends to calculate an accurate return. The success of any investment is its ultimate level of return.

Liquidity As we get older this becomes a priority because we normally don't want to tie up money beyond the time we will enjoy using it. The easier your investments can be converted to cash, the more liquid they are. For example, anything you can sell easily is considered liquid. This includes stocks, bonds, or money invested in any "no-penalty" fund. The most liquid of all investments is money drawing interest in a chequing pass-book, or money-market account. Real-estate investments are usually considered nonliquid, because it can take months to dispose of property even if priced below what you paid for it.

Convenience This also becomes an important consideration after retirement. We don't want to use up too much of our time doing business things. Also, we may be away from home for longer periods on trips or vacation, and we don't want investments such as rental real estate to tie us down.

Diversification You have probably heard "don't put all your eggs in one basket." You should plan your investments so you can handle a few small losses but avoid any one big loss that could wipe you out. The idea behind diversification is to spread your risks. If your stocks go down, interest rates may go up. If interest goes down, stocks might go up.

Our economy is volatile, and even today's experts are having trouble predicting the future. Diversification is a sound practice.

Tax Advantages
The more a retiree has to invest, the more tax considerations might come into play. Once a person reaches above the 30 percent bracket, tax advantages are critical. For example, a retiree in the 50 percent bracket (all income beyond that point is taxed 50 percent) might consider capital gains, which could be tax free. If a security appreciates by 10 percent, it would be the same as 20 percent to an investor in the 50 percent bracket because the tax would not apply. For investors with high incomes, tax factors can overshadow all other considerations. Investments should, however, be for sound principles first and tax savings second.

Investment Decisions
The more money you have after retirement, the more investment decisions you will have to make. The good news is that you have a larger security blanket. The bad news is that you must ensure that your decisions are appropriate. When it comes to making difficult investment decisions, the procedure explained in Chapter 5 works well so long as the five factors (liquidity, diversification, return, convenience and tax) are taken into consideration. Financial decisions can be complex because of different needs and personalities. This is why some investors, in one comfort zone, may find it difficult to fully understand the decisions of others in another zone.

Investment Portfolios
Some retirees become financial experts because they have considerable money to invest and the time to spend on it. They often have a large portfolio of investments. A portfolio is simply a list of the places where your money is working. A typical portfolio would include stocks, bonds, money-market funds, plus other investments. You should make an analysis of your portfolio at frequent intervals to determine if some of your investments should be changed or modified.

Some investors keep in touch with what is happening via newspapers, newsletter, and magazines. Others like to watch more immediate market developments through cable television services that bring the information into their homes. A few use personal computers to keep track of their investments. Individuals who buy and sell frequently, constantly monitoring their portfolios, make investing a part-time career (Plan B). They may spend several hours each week controlling their money.

Rose Learns the Ropes
When it comes to keeping our money busy, none of us can afford to be observers. We should get our "investment feet" wet sooner or later.

This happened rather suddenly to Rose after she lost her husband. She discovered she had $60,000 to invest, most of it from her husband's life-insurance policies. She was nervous at first; but after some research, a discussion with two investment brokers, and attendance at an investment seminar for beginners, she now feels more competent. She placed herself in the "low" category on the Financial Comfort-Zone Scale. After six months of decision making, her portfolio looks like this:

* *Fixed-Rate Term Certificates—$20,000*
  Rose lives close to a branch of a local credit union. Her first investment was in a fixed-rate (11 percent) term (30 months) certificate. The $20,000 is totally insured by the Canada Deposit Insurance Corporation (CDIC). Rose understands there is a substantial penalty to withdraw money from this account before the 30-month term ends. This is within her comfort zone, and she feels it will help keep her ahead of inflation. Interest in this account is compounded daily, which means that interest is added to the rest of her money on a daily basis. Her interest starts working immediately, and her total grows bigger each day.

* *Government Bonds—$5,000*
  Because of their high level of safety, Rose decided to invest in Government of Canada bonds. Two things about government bonds appealed. First, they were easy to purchase at her bank or brokerage house. Second, she discovered that income tax could be deferred on the appreciation (not the interest) part of each bond until it was redeemed.

* *Utility Stocks—$15,000*
  After much deliberation, Rose decided to invest $15,000 in utility stocks. She selected the companies that supply her with both gas and electricity. She got the idea from an investment counselor after he informed her both were highly rated companies recommended by experts. She knew everyone needed these energy items; and knowing she was a stockholder (part owner) make her feel better when she paid her own bills. She decided that instead of receiving a dividend cheque every three months, she would ask the companies to automatically reinvest her dividends to purchase more stock. She learned there were two advantages to this. First, no brokerage fees were involved, and stockholders received a slightly lower

price than that quoted in the market. Second, unlike most stock dividends, no income tax was due on these stocks until they were sold. Rose also hopes to use the capital gains exemption to pay no tax at all.

Now Rose enjoys watching the prices of her stocks in the daily paper, especially when they go up. She knows there is some risk involved, but she believes it is within her comfort zone.

* *Money-Market Mutual Fund Account—$10,000*
This was a difficult investment for Rose to make because, at first, she did not understand the risk. Now she does. She recognizes she has no direct control over how her money is invested since professionals handle it not only for her, but for thousands of other investors in the fund. Most mutual-fund investors send small amounts of money into the fund, where investment specialists use these combined assets to buy and sell. These professionals spend full time maintaining the fund portfolio in an effort to make money for small investors. Some funds regularly outperform others, so Rose was careful about the one she selected.

* *Treasury Bill—$10,000*
Rose surprised herself when she decided to buy, through her local bank, a treasury bill at the regular Thursday auction. Once the process was explained to her, she decided it was a convenient low-risk investment that was within her comfort zone. Her bank acted as a broker and bought a $10,000 treasury bill in her name, discounted. In other words, the interest she was entitled to at the end of six months was deducted from the $10,000 when the bill was acquired; so she paid less than $10,000. She paid the bank a $30 fee. The bill Rose purchased will be held by the bank; so at the end of the six-month period she can either ask for the money or inform the bank she would like to "roll the bill over" for another period of time (six months or a year).

One reason Rose likes treasury bills is that she feels it makes her a little more diversified and sophisticated. She sometimes mentions she owns a T-bill to a few of her close friends.

Preretirement Portfolio

Mr. and Mrs. Spencer spent a great deal of time developing their investment portfolio before retirement. They worked on the plan together, and each contributed part of their income. Now that their retirement date has arrived, they feel they have accomplished their goal. They refer to their fixed income (pensions, CPP and OAS) as security blanket #1 and their investment portfolio as security blanket #2. On the date of their retirement, their portfolio included their home, owned free and clear and valued at around $100,000. (They intend to sell it sometime during the next 10 years and move into a condominium.) Their other investments include:

* *Company Stock—$40,000*
  For the last 15 years, they have taken advantage of a stock plan offered by Mr. Spencer's firm. He purchased his limit through a payroll deduction plan. By taking advantage of this offer, his stock was purchased at 15 percent below market price, and all brokerage fees were waived. The dividends were reinvested to buy additional stock. The market price of the stock is now $40,000, which is pretty good considering Mr. Spencer invested less than $20,000 over the years to accumulate it.

* *Diversified Stock—$40,000*
  Over the last eight years they have purchased common stock currently valued at $40,000. The cost of this investment has been $38,000, so they have not been highly successful. They have, however, enjoyed spending the dividends that arrive each quarter. Also, Mr. Spencer enjoys buying and selling stock. His decisions have mostly been the result of discussions with colleagues. He hopes to be more successful now that he has more time to study the market. So far only common stock has been purchased, but he intends to buy some preferred stock because it is more secure. Mr. Spencer also enjoys deducting the dividend tax credit each year on his income tax return. He knows that a 9% dividend is equivalent to 12% interest return and always compares dividend and interest payments using this one and one-third multiple.

* *Real-Estate Investment—$120,000*
  The Spencers feel fortunate. They purchased a business property as an investment before real-estate prices escalated so much during the 1970s. After a small down payment, they have reinvested all rents plus some additional money of their own, so their current equity is $120,000. They are still paying on a modest first mortgage. This investment has some important tax advantages for the Spencers, because they deduct all interest on their loan, claim a depreciation allowance, and write off their expenses. They have continually

upgraded the property and, as a result, have shown a cash loss each year. Both feel that this property, along with their home, provides diversification and makes up a major part of their total portfolio. They do not resent the time, energy, and problems that come with this type of investment. They also realize that the appreciation from their original purchase price can be received tax free as a capital gain if they sell the property.

* *Corporate Bonds—$20,000*

As something of a balancing factor, the Spencers recently acquired two corporate bonds. These are long-term bonds issued by well-regarded national firms. The interest is paid twice each year and will be spent on entertainment after retirement. The bonds can be sold at any time, so the Spencers are getting not only a high return but also liquidity, convenience, and diversification. They are required to pay income tax on their interest, so there is no appreciable tax advantage. They do, however, feel secure about having the bonds in their safety-deposit box.

* *Precious Metals—$10,000*

Mrs. Spencer was the one who encouraged the purchase of some gold coins and silver bars to enhance their portfolio. Her rationale was that, if everything else fell apart, they would still have $5,000 worth of gold and silver to start over again. Unfortunately, these precious metals were acquired at a high price, so currently this investment has not worked out. Although they are not getting a return and the price continues to deteriorate, both still feel that they will eventually come out ahead. Each time they visit their safety-deposit box, they admire their gold and silver.

* *IRA Account—$8,000 (plus interest)*

Mr. and Mrs. Spencer only took advantage of the RRSP legislation two years before their retirement. They each contributed their maximum of $2,000 per year for two years. The maximum was calculated at $3,500 less their personal pension contributions to their company pension plan of $1,500 annually. They know tax shelters accumulate more money because interest is compounded daily and taxes are deferred. They are also realistic about the requirements for making withdrawals. The law dictates money must be withdrawn when they become 71 years of age. When this time arrives, Mrs. Spencer expects to use this money for travel.

In all, the Spencer's portfolio, not including their home, totals approximately $248,000. The current return on their investments is almost equal to their fixed income from pensions and CPP and OAS. This is exactly what they hoped for when they made their financial plans years ago. In the years ahead, they expect to allow their rental property to pay itself off, so they can continue to maintain the tax advantage. They want to spend both their fixed and investment income at a slightly accelerated rate with more vacations and some international travel. They expect their money to continue working for them at the highest possible level. With this in mind, Mr. Spencer will spend increased time evaluating his portfolio to ensure it continues to fit their financial comfort zone.

Other Investment Possibilities

The two investment scenarios presented do not even begin to reflect available investment opportunities. For example, here are two others:

Municipal Bonds

You may purchase, through a broker, municipal bonds that pay attractive rates of interest. The larger your investment portfolio, the more attractive they may become. Municipal bonds are sold by cities to finance improvements. New bonds reflect current interest rates, but you can also purchase older bonds at discounts created by their lower interest rates.

To receive interest from such a bond, you "clip a coupon" when it matures and turn it into a bank or savings and loan for redemption. You can almost always sell such bonds, so they are quite "liquid." Municipal bonds are rated like corporate bonds, so make sure you get a high enough rating to fit your financial comfort zone.

Mortgages

You can, if you have the money, make loans to individuals at any interest rate and pay-back period agreed upon. This investment is normally secured by the borrower's property. In effect, you become your own banker. Instead of depositing your money in a savings and loan (for them to lend), you act as the financial institution and lend your money directly. Your security is often a mortgage; when properly recorded, this shows the money owed to you and, in case of default, makes you owner of the property secured. It is also possible to purchase a second or third mortgage. Keep in mind the person with the first mortgage is always given first consideration in a default. Most people feel comfortable only with first mortgages. Another idea is to lend against a short payment schedule, where payment can be set within a specified number of years.

There are yet other investments you may want to explore such as:

    * Stock options (which can be used to insure gains on stocks which have not been sold)

    * Self directed registered retirement savings plans (where you manage your retirement funds)

    * Registered retirement income funds (RRIFs)

The opportunities and variations are endless.

Investment Tips   It takes capital, time, and professional advice to build a good, individualized portfolio. Some retirees are better suited to do this than others. Here are some tips to keep in mind as you put your extra money to work.

Tip #1   Stay within your own financial comfort zone. To most people, sleep is more important than gambling for a higher return on an investment.

Tip #2   When it comes to investments, no one has all the answers. Financial markets are influenced by so many factors (national and international) that you cannot predict beyond an element of educated guesswork.

Tip #3   Seek professional help, but make your own final judgments. As with a medical problem, second opinions are valuable. Refrain from becoming overdependent on a single adviser.

Tip #4   If married, work as a team. Two heads are often better than one. Also, should anything happen to one spouse, the other is better prepared to take over.

Tip #5   Stay current with regard to your investments. If changes are required, you will be in a position to take action before you get hurt. You cannot tuck your investments in a safe-deposit box and expect them to take care of themselves. They require more monitoring today than ever before.

Tip #6   No matter how much you know or don't know about investments, keep learning. What was a good investment last week might be a poor one today. The financial world is always changing. If you can't keep in touch, make certain you have financial advisers who do.

Keeping your money hard at work with good results is not easy. If you are not careful, minding your funds may require more time than you are willing to give.

Summary   In making investments, it is important to discover and stay within your financial comfort zone.

Return on investments, liquidity, convenience, diversification, and tax advantages all are factors that must be considered.

Investment of personal funds will become more complex in the future, thus requiring more professional help.

PROBLEM TO SOLVE **Turnover**

Mrs. Z has been getting acquainted with the investment portfolio prepared and put into operation by her husband before his death. Although he never discussed the intricacies of investing with her, he did leave everything in good order. His current investments were listed in precise order, including the stockbrokers and investment counselors he dealt with in the past.

Although Mrs. Z is intelligent and well educated, she does not feel capable of maintaining the portfolio, even with the advice of professionals. She would like to turn it over to a single financial counselor whom she trusts. In this way, her $250,000 could work hard for her, and she would only need to deal with a monthly accounting from her counselor. She is willing to pay a reasonable fee for such a service.

What precautions do you feel Mrs. Z should take in making this move? How can she be sure about the honesty of such a counselor? How does she know he will understand her comfort zone? How does she get started?

See the author's comments in Appendix C.

SELF-QUIZ

True   *False*

_____   _____   1. Liquidity in investments becomes less important as we grow older.

_____   _____   2. It is a good idea to keep at least a few thousand dollars in a savings account so that it can be withdrawn at any moment.

_____   _____   3. A self directed RRSP does not have tax-shelter benefits.

_____   _____   4. The dividend tax credit will generate a tax refund if no tax is otherwise payable.

_____   _____   5. Return is the amount your money will earn for you in a year expressed as a percentage of the amount invested.

(Answers in Appendix C.)

19

Financial Strategies

At my retirement party, an old friend proposed what I thought at the time was a very odd toast: "I hope you outlast your money." At first, I thought it was nothing more than a humorous twist on the overused phrase: "You can't take it with you." Later, I began to think about my friend's words.

Was it possible, I wondered, to plan my retirement income so I could live with style and still break even at the end? Could I have my cake and eat it, too? All I would need to do is spend my income and nest egg at just the right rate. Intriguing!

Most of us want our money to outlast us—at least part of it—to provide a cushion for late-in-life contingencies. Under no conditions do we want to be dependent on others. To achieve the balance that is right for us requires some clever planning and a little luck.

209

Everything I've read on financial planning has dealt with creating and enhancing retirement income. The emphasis has been on having *enough* money. This is Phase I. At some point after retirement, we need to plan for Phase II. We need to know how to use what we have accumulated (no matter how small) to enrich the last phase of our life cycle. Wise spending, not saving, is perhaps the real financial challenge of our later years.

To start you thinking about Phase II, the following strategies may be worthy of consideration. Read all ten before deciding which strategy is best suited to your desires, philosophy, values, and financial situation. The more you discuss options with friends and spouse the better. To be happy with your ultimate choice, it should fall within your personal comfort zone and have a positive impact on your lifestyle.

The Squeeze-and-Spend Strategy

Retired people with limited incomes and small nest eggs do not have a wide range of strategies. Nevertheless, one is required. In fact, it could be argued that the less money accumulated in Phase I, the more a good plan for Phase II can accomplish. The squeeze-and-spend strategy says that you should make renewed efforts to squeeze out more disposable income from your present income (Chapter 17) and what you save should be spent on things that put more style in your life. Live it up within your limitations. This approach may appear to be high risk, but remember you are spending money you would otherwise not have had unless you economized. Therefore, enjoy!

Al and Harriet

Al and Harriet have a combined CPP and OAS of $780 each month. Nothing else. They sold their car three years ago to reduce expenses. They are very successful at holding their spending to $700 per month. This provides discretionary income for them of $80 every 30 days. They spend this money to have fun. They have wine with dinner, play bingo at a local center, and use public transportation to go to nearby events. Their attitude is: "If we started to save what little money we are able to squeeze out of our limited income, we would also squeeze out the fun of living. A little extra money to spend as we wish keeps life interesting."

Check if you agree.

Advantages to this strategy:

 Fun to live dangerously. Not all retirees are conservative. Many enjoy living it up.

Provides a motivating goal. Saving money to receive immediate rewards is motivating to some people.

☐ *Nothing to lose.* When your retirement income is modest and you cannot do anything about it, why worry?

Disadvantages to this strategy:

☐ *No feeling of security.* To live without a small cushion falls outside the comfort zone of many retirees.

☐ *No contingency fund.* If the TV needs repair, you can't pay the bill until you save something.

☐ *Dependency on government.* Without a cushion, it might be necessary to ask for help from an agency.

The Squeeze-and-Save Strategy

This plan is similar to squeeze and spend and also applies to retirees with modest incomes. It is specifically designed for those who enjoy saving more than spending and are happy building a nest egg. Splurging is not their style. They prefer to cover themselves with a security blanket of savings. Some go to extremes and deny themselves necessities like a proper diet. Spending money hurts these people, especially when they worry about inflation. Often these people are victims of the Depression and are dominated by fear.

Ruth's Strategy

Ruth is lucky to live in a small town where expenses are low and her CPP and OAS cheques go further. If desired, she could enjoy a few luxuries, but she refuses to spend the money because she gets more pleasure adding to her financial cushion. Her goal is to save a miniumum of 10 percent each month out of her cheques. Some months she saves 20 percent. Although she has an adequate diet, her home is often so cold in the winter that she is embarrassed to have visitors. Still, Ruth considers herself happy and looks forward to many additional years in her present lifestyle.

Check if you agree.

Advantages to this strategy:

☐ *Provides a feeling of financial security.* Money in the bank provides peace of mind.

☐ A *motivating goal for some.* Saving money is a reward in itself for some individuals.

☐ *Money available for emergencies.* Provides a sense of independence no matter what happens.

Disadvantages to this strategy:

☐ *Loss of immediate rewards.* People who save rather than spend lead more restrictive lifestyles.

☐ *Possibility of fewer friends.* A few individuals are so motivated to save that they chase their friends away. They often turn down social events because of the cost.

☐ *Money saved may be worth less later.* Under inflationary conditions, money saved now will buy less later.

The Modest-Cushion-and-Relax Plan

It's easy to envy those adopting this strategy. Frequently these retirees calculate how much money they think they will need for a comfortable cushion. They then invest or bank that sum and relax. Once they have their personal cushion, they cease to worry about money. From that point on they buy necessities, pay bills, and enjoy life. They tell themselves: "I had a savings goal in mind and reached it. That plus my income (from government or corporate pensions) will have to suffice. I'm not going to change it."

There are psychological advantages to this worry-free strategy. The critics, however, call this the Ostrich Plan, claiming that today it is unrealistic to count on anything but a very large cushion. These people, say the critics, have their heads in the retirement quicksand.

Jake and Sally

Jake and Sally started building their cushion long before retirement. It was still inadequate when the time arrived. They had agreed on $100,000 as a goal, but they had only $80,000 at retirement. As a result, both took part-time jobs. In three years they reached their goal. At that point, Sally and Jake started to enjoy themselves. They had sufficient income to provide $300 in discretionary income each month. They spent every cent of it. They still had financial peace of mind because of the $100,000 they had invested. They had enough spending money to give their lives flexibility and were pleased with their strategy. They did not share their plan with their children or friends because keeping it secret was part of the fun.

*Check
if you agree.*

Advantages to this strategy:

☐ *Provides both security and discretionary income.* For many it seems to be the right combination. You can have your cake and eat it, too.

☐ *Cushion earns additional money.* Properly invested savings should grow.

☐ *Spending discretionary money is more fun.* With a cushion, it's easier to enjoy spending money foolishly.

Disadvantages to this strategy:

☐ *Cushion investments can turn sour.* Some people lose a good cushion through unwise investments.

☐ *Figuring the right amount may be a problem.* Some retirees keep changing their minds when they get close to a predetermined cushion amount. They never reach a point where they can relax and start spending.

☐ *Spending cushion money for emergencies is difficult.* A cushion is designed for unexpected expenses, but many find it painful to use when the time comes.

The Big-Cushion/ Save-Save Strategy

Retirees subscribing to this strategy often do so with little forethought. They probably had good luck during Phase I (accumulating wealth). They enjoyed the process so much (very ego gratifying) that they have trouble switching to Phase II. No matter how large their cushion, it is never enough. As a result, they spend their retirement investing and reinvesting. They frequently live very frugally. Even though they know they can't take it with them, they enjoy making it too much to give it up. Investing and saving becomes not a means to an end but an end in itself. Often these people are wealthy and, ultimately, wish they had given more consideration to other strategies.

Harry's Cushion

Harry is 82 years old and known among his friends as tight-fisted. Although he will sometimes surprise everyone by making a big purchase (new car), he then turns around and embarks on another saving spree. Harry enjoys adding up his cushion and watching it grow. It pleases him to make good investments. Money is something of a game—the more you accumulate, the more you win. Harry keeps telling himself that, if he makes it to 85, he will start spending his cushion. If he survives until then, chances are he'll probably change his mind.

Check if you agree.

Advantages to this strategy:

☐ *Excellent sense of security.* Although big-cushion people frequently admit they are hooked on money, they say the size of their security blanket is responsible for most of their happiness.

☐ *Ego rewarding.* Making and saving money is a form of personal fulfillment for some. It is how they get their "kicks."

☐ *They are usually happy with their lifestyles.* Spending more money on themselves would not fall within their comfort zone.

Disadvantages to this strategy:

☐ *Overconcentration on money.* Many use valuable leisure time to earn more money than they can ever spend.

☐ *Money has a destructive hold on some people.* A few miss out on the special rewards of retirement because their lives are centered around making more money instead of enjoying it.

☐ *Excessive worry.* The bigger the cushion the more some people worry. They worry about losing it or what to do with it. A few agonize over leaving it to those who either don't deserve it or won't appreciate it. Money can be a burden to some.

The Capital-Protection Package

Members of this group seek a balance between saving and spending during retirement years. This strategy is a variation on the previous one, but the differences are significant. Those who adopt the capital-protection package enjoyed success in Phase I. They establish a cut-off date on earning and saving, however, and promise themselves to begin spending their income without disturbing their capital.

No matter how large or small their capital (cushion) may be, it is sacred. It is their security blanket. Those who adopt this strategy can often be found on cruise ships or the golf course. The moment they return from one trip, they calculate next year's return on their capital and plan the next trip accordingly. These people are often happy with their solution, feeling they have the best of both worlds. It seldom occurs to them that they could begin to dip into their capital and take an extra trip or buy a luxury item they have always wanted.

Opal's Choice

Opal's husband left her a small estate—their home, some savings, considerable stock, and a tax-sheltered annuity. She also receives Old Age Security. Opal steadfastly refuses to touch her capital. Each month she totals her interest and dividends and finds a way to spend it. She puts her interest and dividends in a special-event account. This strategy fits her comfort zone perfectly. Her cushion is adequate and its earnings enrich her life. Opal feels she has the best of both worlds.

Check if you agree.

Advantages to this strategy:

☐ *Right combination for some.* Those who don't mind having their capital grow smaller because of inflation and want more money to spend now have a good solution.

☐ *Easy decision.* It is not a complicated strategy, requiring constant review. It is simple to implement.

☐ *Cushion can be any size.* This strategy makes sense for a millionaire or a person with only a few thousand dollars.

Disadvantages to this strategy:

☐ *Inflexible.* Investment portfolios need to be updated. Those who adopt this plan often see their investments deteriorate.

☐ *Capital might disappear.* If a retiree neglects the portfolio long enough, and if inflation is great enough, the cushion could become insignificant.

☐ *Insecure without it.* Some are so hooked on this strategy that they never spend any of their capital.

The Actuarial Strategy

Recently I noticed a bumper sticker that read "We Are Spending Our Children's Inheritance." This plan probably suited the owners of that vehicle. Known as the "come-out-even" strategy, the actuarial strategy involves spending money so that little or nothing is left in the estate for children, friends, or charitable institutions.

For example, as a widow of 65, you can, according to the actuarial tables, anticipate 18.4 more years (this figure will probably increase in the future). Your income from government or company pension will remain relatively constant no matter how long you live. It is possible for you to plan on spending your capital (and the income it produces) over a specified time period. You must take into account that as you dip into your capital, the income it produces will diminish. For a 17-year calculation, simply total your assets and divide by 17. This strategy can be a high risk. If you have a spouse, the calculations are more complex, and you may want to talk to a financial expert before embarking on the actuarial strategy.

Mary's Decision

Looking at the statistical tables prepared by her insurance company, Mary decided she had a good chance to reach age 83. Her total cushion (capital) was $40,000. Her age is 68. She decided that rather than save her cushion, she would spend it at a rate of $3,000 per year until it was gone. Mary decided on this strategy because she had no family and no special charities. Her attitude was to treat herself by spending her money as she wished. She had no logical reason for saving it.

Check if you agree.

Advantages to this strategy:

☐ *Retirement years more enjoyable.* If spending money will make you happier, then the advantage is you can spend it while you will enjoy it most.

☐ *Might eliminate estate taxes.* The government can't take something from you if it is spent in advance.

☐ *Excellent plan if it works.* Winding up close to breakeven is a dream of many. If this is your dream and it works, you can take satisfaction from beating the system.

Disadvantages to this strategy:

☐ *Plan might leave you stranded.* You could wind up broke and insecure.

☐ *You might want your security blanket back.* Once you spend most of your capital, remorse might set in and ruin your later years.

☐ *Actuarial tables are for large groups.* As an individual you may outlive the tables by many years. If this happens, you will have lost your security blanket.

The Big-Scare Contingency Plan

This strategy is a supplemental strategy frequently called into play when something unexpected happens. For example, if a retiree who is an advocate of the big-cushion/save-save strategy encounters a serious medical problem, he might decide to spend part of his cushion while he will still enjoy it. "Why not live it up in case I won't be around?" You may know members of this group who take hurry-up trips around the world. The big-scare plan is, in essence, a speed-up strategy. You do some things you had always planned to do, but you do them sooner and faster. As with all strategies, some risk is involved. You might, for example, go on an all-out, once-in-a-lifetime spending spree and then discover your medical condition was a false alarm. Should this happen, a reverse contingency plan might be required.

Mrs. W

Mrs. W had protected her sizable capital for 15 years when the doctor gave his diagnosis. It was hard for her to take. She often wondered what she would do if she had only a few months to live. With the diagnosis, she made some quick, hard decisions. She first revised her will. Next Mrs. W decided to take a series of expensive trips she had delayed earlier in life. She was amazed at how much fun it was to spend money. Fortunately, she felt well enough to enjoy five trips before she became confined. When this happened, she still had enough capital to maintain her independence.

Check if you agree.

Advantages to this strategy:

☐ *Dreams can still come true.* A few people seem to have a delightful last fling by spending their savings quickly.

☐ *Satisfaction in living an accelerated lifestyle.* Even under such circumstances a big splurge can be fun.

☐ *Going first class for a short time is better than never going first class at all.* Sitting on your capital under these circumstances is not a good alternative.

Disadvantages to this strategy:

☐ *The uncertainty of it all.* How much better it is to speed up without a health problem.

☐ *Money not spent as well.* People are more likely to make poor choices under such pressures.

☐ *Too much pressure.* The danger of trying to crowd too much into a short period can be counterproductive.

The Spread-Around-Ahead-of-Time Pattern

This happy plan can easily be incorporated with others. It is popular for all retirees, but especially appealing to those more advanced in years. This strategy advocates giving away money or belongings while the donor is still around to enjoy the process. Used in a sensible way, this strategy can provide gratification to the giver and a special reward to those who receive the gift. My wife still talks about a $100 gift she received as a teenager from a distant but favorite aunt. There are also tax advantages when you give your money away to registered charities or athletic organizations.

Some people wait until a scare of some sort before embarking on this strategy. Some risks are involved. For example, some individuals might enjoy the process so much they get carried away. Also, it can be a mistake to give children too much too soon. Finally, it is not a good plan for those who might get upset watching how some of their gifts may be used.

Mrs. M's Dilemma

Mrs. M decided a few years ago she could get more attention from her four children if she gave them a small part of her estate ahead of time. It worked. She then had some unexpected expenses, and her capital was not sufficient to cover them. As a result, she started to worry. Unfortunately, her children did not respond to her problems, and Mrs. M was soon back where she had been before—only worse. By giving away her capital prematurely, she lost some of her freedom and control.

Check if you agree.

Advantages to this strategy:

☐ *Protects estate.* Under the tax laws, it is possible to give 20% of net income to charities and get a tax reduction. There are other savings.

☐ *Gain more attention.* Those who receive money often show appreciation while you are still around.

☐ *Life plan more complete.* The distribution of money ahead of time provides most with a feeling of fulfillment.

Disadvantages to this strategy:

☐ *May be premature.* Some retirees get carried away with their generosity and discover they have needlessly lost some freedom and control.

☐ *May not be fully appreciated.* If you give money and it is not fully appreciated, remorse can set in.

☐ *May do children more harm than good.* Giving money too soon can cause children to not reach their potential because they have too much protection.

The Formal-Trust Program

This is a strategy you may already know. Many people with sizable estates establish a legal master plan that provides control over their funds under a trust while they are alive and then distributes their wealth after they are gone. This traditional approach has many advantages. For example, it permits leaving funds to loved ones under certain conditions. Most who elect this route claim that, once they have divided their estates, they relax and enjoy life more. Others may worry about whether they have made the right decision.

Mr. and Mrs. Franklin

Mr. and Mrs. Franklin had accumulated a sizable estate. When they were 70, they decided what they needed and put the rest in an inter vivos trust for their three children and seven grandchildren. Once this was accomplished, they felt more relaxed and satisfied. Their trustee (a local bank) took care of all investment matters, and the Franklins devoted their time to entertaining and creative efforts.

Check if you agree.

Advantages to this strategy:

☐ *Plan is carried out no matter what happens.* A trust permits people to have control over the expenditure of their money when they are no longer around.

☐ *Relieves the pressure.* Once the trust is completed, many feel they have done their best, and there is no need to continue making investments themselves. Let the professionals do it.

☐ *Everything is legal ahead of time.* A good trust agreement makes it easier on those who inherit the money (fewer bad feelings).

Disadvantages to this strategy:

☐ *Inflexible.* Once a trust is set up, it is often difficult and expensive to change.

☐ *Decisions are difficult.* Dividing up a pie can be difficult and taxing. Many avoid it as long as possible.

☐ *Trustees may not be competent.* Turning over business matters to others involves risk.

The Delay-Option Strategy

Some people consider all the various retirement strategies but never seem to make a choice. They always seem poised to make a decision, but they delay and delay. Their rationale is that life changes too fast. "Why adopt a strategy today that may not meet my needs tomorrow?" "Why lock into a plan that I'm not sure I'll be happy with?"

These people point to new tax laws, family realignments, and their own changing lifestyles as justification. You hear them say: "The best way to stay in control is to remain flexible—and change with the times. The best strategy of all is knowing the available options in order to make the best decision when the proper time comes."

Warren's Worries

Warren accepted his firm's offer to stay on the payroll as a consultant after he was 65. He wanted to keep his income as high as possible until he developed a financial strategy. The one thing he did not want was to lock himself in too soon. Inflation worried Warren. The state of the economy worried him. He knew he needed a plan, but he didn't think the time was right. One afternoon Warren had a heart attack; and three months later, he realized it was essential that he develop a plan. He almost delayed too long.

Check if you agree.

Advantages to this strategy:

☐ *You don't lock yourself in.* You can adjust to changing conditions on a monthly basis.

☐ *No plan is better than a bad one.* Some become disenchanted when their plans don't work. The longer you wait the less chance of disappointment.

☐ *No plan can still be a running plan.* Those who think a good deal about financial strategies have, in effect, a running plan. That is, they are thinking as they go. Because of this, they can come up with a plan quickly if necessary.

Disadvantages to this strategy:

☐ *Plan needed for ultimate fulfillment.* The purpose of a strategy is to help you enjoy retirement years more, not less.

☐   *Quick plans are risky.* Those who wait too long may be forced into an ill-advised emergency plan.

☐   *Procrastination creates inner pressure.* Those who delay continue to carry the problem with them. Those who design a plan release these pressures and enjoy life more.

Your Long-Range Financial Strategy

Now that you have reviewed the various strategies, you are invited to design your own. It's unlikely that one single strategy fits your special needs or desires. Based on your comfort zones, some adjustment is probably necessary. You might want to combine two or more of the plans into a strategy you can live with. To assist you to develop the best plan, respond to the following:

* Phase I is preretirement financial planning. Phase II is a strategy to spend money after retirement.

* Everyone should design their own strategy to meet their needs, philosophy, and comfort zone.

* How you learn to spend money after retirement is critical to the quality of life enjoyed.

PROBLEM TO SOLVE   **Time Conflict**

Mr. and Mrs. Trent are 65 years old. Both are in good health. They sold their farm last year and only recently realized the extent of their estate. Mr. Trent has devoted considerable time to the development of a financial strategy, and he describes his three-part plan to his wife in this way:

Part I   Continue to build an even bigger cushion until age 70. Devote substantial time to the investments until then. Little change in lifestyle will take place before this point.

Part II   At age 70, all interest and dividends will be spent on trips and a better lifestyle.

Part III   At 80, begin using the capital and divide the estate among the children to avoid taxes.

Mrs. Trent does not like the strategy her husband developed. She not only wants to spend all interest and dividends immediately, but also to start reducing their capital. She worked hard all her life and wants to make up for things she has denied herself. She wants to travel, buy a new car, and have a more exciting lifestyle. She would like to divide the estate not later than age 70. Mrs. Trent does not want to deal with plans beyond that point. Until then, she wants to spend money on things they have talked about all their lives.

Think about a compromise plan that you feel would satisfy both parties and compare your answer with that of the author in Appendix C.

SELF-QUIZ

True	False	
_____	_____	1. Following retirement, switching from a philosophy of saving to spending is easy.
_____	_____	2. Most retirees quickly dip into their capital.
_____	_____	3. A tailored plan will probably incorporate ideas from more than one of the strategies found in this chapter.
_____	_____	4. The actuarial strategy has the least risk.
_____	_____	5. Generally, the older one gets the more likely that one wishes more money had been spent for personal enjoyment sooner.

(Answers in Appendix C.)

20

Estate Planning

The power of perpetuating our property in our families is one of the most valuable and interesting circumstances belonging to it.
Edmund Burke

When my great-grandmother died, my father explained it to me and my sisters by saying "she took the ferry." This soft, poetic expression is still in use in our family.

Leaving a Will When most people "take the ferry," they leave some valuable properties behind them. Those who plan well also leave a will or trust that describes how they want their estate distributed. Most people gain considerable satisfaction after preparing this document.

* "After I struggled through the preparation of my will, I found peace of mind."

* It's a great feeling to have things in order."

223

* "When we finally got around to creating our will, we discovered it brought us closer together."

By contrast, the poor planners or nonplanners usually leave a disorganized, unpackaged, legal mess. You can tell when this is going to happen by flippant expressions such as:

* "Wish I could be around to watch the fight over my estate."
* "If I spend all my time planning, I won't have any fun getting there."
* "I've found a way to take it with me."

People who prepare wills or trusts often fall into one of the following classifications.

The Delayers
These people dread the process so much that they either postpone it too long or handle it in such a cursory way that it brings little or no satisfaction. They say: "It's such and ugly subject that I just can't get around to doing anything at this point. Besides, what's the hurry? Laws keep changing, and I'll have plenty of time later. All it takes is a few hours, and I'm going to be around for a while."

The Worriers
These individuals agonize over every detail of the will until they drive themselves and their lawyers to distraction. Then, once the will is complete, they continue to make unnecessary changes. "Since making a will 10 years ago, I have changed it six times myself, plus one major overhaul suggested by my lawyer. Now I wish I had waited longer. Think of the money and agony I would have saved." Worriers include those who make too many (but sometimes necessary) changes and those who make temperamental changes. Unfortunately, some people adjust their wills based on the current status of their relationship with beneficiaries. Lawyers who deal with estates can provide juicy examples.

The Realists
These people accept the need for a will or a trust and deal with it in an open, forthright manner. They see the process as important and don't delay beyond a reasonable time. They understand there is no such thing as a perfect instrument and therefore don't agonize over it. Realists recognize changes should be made only when necessary. "I feel good that our will is made, but we still have to be realistic and change it now and then. It will be easier when our adult children settle down. Every time there's a divorce, we are forced to rethink the distribution of our estate."

The Opportunists
It is possible to be realistic yet still make the process a once-in-a-lifetime opportunity. These individuals view the preparation of a

will or trust as a chance to pull their families closer together. They do this through open communication with the beneficiaries ahead of time. They state their views and then listen. In doing this, they accomplish their estate-distribution goals and strengthen relationships at the same time. Once completed, the will is more meaningful to all. "You can't imagine the difference in the relationships with our children since we started talking openly about our estate. They know our feelings and desires, and we know theirs. For example, they want us to enjoy ourselves first; and whatever is left, they will use wisely. Best of all, we have avoided holding money over their heads to gain a change in their behavior. They seem to respect us for this. We are still in control, but they know they are part of the family and have a voice. When it comes to estate planning, it's the best approach."

If you have yet to make arrangements for the distribution of your estate, or your present will needs revision, now is the time to act. Obviously, the more you know about the legal aspects, the better you will be able to communicate to your lawyer and the more you will satisfy your special desires and dreams. The following will help you get started.

Estate Planning The purpose of this section is not only to determine what you know about estate planning but also to prepare you for material to come in the chapter.

Shortly you will have an opportunity to prepare a form you can use as a planning device. Completing this form in advance could save you money if you visit a lawyer who charges by the hour. It will also demonstrate that you are not an ordinary client, but one who is more in charge. This may result in your receiving better attention. Finally it should mean you wind up with a better will.

Here are some ideas to help you to prepare your form.

List Your Assets Refer to your financial statement prepared in Chapter 16 and record all assets at current market value. List any insurance policies at face value rather than cash-surrender value.

Know Form of Ownership Knowing the form of your assets' ownership will save you considerable time. To discover this, you may need to make a trip to your safety-deposit box. Some forms of ownership include:

* *Community property:* If an asset is held in this manner, you can dispose of only your share (50 percent) through your will. Once

PRETEST FOR ESTATE PLANNING

Check your responses with the answers provided to ensure any mis-understandings are immediately corrected. If wills and trusts are new to you, you may miss several questions. You may also surprise yourself with how much you already know.

True   *False*

——————   ——————   1. Only the wealthy need wills.

——————   ——————   2. A primary purpose of a will is to help you specify and delineate your bequests.

——————   ——————   3. "Intestate" is the legal phrase for dying without a will. It means the court will process your estate according to the laws.

——————   ——————   4. Once you have a will, nothing you own can pass to a person outside it.

——————   ——————   5. A holographic (hand-written) will does not require witnesses.

——————   ——————   6. In a joint-tenancy arrangement, one party automatically becomes sole owner upon the death of the other party.

——————   ——————   7. A no-risk approach to preparing a will is to buy a standard form from a stationery store and fill it out yourself.

——————   ——————   8. If you have an attorney draw up your will, it's a good idea to settle on the fee at the first meeting. For existing clients, attorneys usually do wills at a nominal sum.

——————   ——————   9. If you are single and have $100,000 in your estate, you should not investigate a trust.

——————   ——————   10. To the courts a "common disaster" means one spouse dies ahead of the other.

——————   ——————   11. A trust is a legal document by which you transfer assets such as money or real estate to a trustee to manage for any beneficiary or beneficiaries named.

——————   ——————   12. A testimentary trust is considered part of your will and will pass through probate.

——————   ——————   13. One potential of a trust is to provide money to a beneficiary in small amounts so they will not make foolish spending mistakes and use their part of the estate too quickly.

PRETEST (*continued*)

True	False	
_____	_____	14. The executor and trustees are one and the same.
_____	_____	15. You cannot change an irrevocable trust.
_____	_____	16. It is always best to have a friend as an executor or trustee because they know your wishes better than a professional.
_____	_____	17. A codicil is the style of handwriting you use to sign your name to a will.
_____	_____	18. Under the new laws, there are no tax advantages to the preparation of a trust.
_____	_____	19. An executor's job is finished once an estate is settled.
_____	_____	20. A trust is never part of a will.

Total Correct _____

Answers: (1) F (a will is equally important in the settlement of any estate); (2) T; (3) T (this you want to avoid); (4) F; (5) T (there are many ways you can do this legally); (6) T; (7) F (it's wise to work with an attorney, and their fees for preparing wills are usually very reasonable); (8) T (don't be afraid to ask—it's a good idea); (9) F (anyone with a sizable estate might benefit from looking into trusts); (10) F (a common disaster is when both spouses die at the same time); (11) T; (12) T; (13) T; (14) F (you'll discover the difference in the chapter); (15) T; (16) F (selecting an executor or a trustee is a personal choice; sometimes it's better to have a professional, but a fee would be involved); (17) F (a codicil is a legal addition to a will); (18) F (there are still many tax advantages); (19) T; (20) F (although independent, it is still part of the will).

listed as community property, a change to another form of ownership will require a mutual decision. You lawyer may suggest you change this at the first meeting.

* *Joint tenancy:* A joint-tenancy ownership allows one party automatically to become the sole owner upon the death of the other party. When one party or joint tenant dies, assets don't pass through probate, although taxation still must be considered. For many, joint tenancy may be the best arrangement.

* *Tenancy in common:* You and the other tenants (owners) in a given asset have certain, not necessarily equal, shares. Your share is part of your estate, and you may dispose of it in your will.

Designate Beneficiary Assets

Some assets can pass directly to your beneficiaries outside your will. You will want to designate these in some fashion. These assets include items such as:

* Property you own in joint tenancy.
* Proceeds from life-insurance policies.
* Pension plans.
* Individual retirement accounts (RRSPs).

Make certain that you review this list with your attorney.

Name a Trustee

This is a person or institution that you designate to manage your property for your beneficiaries. A trustee and an executor can be the same person. You can be your own trustee.

Name an Executor

This is the individual or firm that will execute your will after you have gone. Your executor can be:

* Family member
* Friend
* Professional (attorney, accountant)
* Trust company

A professional or trust department is likely to have more expertise than a relative or friend and may be more capable of dealing impartially with sensitive issues that develop. Executors get one fee; attorneys get another.

With this minimal background, you are now ready to complete the following form. If it means digging out papers and policies, it will be time well spent. Once the form is complete, you can look forward to a more fruitful meeting with your attorney because you have done your homework.

PRECONSULTATION FORM

This form is to be completed by those preparing or updating their wills before the first appointment with a lawyer. Do it in pencil so changes can be made easily.

1. Refer to your financial statement in completing the following:

Asset	Value	Date Acquired	Marital Status at Time	Form of Ownership

2. List names of intended beneficiaries and other data. For tax purposes, it is important for your attorney to know the line of succession between you and your beneficiaries. Normally, but not always, people list their lineal descendants in order and then add others. Your attorney's advice will be significant here.

Beneficiary	Relationship	Amount of Money or % of Estate	Specific Assets*

* You may list separate pieces of property, specific jewelry, automobiles, or any tangible asset you may have. Your lawyer may suggest this be consolidated on a separate list outside the actual will. If you do this, keep in mind that specific bequests are not only difficult to list but also subject to whimsical changes that annoy attorneys. Give your list careful thought to avoid unnecessary changes. Many people simplify their lists by giving things away ahead of time.

_____

_____

_____

_____

_____

3. Alternative distribution in case both spouses are killed in a common disaster or something happens to a primary beneficiary. This is optional but a good idea to plan for in the unlikely event it might happen.

Beneficiary	Relationship	Amount of Money or % of Estate	Specific Assets

4. After careful investigation, list the names of your executor and alternate in the spaces below.

Executor: _____

(Name)

_____

(Address)

_____

(Telephone)

Alternate
Executor: _____

(Name)

_____

(Address)

_____

(Telephone)

Congratulations! You are now ready to make an appointment with the lawyer of your choice. Your meeting should be viewed as positive and educational. Keep in mind the Mutual-Reward Theory applies to all relationships—even those of a professional nature. Once satisfied with all aspects of your will, you will have your primary reward. Your affairs have been arranged satisfactorily.

Once your will has been completed, keep it in a safe place where your executor, spouse, or closest beneficiary can get to it easily and quickly. Your safety-deposit box may or may not be appropriate. Check with your attorney on this. Copies may be desirable for your spouse or others directly involved.

Keeping a Will Updated

Soon it will be possible for people, in concert with their attorneys, to maintain wills on a home computer. This would make them easily changeable and provide other advantages. Even though not presently realistic, your will should be viewed as an ongoing document and not a once-in-a-lifetime creation forever sealed and stored in a secret place. Wills need to be updated every so often because of such possibilities as:

* You might have a change of mind.

* You might receive an inheritance or other asset not covered in your previous will.

* A marriage, birth, adoption, divorce, or death may dictate a revision.

* New laws may mandate change.

Life is not predictable, especially among beneficiaries. Your life may seem predictable to you, but this may not be so with younger members of your family. They may be more realistic about the probability of divorce. They may also be more conditioned to the fact that divorce can happen in all age groups—even yours.

Caution: Never make changes directly on the face of your written will. Such changes could invalidate it. The best way to make an addition is to use a typewritten, legal codicil (an extra page or more that can explain, add, or delete provisions in the will itself). To be valid, it must meet the same legal requirements as the will. This is another reason to maintain a good, ongoing relationship with your lawyer.

Protecting Your Estate from Unnecessary Taxes

You have worked hard to accumulate and protect your estate, so you probably want to pass much of it to your heirs or beneficiaries. Protecting your estate normally moves you into a higher level of money management and often requires the advice of professionals—tax specialists, lawyers, or trust officers. Keep in mind that although you can obtain good information from an accountant or trust officer, only a lawyer can draft a will. To avoid extra expenses, you may want to go directly to an attorney.

Retirees can learn from lectures, forums, and articles that discuss how to avoid probate. They seem interested in any technique that will help them beat the system. The more you can learn about legal ways to accomplish this, the better. Be careful, however, because estate-tax planning is complex. A major decision will be to find the right professional to help you. This person should know current income tax laws as well as recent applicable court cases. The right person will help you develop the estate plan you want—a plan that both takes advantage of tax provisions and accomplishes your wishes in the disposal of your estate. No easy assignment!

Setting Up a Trust

A trust is a way to leave your money so that it will avoid probate, take full advantage of tax benefits, and accomplish what you desire either before or after you are gone. In a trust, you assign part or all of your estate to a trustee or trustees to manage and distribute in a manner prescribed by you. It is a way to control the release of your money after your death. This can be done to protect and enhance the lives of others, usually those dear to you. Things are prearranged for your beneficiaries because you won't be around to do it yourself.

Mrs. K's Solution

Mrs. K's later years were made beautiful by her granddaughter, Ruth, who took time to know and enjoy her only grandmother. Mrs. K loved her daughter, Ruth's mother, but did not want her to be in charge because she had been married three times and never demonstrated she could manage money. Mrs. K's answer: A trust arrangement would provide Ruth a sum of money each month until she was 25 years of age, at which time she would receive the balance in a lump sum.

Mr. and Mrs. Graber

Mr. and Mrs. Graber have four children. All are self-sufficient except Beth, who was retarded at birth and has required special care all her life. How could Beth be cared for best? Answer: A special trust arrangement. The other children were a part of the trust, and they were consulted about the special provisions for Beth.

Mrs. Jackson

Mrs. Jackson could not have been happier with her 12 grandchildren. She spent much of her time traveling to see them. They were the center of her life for more than 15 years. What might she do to help them later? Answer: A trust that would equally distribute Mrs. Jackson's estate among all 12 grandchildren when each reached a certain age. The details were worked out with a lawyer and administered by a trust officer in a local trust company. An annual fee was charged for this service.

In other words, a trust can be any arrangement you choose to maintain and distribute your estate. It is your money, so it is your responsibility to call the shots. Arrangements, however, can be highly complicated.

Testamentary Versus Inter Vivos Trusts

A testamentary trust is a separate, sophisticated addition to your will. You designate the purpose and specifics in your will and also designate a trustee. When you die, the testamentary trust goes into effect and carries out your wishes.

A so-called inter vivos trust is not a specific part of your will. You draft it outside your will, but refer to it inside your will so that both work in tandem. A trust can be designed to either end after a period of time or continue after your death. It is whatever you wish as long as you understand the tax implications. An inter vivos trust can be either revocable or irrevocable. If revocable, you retain the right to change the terms of the trust, or even end it, during your lifetime. In other words, you remain in charge. If you establish an irrevocable trust, you cannot change the terms or end it.

Structure Versus Flexibility in a Trust

The basic problem in setting up any trust is the uncertainty of what will happen in the future. It is possible to spend hours developing an arrangement that does not ultimately accomplish your desires because of some unanticipated change. On the other hand, if you simply leave your estate to beneficiaries hoping they will spend the money according to your wishes, it might not happen that way either.

Many people like trusts because it is possible to make a more direct contribution to their grandchildren. It is not that they mistrust their children; they simply feel better knowing provisions are made for grandchildren in the event of a divorce or if their children are unsuccessful in building estates of their own.

Once again, the more advance thinking you do, the better prepared you will be when you consult your lawyer. Spouses need to discuss things ahead of time to avoid arguments in the presence of their attorney. No one, including your lawyer, should do your thinking for you.

Naming a Trustee

The individual you designate as an executor can also be designated as your trustee. Selecting a trustee involves many of the same considerations as selecting an executor. However, there is a difference between the two. An executor's job is finished once an estate is settled. This usually happens within a year or two. A trust can continue for many years. This means that the trustee acquires an almost permanent obligation.

You can choose a personal friend, a relative, a professional, or the trust department of a institution as your trustee. There are advantages and disadvantages to each. A personal friend may know and understand you and the beneficiaries, but may not be experienced with investments. A professional may not know you or your beneficiaries but has the experience. A trust department in a bank won't move away or die. It also has a staff of professionals. Finally, the cost of a trust must be taken into consideration. The choice is yours.

If you name a personal acquaintance or relative as trustee of a living trust, the fee will be whatever is agreed upon—often no fee at all. Professional trustees, however, receive fees that are either a set amount or a percent of the trust's assets. Fees should be discussed and negotiated ahead of time.

Letter of Instruction

Once you have completed your will and trust arrangements, you will probably want to prepare a letter of instruction for your beneficiaries. This letter is a guide to make it easier for your family to close out your affairs. Although not a legal document, it should be in agreement with the terms of your will. You may want to check with your attorney on this matter. This letter of instruction may be written or placed on audio or video tape. Most people write a letter.

Here is some information you may want to consider as you prepare your letter of instruction. Use it as your outline.

* *People to be notified of death:* Certain people and institutions need to be notified of your death, including your attorney, your executor, your trustee, and your tax specialist, to name a few. Also your Canada Pension Plan office needs to know. Special friends will want to know as soon as possible. Providing names, titles, addresses, and telephone numbers will make it easier for the individual who assumes this responsibility. Take time in preparing this list. You will probably include your inner-circle support group of relatives and close friends. These individuals can provide emotional support if needed.

* *Advance funeral arrangements:* You have the freedom to make all your own arrangements. Make sure you communicate them, providing all necessary details. Include a reminder that the

funeral director provide multiple copies of the death certificate for processing insurance and Canada Pension claims.

* *Location of personal papers:* Provide all the help you can here. Give the exact location of your personal documents. These documents include birth certificate, marriage certificate, diplomas, military papers, and so on. It's a good idea to gather these in a single location.

* *Bank accounts:* List all checking and savings accounts by name of institution, address where the account is located, type of account, and account number. Also give location of canceled cheques and statements.

* *Credit cards:* List by issuer and card number. Make sure payer is provided access to accounts. Ask that these accounts be paid immediately and cards destroyed.

* *Deed and mortgage papers:* Most people keep these vital documents in their safety-deposit boxes. If you do, also provide location of the box, key, and a list of the box's contents.

* *Insurance policies:* List all life, auto, home, veteran's, medical, and other insurance policies. Name the agent(s) and give the location of these documents. Describe any loans you may have taken out against said policies.

* *Vehicles:* Tell where registration and other papers may be found for all motor vehicles or boats you own. Provide location of all keys and special instructions.

* *Taxes:* Provide the location of your income-tax returns for the past three years. Name your tax consultant. Give special instructions if necessary.

* *Investments:* For some people, this can be most important. List all stocks, bonds, certificates of deposit, RRSP or RRIF accounts, and other investments. Include name of issuer and the cost to you. Also indicate where items are located. Identify your stock-broker and other agents. If you have any gold coins or silver bars that constitute an investment, provide location and details.

* *Valuables:* Make certain you have a complete list of all jewelry and other valuables (china, glassware, art pieces, etc.). Tell where things are located. This list may also include the names of those to whom articles should be given. Often this list is a part of the will itself (on separate list of personal property).

* *Trusts:* List any trust you have established and give the name and address of the trustee. Very important!

NOVEL IDEA

If you are looking for an enjoyable way to distribute your personal possessions ahead of time, you might consider throwing a "label party." It works like this. Invite your children (or perhaps special friends) to your home for a party. Provide a stack of gummed labels with their names printed on them. After preliminary instructions, ask them to work out, through discussion, who wants what property you wish to pass along. Once agreements have been reached, they can place their label on each item (where it cannot be seen). After the party, you can enjoy their choices and back up their selections with a list.

---

* *Loans:* List all loans and other accounts payable by lender. Give full information on terms, payments, collateral, and so forth.

* *Money owed you:* List all debts, first trust deeds, and other forms of loans owed to you. Provide all details.

* *Special survivor's benefits:* List possible sources of benefits not named in will—Canada Pension, veteran's, employee, pension, retirement, fraternal associations, and so on. Others may not think of these benefits as they go through your papers.

* *Miscellaneous:* There will be other documents you should include. Think of them and prepare a list.

Even if you review the foregoing items with your executor or chief beneficiary, a letter of instruction is still advisable.

My wife has always made an effort to leave our home in tiptop shape before vacations or trips. Often I felt she overdid it; but, looking back, I think her efforts enhanced our trips. We knew things were in order at home, so we were more relaxed. These same psychological forces should encourage you to get busy on your estate planning. Your rewards will be the comfort of knowing your affairs are in order. The completed documents will provide peace of mind. You could view this as infusing more gold into your so-called "golden years." Not a bad investment.

Summary A will or trust is a way to distribute an estate among beneficiaries with tax savings.

Those who do homework before seeing a lawyer can often save time and money and build a better relationship.

The process of developing a will and/or trust can be a positive experience and add to your quality of life.

| PROBLEM TO SOLVE | **To Trust or Not To Trust** |

Mr. and Mrs. Laval consider themselves fortunate. They are in excellent health, have accumulated a sizable estate, and, best of all, have a devoted family. Their two sons and daughter are happily married and are well off. They have seven grandchildren.

There is no question that they want to divide their estate in a fair and equitable manner. When they started to think about the situation two years ago, they initially believed a simple will would suffice, where each of their children would receive one-third of the estate. No provisions would be made for grandchildren. It seemed fair. Why make it complicated?

Then they started to think about some penetrating questions:

* What if one adult child died after the distribution of the estate? Could this leave grandchildren unprotected?
* With adult children receiving the inheritance equally, how could grandchildren be treated equally because of different-sized families?
* Can trusts accomplish individualized goals similar to those Mr. and Mrs. Laval would like?

These and similar questions surfaced. Each new question raised other questions.

What is your opinion? Should they settle for a simple will and divide their estate equally, or should they construct a legal trust that specifies certain provisions? (See author's views in Appendix C.)

SELF-QUIZ

True	False	
_____	_____	1. Preparing a will can and should be a positive experience.
_____	_____	2. Although separate and independent, a trust can be an integral part of a will.

———— ———— 3. A primary purpose of a trust is to avoid taxes.

———— ———— 4. A letter of instruction is a legal document.

———— ———— 5. A fee paid to a lawyer to prepare a will can be worth the greater peace of mind.

(Answers in Appendix C.)

21

Insurance: Protect Yourself First and Your Possessions Second

Science may have found a cure for most evils; but it has found no remedy for the worst of them all—the apathy of human beings.
Helen Keller

* "Nothing—just nothing is more frustrating than dealing with insurance matters."

* "I throw all those insurance mailings into the wastebasket without reading them."

* "I spend too much time and money protecting things and not enough kicking up my heels."

Even though you may sympathize with these thoughts, you should recognize that, as you near retirement, protecting yourself and your possessions takes on a new dimension. For example, health insurance becomes increasingly important. Although you may take fewer risks, you still need more insurance protection because accident and health problems tend to accelerate as you grow older.

239

Insurance Goals   Recently a retiree said to me: "When I start thinking about insurance, I want to crawl to a corner and pull a blanket over my head." This is not a bad idea providing one is sleepy and the blanket is an *insurance blanket*. The objective is to develop an insurance package (blanket) that accomplishes the following goals.

Goal 1:
Greater Peace of Mind   The secret is to be able to look down the road recognizing real risks but not creating ones that are not there. When we identify a risk, we should pass it along to an insurance company. After doing this, we should relax. No part of life, especially retirement, is totally worry-free; but the more worries we can transfer to insurance companies the better.

Goal 2:
Less Confusion and
Frustration   For most people, insurance contracts are hard to understand. There are too many clauses, too many exclusions, and too much small print. Many capable people throw up their hands in defeat. This chapter should help simplify the problem.

Goal 3:
Save Money   Senior discounts provide opportunities to stretch insurance dollars if you select the right policies and avoid duplication. Saving dollars in areas where you need less insurance means you get more protection where your need is greater.

Goal 4:
More Help from
Insurance Agents   Among professional people, your insurance agent should stand beside your medical doctor and lawyer. The more you learn about insurance, the more effective you will be in building a sound, rewarding relationship with your agent. The better your relationship, the more help you should receive.

**A Definition of
Insurance**   Insurance is accepting a small loss now (premium payment) to prevent a potentially larger loss in the future. If you take out a policy to protect yourself against a loss (such as theft), then, in a sense, you win if you are robbed. You were smart enough to protect yourself. On the other hand, if you paid the premiums for 20 years and were never robbed, you still won because you transferred the risk at a small cost and gained peace of mind. Insurance is a way to transfer risk and worry to another so you come out ahead. No time is more important to transfer worry than after you retire.

Dealing with Risks   There are three ways to deal with risks.

Take All Possible
Preventive Measures   If the time comes when you become a little unsteady on your feet, you should have enough common sense to stay off roofs and out of

slippery bathtubs. If necessary, buy a cane and use it with style. If your eyesight begins to dim, recognize that driving at night will be more risky and plan daytime driving trips when possible.

Unless you take commonsense precautions, all the insurance in the world can be meaningless. Insurance only cushions risks with money *after* something bad happens. To live with style, your objective should be to keep accidents and illnesses from happening in the first place. Take a "risk management" approach—that is, avoid risks without hurting your lifestyle and then transfer the remaining risks to others. Like other aspects of life, risks can be managed.

Insure Yourself

The more money you have, the easier this is to do. For example, you might buy dental insurance. But perhaps your dentist bills in excess of the provincial fee schedule. The policy would be good only if you switched dentists. Solution? Insure yourself. Instead of paying, say $15, into a policy each month, use the money to build a "kitty" for future dental bills. Such a fund becomes a self-insurance policy. Of course, it doesn't work in all cases. For example, you would probably not have enough money to self-insure against a catastrophic illness. Self-insurance works best when the risk is small.*

Transfer the Risk to an Insurance Company

Do this by entering into a contract that costs a little each month as protection against a possible loss. You might never have enough money to rebuild your home if it burned, so you pay a company each month to assume that risk. When thousands of others do this, you receive the protection you seek at a low cost.

Transferring risk may sound easy. All you need is to find the right policy, for the right need, at the right cost. Write a cheque once a year and hope nothing happens. Of course, it is more complicated than this. When we retire, we must find policies that cover new risks or close gaps in existing ones. Policies can be deceptive. You may think you are fully covered when you are not. There are sometimes exclusions that limit your policy. Also, you must consider cost. It's impossible to live with style if you spend all your discretionary income on insurance premiums.

Getting Started

Before you move further into this chapter, please take time to go over the warning tips in the following exercise. These tips will prepare you for the challenging material ahead.

---

*Deductibles are, in a sense, self-insurance. The more money you have, the higher the deductible can be.

Tips for Selecting Your Insurance

If you agree with the tip, place a checkmark in the square on the left of it.

☐ *Always compare.* In buying any new insurance policy, compare the two that you feel provide the best protection. Only after a step-by-step comparison should you make your choice.

☐ *Buy only what you need and can afford.* Duplicate coverage is not only costly but confusing as well. Keep your insurance program as uncomplicated as possible, but still get the protection you need. Don't fill the same gap twice.

☐ *Look for major exclusions.* Unless you cover the big risk you want to eliminate, forget it. You've got to get what you buy, or you've been misled. *Ask your agent to write out exclusions.*

☐ *Beware of a replacement offer.* If someone tries to replace your policy, be suspicious, especially in health insurance. Have someone who is qualified help you make a comparison.

☐ *Question policies with maximum ceilings.* If a company puts a low limit on how much they will pay, they are, in effect, leaving the risk with you. If their payoff is low, it may not be worthwhile.

☐ *Renewal rights.* If you cannot retain a policy as you get older, then you are only buying temporary protection and have not effectively transferred the risk.

☐ *Only private companies supplement provincial health insurance plans (PHIP).* Do not be misled that the government is protecting you when you deal with private companies. Federal insurance departments provide standards for insurance firms, but you are on your own when you deal with anything other than PHIP.

☐ *Take enough time to do research.* We sometimes buy something just to get it done. This frequently creates more stress at a later date. Be sure of what you are buying before you act.

☐ *When possible, deal with a single, reliable insurance agent.* Choose insurance agents the same way you choose lawyers or doctors. Seek one who enjoys working with people. Do not deal with anyone who is not sympathetic to your special needs as a retiree.

PROVINCIAL HEALTH INSURANCE PLANS (PHIP)

If you are 65 your premiums are paid by the province.

How much do you know about this government-sponsored program? The following test will give an indication. To learn your PHIP knowledge, complete the test and score yourself by checking the correct answers.

True	False	
_____	_____	1. PHIP has a hospital-insurance deductible for each benefit period.
_____	_____	2. PHIP pays for a private room.
_____	_____	3. PHIP does not cover operating and recovery-room costs.
_____	_____	4. PHIP does not pay for the first three pints of blood received.
_____	_____	5. PHIP cannot generally pay for hospital and medical services outside Canada.
_____	_____	6. PHIP can help pay for care in a participating psychiatric hospital on an indefinite basis.
_____	_____	7. Hospitals will submit PHIP forms for you, but medical doctors may not.
_____	_____	8. PHIP has a $100 deductible for each calendar year.
_____	_____	9. PHIP cover only fees up to a reasonable charge established in a fee structure.
_____	_____	10. Based on reviews by officials, new reasonable charges are put into effect periodically.
_____	_____	11. It is illegal for those protected by PHIP to have additional, private supplemental insurance.

PHIP *(continued)*

True	False	
_____	_____	12. The premium for PHIP is deductible for income tax purposes.
_____	_____	13. Annual checkups are covered by PHIP.
_____	_____	14. PHIP does not cover dental care.
_____	_____	15. You may submit a number of bills with a single Request for PHIP Payment form.
_____	_____	16. If you disagree with a decision on the amount PHIP will pay on a claim, you have the right of appeal.
_____	_____	17. PHIP does not usually pay for home health care.
_____	_____	18. Ambulance transportation can be paid for by PHIP.
_____	_____	19. Request for PHIP payment forms can be obtained from your medical doctor.
_____	_____	20. For any help you may need regarding PHIP, call your local insurance agent.

Total Correct _____

Answers: (1) F; (2) F; (3) F; (4) F; (5) F; (6) T; (7) F; (8) F; (9) T; (10) T; (11) F; (12) F; (13) T; (14) T; (15) T; (16) F; (17) T; (18) T; (19) T; (20) F

**Part I:
Protecting Yourself**

You are now ready to develop a protection package that is best for you. Part I deals with protecting yourself by designing a health-protection package that fits your income and needs. You may have taken health insurance casually up to now because your company took care of it automatically through payroll deduction. Those days are over. You have a whole new challenge ahead of you — one that has some difficult wrinkles you must iron out.

For most retirees, health protection is built around provincial health insurance plans. It is advisable, therefore, to know as much about PHIP as possible. The PHIP test is designed to help you do this.

If you scored high in the self-test (16 or more correct answers), you are well informed. If you scored substantially lower, write the provincial authority for free literature.

The more you know about PHIP the better. It will help you decide what additional coverage you want. Armed with information about the provisions of PHIP, you are in a position to supplement it as you see fit. The term "medigap" might be appropriate, because as you evaluate your health-care needs, you will learn PHIP cannot do it all.

You can close these 'medigaps' with individual health policies. You should investigate alternative private programs such as Blue Cross/Blue Shield or a health-maintenance organization. Sound programs, though expensive, can fill the medigaps in provincial health insurance plans.

Part II:
Protecting Your
Possesions

Part II deals with protecting what you own, namely property insurance. You worked hard to earn your retirement nest egg. Now you want to enjoy it. You don't want to see it disappear because of some calamity, especially if you can transfer the risk for a reasonable price. To increase your knowledge in the general insurance area, complete the pretest on the following pages.

Please continue by completing the Exercise on General Insurance Protection.

General Insurance
Protection

You want to protect what you own in the best way at the least cost. This exercise will help you find gaps in your current protection. Naturally, the more money or property you have, the more extensive your coverage should be.

Check the appropriate box in each category and take the results to your insurance agent(s) if you desire further investigation.

1. *Homeowner's policy:* If you own your home, it may be time to review the kind or protection you have. View your homeowner's policy as a blanket that provides protection from anything that could happen—fire, theft, accidents to guests, wind damage, or anything else. Check one of the following.

☐	☐	☐
I don't own a home or other real-estate property	I'm fully aware of my homeowner's policy and no action on my part is required—it's complete	It's time for a review so constructive changes can be made

2. *Renters only.* If you rent or lease and someone else insures the structure, you still should protect personal possessions from fire and theft. Are there any gaps in this protection? Is it time to take a new look? Can you save money?

PRETEST ON GENERAL INSURANCE

Insurance has always been complicated. It is even more complex today. The more you know, of course, the better, because it helps you make better decisions. The following questions indicate your present knowledge. Before deciding to buy a new policy or discontinue an old one, you should get advice from a professional

Correct answers are provided. Please complete the work before you check the answers.

True   *False*

1. Some policies make more money for insurance agents than others.

2. An insurance policy is a legal contract.

3. Mutual insurance companies are owned by stockholders, not policy holders.

4. Basically, an insurance policy transfers a risk from you to the company.

5. If you have enough money, you can insure yourself against all risks.

6. You can insure anything you possess that has a determinable value, including land.

7. A personal-property inventory you prepared yourself has no value in substantiating a claim.

8. A homeowner's policy normally covers the home itself and all personal property within it but does not include liability.

9. A floater policy covers property anywhere as long as it is over water.

10. Flood insurance is normally included in a homeowner's policy.

11. You can usually save money by buying a package policy as opposed to individual contracts.

PRETEST (continued)

True	False	
_____	_____	12. You cannot purchase a catch-all, umbrella liability policy unless you first maintain a basic underlying coverage through other policies.
_____	_____	13. Automobile medical-expense coverage applies to anyone riding in your car regardless of fault.
_____	_____	14. Safe-driver plans do not apply to people over 65.
_____	_____	15. The size of the car has nothing to do with the cost of insurance.
_____	_____	16. As far as immediate risk is concerned, life insurance is more important when you are young.
_____	_____	17. If you reach a point of financial independence, you outlive your need for life insurance.
_____	_____	18. Term insurance (no cash value or annuity payments) is pure insurance.
_____	_____	19. You can borrow from a cash-value policy if you have built up enough equity.
_____	_____	20. The trend in Canada is towards more and more civil liability suits.

Total Correct: _____

Answers: (1) T (back away from any agent who gives you a signal that he or she is more interested in a quick buck than in your future); (2) T (sign one only after careful evaluation); (3) F (the other way around); (4) T; (5)T; (6) F (not land); (7) F (of substantial value); (8) F (includes liability); (9) F (anywhere you transport it); (10) F; (11) T; (12) T (umbrella liability policies are complex—see your agent): (13) T; (14) F; (15) F; (16) T; (17) T; (18) T; (19) T; (20) T.

☐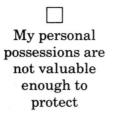
My personal
possessions are
not valuable
enough to
protect

☐
I'm fully
satisfied with
my present
protection—it's
complete

☐
It's time for a
new look and
review—there
may be gaps

3. *Inventory of personal possessions.* Whether you own your home or rent, it's an excellent idea to inventory your possessions so you know what was lost in case of theft or fire. It's also a good idea to take this list to your insurance agent to learn what is covered and what is not. Your agent may provide inventory forms and suggestions. Photographs and bills of sale are helpful. Highly valuable items should be appraised.

☐
I really do not
have enough
personal
possessions to
need an inventory

☐
Good idea—I'm
going to get the
forms and do it
immediately

4. *Automobile insurance.* Most retirees are knowledgeable about automobile insurance. They need to understand laws and requirements that relate to bodily injury and property damage insurance. The "other driver" may not have insurance, so all companies must offer coverage for uninsured motorists. Also, comprehensive coverage is needed if someone steals or vandalizes the car.

Why is a review necessary? Here are two examples. If your car is more than five years old, collision insurance may not be a good buy anymore. Also, many firms now offer "55 and over" discounts for those with safe driving records. It might be worth looking into. Finally, higher deductibles save you money "off the top" without jeopardizing basic protection.

☐
I've got the best
protection
available for the
money

☐
It is time for a
review; if I don't
save money, I will
at least be better
protected

5. *Towing and roadside coverage.* Many retirees travel. To worry less they join the Canadian Automobile Association (CAA) which provides towing service and other benefits. It is possible, of course,

that your present policy gives you this protection. If not, getting a policy to fill this gap may be wise.

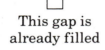

I'm adequately protected in these areas	This policy may fit my needs—I'll investigate

6. *Accident medical insurance.* Anyone who rides with you can collect under the bodily injury part of your automobile policy, so this is insurance on top of insurance. If you feel better having it, the cost is usually nominal.

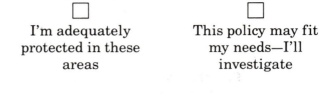

This gap is already filled	Good idea—I'll talk it over with my agent

7. *Extra liability insurance.* You should make certain your home-owner's policy protects you in case someone is injured in your home or on your property. The same is true for rental property you own. Also, you may want extra liability coverage on your automobile insurance. If you wish, all your liability protection can be covered under a single umbrella policy. The more you are worth or the more you are exposed to risk, the more protection you need. Many people feel this type of insurance is a must. It is not expensive.

I am adequately covered for liability	I will talk this over with my agent

8. *Life insurance.* As we grow older, our need for life insurance normally will decrease. Life insurance is intended to protect a family from the premature death of the person who earns the income. Upon retirement, life insurance should be viewed in a different way, especially when enough wealth has been accumulated to cover most needs. After retirement, the best argument for new life insurance would be to take care of income taxes at death or funeral expenses.

For policies currently in effect, most experts recommend a careful review. In some cases, it might be best to cash in a policy. Life insurance has been going through such a revolution recently that a look at all your life insurance is strongly recommended.

☐

I agree—a study of
my life-insurance
program is
necessary

☐

I'm going to stay
with what I have

9. *Miscellaneous protection.* As with medical insurance, there are certain gaps you should make sure are filled. For example, you may want insurance that would pay the mortgage balance on your home in case of your death or that of your spouse. Depending on where you live, you might want to investigate flood insurance. Everyone has special needs which require consideration.

☐

I am satisfied that
there are no gaps
in my insurance
package

☐

I should see an
insurance agent
for a review

If you feel your insurance needs are ready for reevaluation, the following steps are recommended:

Step 1: Inventory and review all your current insurance policies. Place them in a single portfolio along with the exercise you just completed.

Step 2: Arrange a consultation with either your present insurance agent or a new one who deals in several types of insurance and has been recommended. It is best to work with a single agent or agency if they offer the services you require.

Step 3: After your consultation, take action to gain the kind of protection that you can afford and that fits your comfort zone. Your primary goal should be to improve the quality of your life through protection that allows you to relax.

Summary   Insurance needs change after retirement.

Generally, we need to switch from protecting our possessions to protecting ourselves. This means filling in all the gaps our income will permit.

Our success in doing this depends on the relationship we build with our insurance agent. The more sophisticated we become about insurance matters, the better the relationship should become.

PROBLEM TO SOLVE   **Too Much Versus Too Little**

Mrs. Starr and Mrs. Grey come from strikingly similar situations. Both are in the same bridge group. Both own and maintain similar homes in the same part of town. Also, both stay in charge of their financial matters. When it comes to insurance protection, however, they differ drastically in philosophy and practice.

Mrs. Starr reflects the attitude of her late husband, who often said: "It's impossible to have too much insurance." As a result, Mrs. Starr is well off thanks to the large amount of life insurance left by her husband. She has continued with the same philosophy and spends over $4,000 in premiums each year. Mrs. Starr's health coverage is approximately $2,500. She has tried to fill every gap. Consequently, there is much duplication in her protection package. In all, she has 17 different policies, several of which were purchased by direct mail. Every time she receives an announcement of new coverage, she buys it without considering what she already owns. Her attitude is: "I have the money, and sooner or later these policies will be necessary. It's inevitable."

Mrs. Grey is the opposite of Mrs. Starr. She has only one health-care supplement policy. Her general insurance package runs much more because she has complete automobile coverage, a substantial homeowner's policy, and three other "fill-in" contracts. She has exactly seven policies at an annual cost of $1,600. Her attitude toward insurance is: "I feel it is possible to be so overinsured you damage your lifestyle because of premium payments. I believe in general coverage, but I'm not concerned with filling every gap. After all, I have savings to fall back on. It bothers me to get brochures in the mail tempting me to buy another policy, because they play on my fears. Some people I know have so many policies it would take a Bay Street lawyer to sort them out. It's ridiculous."

Which person do you side with? What suggestions would you make to each party? Is there a middle road between the two extremes? What is your position on insurance protection?

Compare your views with those of the author in Appendix C.

SELF-QUIZ

True	*False*	
_____	_____	1. It is never financially wise to self-insure.
_____	_____	2. It is a good idea to question policies that have a maximum or limited pay-off ceiling.
_____	_____	3. Choosing not to insure a risk is never a wise decision.
_____	_____	4. Supplementing PHIP requires nothing more than finding a single, standard policy designed for that purpose. Taking this action will close all gaps.
_____	_____	5. There is no such thing as a special insurance policy covering floods.

(Answers in Appendix C.)

VI

PERSONAL FULFILLMENT

Do you live in the best possible environment? Should you make a change? What kind of a senior do you intend to be? This section deals with these issues. When you finish it, you should be able to: choose the best living situation available to you; decide whether or not you want to become a Master Senior.

22

Choosing Where to Live

Doubt is not a pleasant state but certainly is a ridiculous one.
Voltaire

One of your biggest retirement decisions will be where to live. Do you stay where you are or move? Have a mobile home in Muskoka or a condo in Toronto? Rent an apartment in your home town? There are many options.

Everything thus far has been leading you to this juncture. By now, you should have a solid foundation on which to make the best decision. The bad news is that you may still have to make it.

Study the accompanying illustration for a moment. The circle shows factors—finances, leisure plans, and so on—involved in your decision-making process. The background map is a reminder that you are free to live anywhere. The other illustrations—mobile homes, condominiums, retirement centers—show that you have many choices of accommodation.

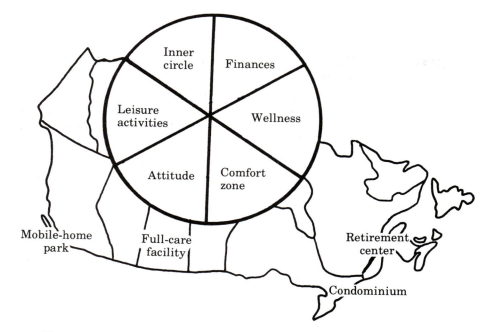

Exciting possibilities, but there is a disturbing finality about it all. Once you sell a home, you might not be able to buy it back. Once you move to a retirement center, there may not be an easy way out. So, as you read this chapter, the primary word is *caution*. Try not to make a move until you are sure. Make your investigation a personal one. As you accept or reject possibilities, keep in mind that what makes sense for some people might not work for you. You are an individual, and you must make decisions about where and how to live based on your background—your comfort zone and what makes you happy. The quality of your retirement years can depend on your decision.

Your First Choice Is Geographical

Ah, exotic Hawaii! Or what about sunny Florida? Perhaps a retirement home in Vancouver (Lotusland)? It's fun to talk about faraway places and to dream. This is especially true before retirement, because you can prepare for your move through preretirement financial planning. There is time to make enough money to facilitate your dream move.

After retirement your choices may be more limited, because your income will probably be more stabilized. Geographical choices may still remain, however. People of all income levels still move from colder climates to the Carribean or the southern U.S.

Retirees migrate like birds. The journey can be fatiguing, and sanctuaries are difficult to assess. For many, it will become a permanent migration, since only wealthy birds can maintain two homes.

Migrating Can Be a Mistake

Although most dream of a distant retirement paradise, some retirees, after careful analysis, wisely opt to stay close to their roots. They discover paradise is in their own backyard.

I know a woman whose personal paradise is in Deep River, Ontario. Her life is wrapped up in the town. She has adjusted to the climate. Her church and her friends are there. It would be a mistake for her to move.

A member of my family, a surgeon, has spent her adult life practicing in Winnipeg. She owns a lovely home, and her many friends are there. She has had a love affair with the prairies for more than 40 years. It would be a mistake for her to move.

What about you? Do you already live in paradise or is it time to consider a new location? Should you move to a warm climate? Should you compare advantages and disadvantages of where you now live with what is available? The following may be helpful. It presents 10 factors that should be taken into consideration before any geographical move.

Step 1: Rate all factors on where you now live. Write a number from 1 to 10 in the appropriate box in the exercise (10 is the highest rating; 1 is the lowest).

Step 2: Select two other locations you have considered in the past or have investigated. Write these locations in the boxes under options 1 and 2.

Step 3: Rate each of these locations and compare them to the rating of the place you now live in. (Before doing this step, you may want to accumulate more information about your other locations. You can do this by writing the city's chamber of commerce, subscribing to the local newspaper, or visiting and talking to people who live there.)

Step 4: Keep in mind that some of the 10 factors could be far more critical to your needs than others and should, therefore, be given more weight in your personal analysis.

EXERCISE ON WHERE TO RETIRE   **Preliminary analysis of geographical locations**

Factors to be rated	Where you live now	Option #1 ___(city)___	Option #2 ___(city)___
1. *Climate from a health point of view.* Is the climate good for you? Less demanding, with less chance of illness? Might it extend your life? A rating of 10 would be the most healthy of all climates.	☐	☐	☐
2. *Climate from a cost standpoint.* Would it reduce your utility bills? Are clothing costs less? Under this category, it is probably more expensive to live in Ontario than in B.C.	☐	☐	☐
3. *Does the geographical area fit your comfort zone?* Do you enjoy changes in seasons? Are mountains more attractive to you than beaches? Would you fit the local culture? Victoria, B.C. is vastly different from Saskatoon, Saskatchewan. Give high ratings to those areas that best fit your personal comfort zone.	☐	☐	☐
4. *What about housing?* Could you afford the kind of housing you want? How do costs compare to where you are now? What would	☐	☐	☐

Factors to be rated	Where you live now	Option #1 ——— (city)	Option #2 ——— (city)

it cost to move? Preliminary housing-cost comparisons may be made by writing for a local newspaper. Make certain you have accurate data before rating this significant factor.

5. *What about other expenses?* The cost of consumer goods or tax rates? Some provinces have lower income taxes. Sales taxes are lower in some areas—Alberta has no sales tax. A high rating indicates lower prices. Local newspapers can provide data in this area. Your library or chamber of commerce can provide even more information.

6. *Are your kind of leisure activities available?* Can you enjoy them year-round? Do they cost less? The quality or your retirement years can depend heavily on your leisure activities.

7. *What about medical facilities?* Would you be close to the best possible help? Would your present medical plan be totally operational? Would you

Factors to be rated	Where you live now	Option #1 _____ (city)	Option #2 _____ (city)

need to change doctors? Do you have a special health problem?

8. *Would you be able to build a new inner circle easily?* Would you be with your kind of people? People in Nova Scotia can be different from those in Alberta. Would you be quickly accepted in a new environment?

☐ ☐ ☐

9. *What about transportation?* Is public transportation available if you need it? Would transportation be a low or high factor?

☐ ☐ ☐

10. *Other factors?* Would you be near friends and relatives you would choose to be with? Would you be closer or farther away from your special vacation spots? Would you be too isolated for friends to visit? Give this a general rating based on what has not already been covered. A high rating indicates you are still enthusiastic; a low rating indicates you may be changing your mind.

☐ ☐ ☐

Totals ☐ ☐ ☐

If you rated where you live now higher than your options, you are saying there may be more advantages in staying where you are than in making a move. If either option is rated higher, this signals that more investigation would be desirable, including perhaps a trip to make specific comparisons.

A geographical move is a decision that should be made only after lengthy, careful, and complete analysis. Several months' time is recommended, including visits during different seasons so you can verify all significant factors. Many retirees recommend living in a new area for several months as renters until you are sure.

Understanding Yourself Better

Once your geographic preference has been selected, what kind of housing or living environment is best for you? What can you afford? What is your comfort zone? Here again, make sure of your decision—a mistake could be costly.

It may help to position yourself on the following scale. To accomplish this, first, complete the Continuum Exercise by circling the appropriate numbers. This may help you understand your needs better in deciding what direction to take in the future. As you complete the exercise, keep the following in mind:

* Your own comfort zones.
* The state of your health.
* Whether or not you live alone.
* Your age.

Total your score for all items and divide by 20. If you scored 100, for example, you should circle 5 on the Continuum Scale. If you scored 60, you should circle 3. The number you circle indicates how much you want independence versus protection. The left side means you want to assume responsibilities; the right suggests you are comfortable turning responsibilities over to others. As we become older, there is often movement toward the right—but not always.

Understanding Your Position

If you averaged 8 or above on the continuum, this probably suggests you should not move from your home (or present living facility) at this time. You want to take care of yourself and remain in charge.

CONTINUUM SCALE

Private homeowner Fully independent	10	9	8	7	6	5	4	3	2	1	Retirement center Full-care facility

CONTINUUM EXERCISE

I'm fiercely independent and need space.	10 9 8 7 6 5 4 3 2 1	I'm highly social—give me people.
I'm happiest alone.	10 9 8 7 6 5 4 3 2 1	I'm happiest with others.
Risks of living alone do not bother me.	10 9 8 7 6 5 4 3 2 1	I want all the protection I can get.
I want pets around me.	10 9 8 7 6 5 4 3 2 1	I'm happier without pets.
I'm happy at home; traveling is not my thing.	10 9 8 7 6 5 4 3 2 1	I love to travel and be free to leave at anytime.
I love gardening and caring for my home.	10 9 8 7 6 5 4 3 2 1	I want to be free of all home responsibilities.
I refuse to give up my possessions to move into a smaller place.	10 9 8 7 6 5 4 3 2 1	I no longer want the responsibility of possessions.
I have a high neighborhood and community identity.	10 9 8 7 6 5 4 3 2 1	I have no deep roots and can live anywhere.
Money is not a problem—I can maintain my home.	10 9 8 7 6 5 4 3 2 1	Money is a problem—I need a cheaper place.
I make friends slowly.	10 9 8 7 6 5 4 3 2 1	I make new friends quickly and love it.
I don't want to be around other older people.	10 9 8 7 6 5 4 3 2 1	I want to be with those my own age.
I hate group efforts.	10 9 8 7 6 5 4 3 2 1	I would ask to be on a committee.
I can take care of my own recreation.	10 9 8 7 6 5 4 3 2 1	I need and love group activities.
I will drive my car until my license is taken away.	10 9 8 7 6 5 4 3 2 1	The less I drive and the sooner I give it up the better.
I intend to take care of my own health as long as possible.	10 9 8 7 6 5 4 3 2 1	Being close to medical help is vital to me.
I'm not concerned with lifelong care.	10 9 8 7 6 5 4 3 2 1	Lifelong care has great appeal.
I love having children around.	10 9 8 7 6 5 4 3 2 1	Give me a pure adult community.
A changing neighborhood doesn't bother me.	10 9 8 7 6 5 4 3 2 1	I can't handle neighborhood changes..
Freedom, to me, is living away from others.	10 9 8 7 6 5 4 3 2 1	Freedom, to me, is not having to worry about tomorrow.
A home of my own is part of my identity.	10 9 8 7 6 5 4 3 2 1	Give me comfort, protection, people, and less responsibility.

Total Score _____

If you are in the middle—between 4 and 7—you seem to indicate you don't want the responsibilities of home ownership, but you want independence. Many facilities can provide this, including adult parks, condominiums, and retirement centers. It will require investigation on your part to decide.

If you are 3 or below, you seem to desire a more protected living environment. You will probably be happier with protection and health care close to you. A full-service retirement center might fit your needs better than simply owning a condominium in a protected environment.

Some General Rules for Choosing Where to Live

Following are seven living environment choices. The possibilities, of course, are vast. Covering these broad choices may help direct you to additional investigation. As you consider which path to take, keep these general thoughts in mind.

* It is usually a good idea to stay where you are happy, comfortable, and near your inner-circle support system.

* Before deciding to move, make sure advantages measurably outweigh disadvantages.

* You alone should make the final decision. Do not be overly influenced by relatives, friends, or promoters. (Remember, the grass always looks greener on the other side.)

* Protect your freedom with a passion. Any move that will cause you to lose freedom or make your world smaller may not be worth the apparent security it brings.

* Take culture shock seriously. Culture shock—the disorientation that occurs when moving from one country to another (Canada to Japan) or one part of the country to another (Quebec to Vancouver)—requires adjustment. There is also a necessary adjustment when you move from your private home to a different living environment. There will be new neighbors, new social situations, and new rules to follow. This culture shock is possible in your own community when you move from your home into a retirement center.

Seven Living Styles

Check the appropriate boxes as you analyze the possibilities.

Is Your Home Still Your Castle?

If you own your home, you might be happier staying there. More and more gerontology specialists advocate this, and there seems to be a trend in this direction. There can be a lot of happiness in your own backyard. Sometimes, though, it is wise to move: neighborhoods change, or we change. Study the following advantages and disadvantages of living in your own home, and check items important to you. Write in any you feel are missing.

Advantages:

☐ Your image is tied to your home. People you love identify you there.

☐ You feel more in charge in your own home.

☐ You have more privacy and space in your own home. You don't have to listen to someone else's plumbing.

☐ You retain more of your possessions.

☐ Appreciation in value is tax exempt when you sell your home.

☐ You can keep your pets.

Other: _____

_____

Disadvantages:

☐ Home ownership is often more expensive (taxes, maintenance, etc.).

☐ Maintenance takes time, and you may do too much yourself or worry about it.

☐ Security risks may be higher.

☐ It may be more difficult to take trips.

Other: _____

_____

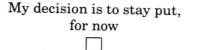

My decision is to stay put, for now	I need to seriously investigate other options
☐	☐

Would You Be Happier Renting? Some retirees are very happy in rented apartments. The reason is that they are not tied down with homeowner responsibilities. They can select the neighborhood they prefer in the community they like. They can also stay close to their inner circle without the problems of maintaining their own home.

Advantages:

☐ Moving to a new apartment is usually easy.

☐ Apartments don't have maintenance problems.

☐ Apartments require no capital investment.

☐ Apartments with special facilities (swimming pools, health clubs, etc.) are often available.

Other: _____

_____

Disadvantages:

☐ Landlords can be uncooperative and difficult.

☐ Rent increases are always possible.

☐ Neighbors living too close can be a problem.

☐ Apartments build no equity.

Other: _____

_____

No thanks—apartment living is not for me	I have an open mind and will investigate
☐	☐

What About a Condominium? If you own your home, you might be able to sell it, buy a nice condo at a lower price, and invest the difference. Many do this and feel they have done the right thing. Condominium life can have style!

Maintenance is normally not required. You are responsible for things inside your unit, but nothing on the outside. You will have a deed and/or mortgage and pay real-estate taxes. But you join with other owners to pay for outside maintenance, including recreational areas, landscaping, and even roofing. There are many elegant condominimum facilities in Canada. All have their own special requirements, and almost all have a homeowner's association in which you automatically become a member.

Advantages:

☐ Usually safer than an isolated, private dwelling.

☐ Easier to leave for long trips because there is less to care for.

☐ Special facilities are often available—pool, sauna, recreation rooms, tennis courts.

☐ More likely to have neighbors your own age and social level.

☐ Easier to make new friends.

Other: _____

_____

Disadvantages:

☐ There are rules to follow and association involvement.

☐ Normally you have less room, which may force you to sell some of your possessions.

☐ Your assessment fees can increase.

☐ Your neighbors are not always compatible.

☐ There are often restrictions on pets.

Other: _____

_____

Condominium is best bet	Much more investigation is called for
☐	☐

Mobile-Home Living Can Be Nifty

A growing number of retirees are living happily in adult mobile parks, some of which are quite elegant. The homes are really prefabricated houses, and some have two or three bedrooms. Mobile homes normally cost less than condominiums or single-dwelling houses. Often you can sell a private home, buy a mobile home, and bank the difference.

Advantages:

☐ Less capital investment is required.

☐ There are many parks from which to select.

☐ Security protection can be excellent.

☐ Your neighbors are often in your comfort zone.

☐ There can be excellent recreational facilities or locally sponsored social events.

Other: _____

_____

Disadvantages:

☐ Neighbors can be too close.

☐ Usually some restrictions prevail—for example, pets may not be permitted.

☐ Park owners can raise rent on space.

☐ Like neighborhoods, parks can deteriorate.

☐ Sometimes it is difficult to get into good parks.

Other: _____

Mobile home living is not my
cup of tea
☐

I need to investigate this
option
☐

Retirement Centers Are
in Vogue

Many retirees are so enthusiastic about retirement centers that
they have closed their eyes to other possibilities. Retirement centers
can come in all sizes, varieties, and prices. Many have medical centers. Large ones often have churches, organized social activities,
golf, swimming, and tennis. Compared to adult condominiums and
mobile-home parks, retirement centers are more self-contained.

Advantages:

☐ Retirement centers offer greater protection.

☐ More facilities are available, especially medical.

☐ You have less worry and feel more secure as you grow older.

☐ You have easier access to inside facilities.

☐ Different centers fit most pocketbooks.

Other: _____

Disadvantages:

☐ There are many restrictions.

☐ Generally no pets are allowed.

☐ Centers are like a closed world.

☐ There are fewer young people around.

☐ Sometimes it is difficult to get out.

Other: _____

I'm not the retirement center
kind
☐

I'm going to do a complete
investigation
☐

Should You Apply for
Government-Sponsored
Housing?

If your income is modest, government housing could be the best step
to take. If you can find a place and the list is not too long, you might
want to act in a hurry.

Advantages:

☐ Lower costs are often adjusted to your income.

☐ Each facility must meet government specifications.

☐ There are few responsibilities.

☐ Government housing is usually close to public transportation.

☐ Government facilities are normally secure.

Other: _____

_____

Disadvantages:

☐ Being accepted can be difficult.

☐ Like most things connected with government, there are many restrictions.

☐ Rooms are usually small.

☐ There is often a hotel atmosphere.

☐ There is some loss of freedom.

Other: _____

_____

Government housing is not for me	I'm going to look into this
☐	☐

Life-Care Centers Have Special Attractions

There are centers that provide full or life care. This usually means that, with a sizable investment, you can enter a community with the intention of staying there the rest of your life. You may be totally able when you enter; but later, when you need greater—even custodial—care, the facility is prepared to care for you. Some are very attractive, and often they are connected with a religious denomination.

Advantages:

☐ You can receive the greatest possible care and security.

☐ Life-care centers can provide peace of mind.

☐ The other residents are usually in the same comfort zone.

☐ The centers potentially eliminate future difficult decisions.

☐ Often less concern is required by your family.

☐ Activities may fit your needs better than other retirement options.

Other: _____

_____

Disadvantages:

☐ Centers cost money. Often a sizable investment is required. In some cases you turn over a part of your estate.

☐ The age level is usually more advanced.

☐ Often people lose more freedom than expected.

☐ The decision can be almost irrevocable.

☐ It is difficult to find the perfect center.

☐ There is a possibility of default.

Other: _____

_____

I could become interested at a later date	I'm going to spend some time investigating
☐	☐

Earlier in this book you were told there would be some major decisions as you approached retirement. Where to live and when to move is the kind of decision we had in mind. You may want to review Chapter 4 ("Decision Making and Comfort Zones").

Take Your Positive Attitude with You

If you decide to make a major move, take your positive attitude with you. Pack it with your most priceless possessions and hand-carry it to your new environment. More than anything else, it will help make your move successful. Here are some further tips:

* Within reason, take your prized possessions with you. They help make a new location seem more like home in a hurry.

* Once settled, engage in a number of civic, athletic, social, or church activities.

* The sooner you make new friends or rebuild an inner-circle support system, the better.

People you meet will do more than anything else to make your new environment a happy one.

Summary The most difficult decision facing those who retire is where to live and what kind of housing facility or living environment to select.

When the advantages of one geographic area over another become apparent, a move should be seriously considered, finances permitting.

It is helpful for people to position themselves on a continuum between having their own home or joining a full-care facility.

Comfort zone is an important consideration in the choice of any living environment.

Housing decisions are not always revocable.

PROBLEM TO SOLVE **To Each His Own**

Mrs. Henry purchased a home in a retirement center and moved in at age 53. She was one of the youngest residents. Her lifelong friend, Mrs. Krouse, about the same age, decided to continue living in her own home. She is emphatic about staying there as long as possible.

During a recent visit, they got into an argument over the two environments and the influence each had on the aging process.

Mrs Henry said: "I realize most of the people are older than I, but they are beautiful, active people, and I can learn from them. By the time I am 65, I will be fully adjusted. In the meantime, this is a safe place to live, and I have excellent medical protection and a wide range of social activities. Being around older people doesn't age an individual. That's ridiculous!"

Mrs. Krouse responded: "You won't admit it, but you are surrounded by older people who will involve you in their older habits without your knowing it, and you will age faster. By moving into the center too soon, you have needlessly aged yourself five years, just by being a victim of your environment."

How would you defend either Mrs. Henry or Mrs. Krouse? Compare your thoughts with those of the author in Appendix C.

SELF-QUIZ

True	False	
_____	_____	1. Fewer retirees are migrating to warmer climates.
_____	_____	2. A geographic move makes it easy to take your inner circle along.

_____ _____ 3. The advantages of staying in your home seldom outweigh the advantages of moving.

_____ _____ 4. Culture shock applies only when moving to a foreign country.

_____ _____ 5. It is a good idea to live a few months in a new geographical area before deciding to make a permanent move.

(Answers in Appendix C.)

23

How to Become a Master Senior

Though pride is not a virtue, it is the parent of many virtues.
M. C. Collins

Have you ever sipped a drink on the Via Veneta in Rome? Or enjoyed the cafés of Parisian streets? There's a similar place in Canada—believe it or not, it's in Toronto. I'm talking about a promenade along Lake Ontario that winds through Harbourfront and Queen's Quay. This public spot provides a great atmosphere in which to study people of all ages and backgrounds.

A few months ago, I was there and made some significant observations. As one might expect, the small children were mostly innocent, the teenagers were exuberant, and young adults sometimes showed the strain of family responsibilities. Most impressive, however, were certain older individuals. Several of them seemed to dress better than those five to ten years younger. They walked with greater authority, and I heard more laughter from them. They communicated a certain dignity and style that made them stand out.

As a recent retiree, I was encouraged by observing this. Only a select few of these seniors stood out; others were lost in the crowd. I asked myself why? What secrets had some found that others had not?

Pride Makes the Difference

I finally concluded that the difference was pride. Those with style were proud of their age. They demonstrated they were active and could communicate. They appeared proud to be involved with life. Beautiful, I thought—that's the way it should be. But I wondered what was the source of their pride? Why did only a select few possess it?

I began watching those who did not transmit this sense of dignity. Most looked worn down, defeated, or disinterested. The most significant observation was that those with greatest personal pride seemed to have set standards for themselves. They apparently were living up to some self-imposed expectations.

Pride Comes from Making the Most of Retirement

That week I interviewed a woman in her eighties, and I asked her about my observation. She responded: "Of course they have pride because they are living up to their expectations of retired life."

I mentioned that many seniors did not reflect any pride. She suggested that in each phase of life, some individuals rise to challenges and others fall to the wayside. Some are not proud because they have wasted their later years. Retirement has defeated rather than strengthened them.

Her thoughts led me to wonder if some kind of designation was needed to separate those who merely survive from those who make the most of retirement—something that would help more seniors achieve the pride I noticed in Toronto. The designation I selected is *Master Senior*.

What Is a Master Senior?

Every phase of life should have special goals, and this includes retirement. I believe it is a serious mistake to retire without certain self-imposed standards. I feel many lose pride because they do not have serious goal replacements. Their sole aim is to let down, which in itself does not provide the motivation that converts to pride. They don't know how to measure themselves as retirees, and thus many deteriorate.

Many of us are programmed to reach retirement, but nothing beyond. We look back to goals already accomplished, but not ahead to new ones. Assuming this is true, I want to propose the following standards.

MASTER SENIOR STANDARDS

Indicate whether or not you agree with the following 10 standards. Write any changes you want to make under "comments" in the left margin. Keep in mind you are establishing standards that you wish to reach yourself. You need not reach all standards to earn the title, "Master Senior"; it is simply something personal between you and what you hope to make of your retirement years.

Agree ☐   *Disagree* ☐

Comments:
_____
_____
_____
_____

Standard 1: To be called a Master Senior, one must live with style. In this case, style means an individual has retained visible personal pride, maintained personal dignity, and been involved in some form of social or group activity.
Those who permit themselves to fall into a careless attitude in which they become inactive or unkempt would not meet this standard.

☐   ☐

Comments:
_____
_____
_____
_____

Standard 2: To become a Master Senior, an individual must find a new role in retirement. This could be anything from a money-making job to a volunteer position. Those involved in individual creative efforts—painting, acting, writing, crafts, gardening, running a business—would also qualify.
Those who have not accepted or developed any postretirement roles would not qualify.

☐   ☐

Comments:
_____
_____
_____
_____

Standard 3: This standard requires that some positive contribution be made to the lives of others on a regular basis. Some people call this paying your human "rent." Others simply say it's being a good person. These individuals make a special effort to bring happiness to others each day. They often demonstrate their compassion by visiting those confined or making telephone calls that bring cheer to others.
Retirees who live only for themselves would not meet this humanistic standard.

Agree   *Disagree*
☐   ☐
Comments:

_____
_____
_____
_____

Standard 4: This standard demands a sense of humor—an ability to laugh at where you are, to see yourself in perspective. To qualify individuals must consistently make a special effort to see the positive, lighter side of life and communicate it to others. If someone is considered good company, they probably have met this standard. If they are known as a positive force, they have qualified. If they consistently make others laugh, they are setting a standard.
Retirees who constantly complain and focus exclusively on the negative side of life would not meet this standard.

☐   ☐
Comments:

_____
_____
_____
_____

Standard 5: To achieve this, an individual must continue to learn. This can mean returning to school, attending educational forums, learning from cultural involvements, or practicing a self-improvement program at home. These folks read books, watch television programs of substance, and enjoy intellectual conversations. They constantly attempt to understand society and improve their minds.
Those who seek only personal entertainment and refuse to stretch their minds intellectually do not meet this standard.

☐   ☐
Comments:

_____
_____
_____
_____

Standard 6: This person must have handled one or more setbacks gracefully and with strength. Retirement years are not always easy. Serious health problems are common. There is always the risk of losing a spouse. There can be a major geographical relocation or an agonizing problem with children. Master Seniors handle such problems without dragging others down. They bounce back and earn their stripes by facing difficulties with style.
Those who permit such problems to destroy their spirit would not meet this standard.

☐   ☐
Comments:

_____
_____
_____
_____

Standard 7: To be a Master Senior, one must maintain personal independence. This can mean "going it alone" under trying circumstances—handling financial matters and making decisions as long as possible. Circumstances vary, but those who put up a strong fight can qualify. Master Seniors stay in charge of their lives longer.
An individual who prematurely gives away his or her independence would not meet this standard.

Agree   Disagree
□   □
Comments:
_____
_____
_____
_____

Standard 8: Those who create and maintain good human relationships meet this difficult qualification. They not only maintain their inner circles but also reach out to meet new people. Some of these new relationships will be with younger people. If a human-relations problem occurs, they repair it.
Those who nurse hurts and slights to the point where they chase others away do not qualify.

□   □
Comments:
_____
_____
_____
_____

Standard 9: To become a Master Senior, retirees must make a major effort not only to maintain their best possible state of health but also to resist complaining about aches and pains. This often means experiencing discomfort in silence without becoming negative. It means controlling diet, exercising, and avoiding excessive medication.
Those who do nothing to maintain good health, and who dwell excessively and needlessly on present health problems do not meet this difficult standard.

□   □
Comments:
_____
_____
_____
_____

Standard 10: This standard requires individuals to remain a positive force within the community as long as possible. They must continue to have an impact on others through speaking up and taking action when called for. Others must sense their presence. In certain situations it may mean becoming a matriarch or patriarch within a family circle. Master Seniors are strong personalities.
Those who lose their individuality and, as a result, permit themselves to be ignored do not meet this standard.

To demonstrate personal pride—and be admired by relatives, friends, and strangers—is to become a Master Senior. What a challenge! If you talk with those who have met the challenge and made the successful journey into retirement, you will hear expressions such as:

* "Looking back, I'm glad I set such demanding standards. The payoff has been worth the efforts involved."

* "It took discipline, but these have been years of creativity and accomplishment."

* "My retirement years have not always been easy, but the respect and recognition I earned have made it worthwhile."

* "You either fight to make retirement work or you give up. I'm proud I made mine work."

* "Nobody told me retirement would take so much self-determination. Nobody told me it would be this rewarding, either."

If you stay in charge and have some luck with your health, you can become a Master Senior. Friends and family may not use this term, but you will see the admiration and respect in their eyes. You will realize that you have met your retirement standards and that your life has been a success.

Summary It may take time and effort, but, by meeting certain self-imposed standards, you can earn the right to be called a Master Senior.

Master Seniors will make the most out of retirement regardless of their special situations.

MASTER SENIOR CARD

You may want to carry the following message with you. It can be a reminder to live up to the Master Senior Standards presented in this book. Good luck!

MASTER SENIOR STANDARDS

* Stay in charge.
* Live with style.
* Pursue activities with enthusiasm.
* Maintain health through exercise and diet control.
* Continue to learn.
* Develop an inner-circle support system.
* Contribute to others.
* Keep a sense of humor.

Being designated a Master Senior by others is the highest compliment.

PROBLEM TO SOLVE   **Master Senior Award Decision**

Ten years ago, Harvey and Hazel sold their farm and purchased a nice home in a retirement community. He was 65 at the time; she was 57.

Since that time Harvey has become one of the best-liked people in the center. He constantly does favors and household repairs for others, and he is an active committee person. Harvey is always willing to help others and expects nothing in return. He enjoys people.

Three months ago the general committee of the center inaugurated a special awards program. Standards were established, and 10 individuals were to be selected each year and recognized at an annual dinner. After several meetings, 10 candidates were chosen, and Harvey was near the top of the list.

At this point, Mrs. Reynolds suggested it would be unfair to give an award to Harvey without including his wife, Hazel. She pointed out that Hazel encouraged Harvey to be active outside the home, never complained, and maintained a positive attitude despite pain caused by arthritis. She did everything she could to support Harvey psychologically. Mrs. Reynolds recommended the number of awards be expanded to eleven so that Hazel could also be honored.

How would you vote as a member of the committee? Why? See the author's comments in Appendix C.

SELF-QUIZ

True	False	
_____	_____	1. Life goals are less important after retirement.
_____	_____	2. A true Master Senior can be an excellent role model for a new retiree.
_____	_____	3. A Master Senior sets high individual retirement expectations and works hard to live up to them.
_____	_____	4. A Master Senior communicates pride of accomplishment.
_____	_____	5. Most retirees become Master Seniors.

(Answers in Appendix C.)

Appendix A

IRA: Inventory of Retirement Activities

This easy, self-scoring survey can help you make the most of your retirement years.

This Inventory of Retirement Activities (IRA) could be an important way to enhance your retirement years. It can help develop interests worthy of your retirement leisure hours—activities that fit your personality and provide satisfaction.

There are three parts to the exercise: (1) ranking your activity preferences, (2) constructing and interpreting your personal profile, and (3) comparing your profile with others—especially a spouse or friend. Complete one step at a time; please do not jump ahead.

285

Part I   Preference Inventory Scale

Rate each statement in each box by circling an appropriate number.

* A 10 indicates that you look forward with great enthusiasm to participating in the activity.

* A 9, 8, or 7 indicates high interest in the activity. You thoroughly enjoy it.

* From 6 to 4 indicates moderate interest. Time permitting, you would enjoy the activity.

* A 3 or 2 signifies limited interest. You would probably engage in the activity only to make another person happy.

* A 1 says you would not participate under any circumstances.

If you are currently working, rate the items as if you were retired. As you complete each statement, assume your financial condition makes the activity affordable.

This is not a test, so there are no wrong answers. Work quickly; first impressions will probably give you the best results.

IRA—BOX 1

Statement	*Scale*
1. Enjoying a sunset from a foreign shore	10 9 8 7 6 5 4 3 2 1
2. Playing competitive outdoor games	10 9 8 7 6 5 4 3 2 1
3. Participating in church or temple activities	10 9 8 7 6 5 4 3 2 1
4. Using a drill, skillsaw, sewing machine, or other craft activities	10 9 8 7 6 5 4 3 2 1
5. Painting, sketching, designing, writing, or other creative activities	10 9 8 7 6 5 4 3 2 1
6. Camping, backpacking, or other wilderness activities	10 9 8 7 6 5 4 3 2 1
7. Demonstrating pride of ownership through home improvements	10 9 8 7 6 5 4 3 2 1
8. Planning a festive party or attending one	10 9 8 7 6 5 4 3 2 1
9. Listening to music alone	10 9 8 7 6 5 4 3 2 1
10. Playing a game for fun, prize, money	10 9 8 7 6 5 4 3 2 1
11. Watching the six o'clock news	10 9 8 7 6 5 4 3 2 1
12. Browsing in a bookstore or library	10 9 8 7 6 5 4 3 2 1
13. Dealing with investments as a leisure activity	10 9 8 7 6 5 4 3 2 1
14. Having fun with children, grandchildren, nieces, nephews	10 9 8 7 6 5 4 3 2 1
15. Earning as much money as the guaranteed income supplement allows.	10 9 8 7 6 5 4 3 2 1
16. Volunteering services to a cause	10 9 8 7 6 5 4 3 2 1
17. Visiting an art gallery or museum	10 9 8 7 6 5 4 3 2 1
18. Having an intriguing conversation with a neighbor or friend	10 9 8 7 6 5 4 3 2 1

IRA—BOX 2

	Statement	*Scale*
1.	Getting away from it all—staying at a resort, taking a cruise, etc.	10 9 8 7 6 5 4 3 2 1
2.	Participating in sports or taking part in a physical-conditioning program	10 9 8 7 6 5 4 3 2 1
3.	Contributing to the welfare of others through a religious organization	10 9 8 7 6 5 4 3 2 1
4.	Working creatively with wood, fabric, leather, or other materials	10 9 8 7 6 5 4 3 2 1
5.	Blocking out time to satisfy creative needs	10 9 8 7 6 5 4 3 2 1
6.	Enjoying nature	10 9 8 7 6 5 4 3 2 1
7.	Working in a garden or other home-related activity	10 9 8 7 6 5 4 3 2 1
8.	Meeting members of the opposite sex in a social setting	10 9 8 7 6 5 4 3 2 1
9.	Reading an interesting book	10 9 8 7 6 5 4 3 2 1
10.	Playing bridge, poker, other inside games	10 9 8 7 6 5 4 3 2 1
11.	Watching television in bed before going to sleep	10 9 8 7 6 5 4 3 2 1
12.	Reading mystery stories, westerns, or historical novels	10 9 8 7 6 5 4 3 2 1
13.	Turning to the financial page first	10 9 8 7 6 5 4 3 2 1
14.	Entertaining favorite relatives	10 9 8 7 6 5 4 3 2 1
15.	Earning money in preference to a retirement leisure activity	10 9 8 7 6 5 4 3 2 1
16.	Participating in community activities	10 9 8 7 6 5 4 3 2 1
17.	Reading about concerts, ballets, or musicals	10 9 8 7 6 5 4 3 2 1
18.	Having coffee or cocktails with a good friend	10 9 8 7 6 5 4 3 2 1

IRA—BOX 3

Statement	*Scale*
1. Participating in an activity in locales such as mountains, deserts, or other scenic areas, local or abroad	10 9 8 7 6 5 4 3 2 1
2. Staying active—walking, jogging, or riding a bicycle in pleasant surroundings	10 9 8 7 6 5 4 3 2 1
3. Attending religious retreats or events	10 9 8 7 6 5 4 3 2 1
4. Building something with my hands	10 9 8 7 6 5 4 3 2 1
5. Taking courses in art, music, writing, or crafts to enhance my creative skills	10 9 8 7 6 5 4 3 2 1
6. Owning a recreational vehicle	10 9 8 7 6 5 4 3 2 1
7. Being a homebody—enjoying crafts, hobbies, television, comforts	10 9 8 7 6 5 4 3 2 1
8. Having people contacts—spending time with a congenial group	10 9 8 7 6 5 4 3 2 1
9. Doing special things alone	10 9 8 7 6 5 4 3 2 1
10. Going to Las Vegas, spending time at a racetrack, playing bingo	10 9 8 7 6 5 4 3 2 1
11. Watching a TV special, sporting event, situation comedy	10 9 8 7 6 5 4 3 2 1
12. Turning to the book section in a publication	10 9 8 7 6 5 4 3 2 1
13. Following the stock market or checking on my other investments	10 9 8 7 6 5 4 3 2 1
14. Attending family gatherings	10 9 8 7 6 5 4 3 2 1
15. Earning dollars after retirement—odd jobs, consulting, self-owned business	10 9 8 7 6 5 4 3 2 1
16. Engaging in community activities—Meals on Wheels, hospital auxiliary	10 9 8 7 6 5 4 3 2 1
17. Attending a play or musical comedy	10 9 8 7 6 5 4 3 2 1
18. Talking privately about an interesting subject	10 9 8 7 6 5 4 3 2 1

Part II   Constructing and Interpreting Your Personal Profile

Now that you have indicated your activity preferences, you have the fun of constructing your personal profile.

Step 1   Study the accompanying profile diagram for a moment. The scale from 0 to 30 on the left will measure the level of your interests; the labels across the top identify your activity interest.

Step 2   Total your responses to question number 1 in each of the preceding three IRA boxes and enter this number at the bottom of column 1 (travel). You may want to use a scratch pad or calculator. *Continue this process until you have entered the correct number at the bottom of each of the 18 columns.*

Step 3   On the scale for each column locate the number equal to your total and draw a line across the column.

It is now time to evaluate your profile. Like personality, it is uniquely yours and should be studied carefully. Here are some tips that will help you interpret it:

* The more high-interest categories you have, the more exciting your retirement can be. If you have only a few, study others you might like to develop.

* Categories 1, 2, 3, 8, 10, 14, 15, 16, 17, and 18 involve considerable human contact; categories 4, 5, 6, 7, 11, and 13 are low-social activities. Often a mix of the two is best.

* Retirement is a perfect time to develop new interests. A higher interest than you expected in any activity could be a signal it is waiting to be developed.

* Significant interrelationships may exist between your interests. High travel and social interests suggest you might enjoy group tours or cruises more than independent travel. A high hobby or home interest may indicate your greatest happiness is at home and not on the road. A high sports interest can reinforce a love for the outdoors. Look for other correlations in your profile. You may find some surprises that will allow you to understand yourself better.

* According to Dr. G. Frederic Kuder, who developed the Kuder Preference Vocational Record, interest patterns tend to be relatively stable. This does not mean medium- or low-interest activities cannot be developed. For example, at a later date, perhaps

ACTIVITY INTEREST PROFILE		High Interest		Medium Interest		Low Interest		Total
PRIVATE COMMUNICATIONS	18							
CULTURE/EDUCATION	17							
VOLUNTEER WORK	16							
WORKING	15							
FAMILY	14							
INVESTMENTS	13							
READING	12							
TELEVISION	11							
GAMES	10							
TIME ALONE	9							
SOCIAL	8							
HOME	7							
OUTDOORS	6							
HOBBIES (Artistic)	5							
HOBBIES (Mechanical)	4							
RELIGIOUS ACTIVITIES	3							
SPORTS/EXERCISE	2							
TRAVEL	1							
		30	25	20	15	10	5	0

when your health may not permit you to pursue a previous high-interest choice, another may be substituted.

If you sense the exercise did not fully identify or highlight a special interest of yours, rely on your judgment. Such an interest can easily be added to your profile.

Part III Comparing Profiles

Common interests

Spouses and friends can discover, through a comparison of their individual profiles, that they share interests they were not aware existed. One wife learned her husband had a higher social interest than she anticipated; with his involvement, she initiated more social situations. A husband learned his wife showed higher interest in outdoor activities than he had imagined. After some discussion, they purchased a camper and enjoyed some great trips together.

Capitalizing on common interests (even when one is high and the other moderate) is the best way for two people to make the most of retirement. A profile comparison can reveal compatible interests that will bring enjoyment to both parties.

Contrasting interests

A profile comparison can also show polarized interests. For example, one person may show a high interest in artistic hobbies while the other shows none at all. However, the person with the low artistic interest might be high in sports or games. Solution? A comfortable tradeoff. To make the most of retirement, one person should permit the other to enjoy his or her favorite activity. Not all interests can or should be shared. For example, one spouse with a high interest in religion, not shared by her husband, spent evenings at her church while he scheduled time at his fraternal club. Each person had the freedom and time to pursue divergent interests.

Conflicting situations

Some retirement activities need to be shared more than others. It is difficult when one person likes to travel but the other does not or when one person likes to go out socially and the other prefers solitude. In these situations, some give and take is necessary. When each person gives a little, often good things happen. Many an individual, through encouragement from a spouse, discovers the joys of social activity or the outdoors. One party learns from the other. When this happens, both individuals come out ahead.

Be enthusiastic about your high-interest activities, and continue to develop those in lower categories. Doing this should provide you with a more fulfilling retirement. Good luck!

Appendix B

How to Approach Retirement with Class

Although not always easy to do, most individuals take pride when approaching retirement. They dig in and make the most of their final months, maintaining positive attitudes and high productivity.

A few preretirees, however, permit their negative attitudes to surface. Instead of completing their careers with grace, they disappoint colleagues and make themselves miserable. Instead of continuing to make a contribution, they take advantage of their senior status and slack off. Instead of maintaining their previous standards, they succumb to the preretirement blues. It's sad.

These negative folks are easy to spot. Whether they have five years or five weeks to go, they generally fall into one of these categories:

* *The Hideouts:* These nonverbal characters sneak in and out of work so quietly that, if they meet a co-worker, the comment often is: "I thought you retired." Most successful in large

293

organizations, these crafty old-timers depart mentally before they do physically. The good news is that they stay hidden in their work stations and produce just enough to get by. The bad news is that they are no longer creative team members. Hideouts seldom have retirement parties because people forget they are around.

* *The Sitouts:* These low producers live by the motto: "I'll hang around until I get everything that I have coming." As a result, they drag out their work assignments until they reach a special benefit date. Others leave the moment they become eligible for the Canada Pension Plan. A few get so comfortable in their soft environments that only a "Golden Handshake" special retirement benefits bonus will get them to make the big decision. For their contributions, they might as well be retired even if they still come to work.

* *The Wounded:* These once dedicated individuals had previously been models of productivity. Through some unfortunate organizational politics, however, their feelings were hurt. They are easy to pick out because their noses are consistently out of joint. These folks enjoy nursing their wounds. You hear them say: "I gave this outfit the best years of my life." The wounded often say they don't want a retirement party, but they will be hurt even more if they don't receive a lavish one.

* *The Downers:* Once high flyers within the organization, these bitter people are now down on their leaders, their careers, and life in general. Even those who continue to produce are often counterproductive because they contaminate other workers with their negative views. The company cafeteria is their soapbox. When the downers finally announce their retirement, there are sighs of relief from all quarters. Sometimes people are so happy to see them go that a successful retirement party results.

You could add to or make up your own list, because each organization produces its own unique crop. Depending on your own age and position, you could either be sensitive or insensitive to the behavior of the modern preretiree. Here are two reasons to be understanding:

* *Organizational changes are more frequent and dramatic today.* Mergers, consolidations, and organizational realignments are more common in the world of work today. Adjusting to these changes is difficult for all personnel, but it's far more traumatic

for those who built their comfort zones during more stable times.

* *New guard/old guard conflicts are often greater.* Sooner or later, in all organizations, a changing of the guard must take place. The process is difficult for the "old guard" because, in many cases, the new guard has a value system that doesn't honor the past. The new guard has the right to initiate change and go about doing things differently. But often, perhaps without meaning to, they step hard on the very people who built the organization that gave them their opportunity.

Even 20 years ago, approaching retirement with class was not easy. It has always been possible to fall into negative, wait-it-out moods—especially when we start thinking that our past contributions are not appreciated. It has always been easy to become overly sensitive—especially when we start thinking there is a subtle conspiracy to push us out. When we indulge in these and similar thinking patterns, we not only make life difficult for ourselves and our co-workers, we also jeopardize our own retirements. Instead of moving into retirement free of resentments and hard feelings, we spoil our journey by taking excess baggage with us and become double losers.

How can you avoid this? Here are some thoughts:

* *Do your retirement planning now.* Nothing will do more to help you retire with class than a sound, detailed plan you can be happy about ahead of time. The following can occur once you have such a plan in place:
  —Negative thoughts about your current situation can be replaced by positive thoughts about where you will be after you retire.
  —Your plan will help you see your present working environment in a better light.
  —Anticipating a well-planned future will enable you to lighten your daily work routine and maintain better relationships with co-workers and superiors.

  Those who approach retirement without a good plan are often riddled with fear and anxiety, which shows in their preretirement behavior.

* *Let your enthusiasm toward retirement show.* One way to do this is to start getting ready for retirement in advance. Start training replacements, turn in some creative ideas you have been mulling over, or computerize your old files. The more you

demonstrate your enthusiasm to "take off," the more fun you will have getting there.

* *Communicate a new image.* Wear the best part of your wardrobe or a different hairstyle. Do whatever it takes to let superiors and co-workers know you are starting to leave work problems behind. Occasionally you might show up in more informal attire. This may sound like strange advice, but it can help improve your attitude toward retirement if there is a little envy from those you are leaving behind.

* *Be mysterious about your plans.* There is excitement to mystery, so consider keeping your co-workers in the dark. When asked about your plan, say something like this: "I have plans to do a lot of fun things. If you will invite me out to dinner in a few months, I'll fill you in." Do all of this with a smile and a twinkle in your eye.

* *Dissipate any hidden resentments.* If you are harboring some bad feelings, dig them out and release them forever. Be your own therapist. Tell yourself: "It's too late to cry over the past. The only way I can free myself of ill feelings is to get them in the open and forget them. If I bury them, they could spring up later an make me unhappy."

* *Restore any broken relationships.* Leaving a wake of battered relationships as you retire is like leaving a party after embarrassing yourself. Guilt feelings follow. You will feel better *after retirement* if you clean your human relations slate before you leave. Say to yourself: "I'm going to demonstrate I can be a big person. I will mend fences and walk with my head held high. Carrying conflict into retirement is like taking a domineering mother-in-law on a vacation."

* *Don't take things too seriously as you approach retirement.* This does not mean to cast off your job responsibilities and lower your personal standards. That would not be professional. It simply means you have a grace period ahead of you, so enjoy it. Tell yourself: "The career game is over, so I am going to turn this last period into a light-hearted time."

* *Accept farewell arrangements with grace.* The "gold watch" days may be gone, but some kind of send-off may develop whether you want it or not. Whatever happens, don't fight it. Show your class by making the most of what *does* occur. Remember that retirement affairs can be awkward for others as well as yourself. It is possible that your friends and fans have already retired and

those remaining have had less time to appreciate you. Be nice. They will have to be at work next week. You won't.

Your attitude is the main thing that will allow you to retire with class. Make the time between now and your departure enjoyable and positive, and your retirement will be more successful.
Isn't it worth the effort?

Appendix C

Suggested Answers to Problems and Questions

Problems at the end of each chapter were designed to encourage individual thinking and discussion. There are no "correct" answers to any of the problems. Only the most essential facts were presented, and it is impossible to give a definitive answer without *all* the facts. Different points of view are not only possible but encouraged.

Therefore, the following "answers" are nothing more than the author's opinion of how the problem might be approached. They are only a guide.

Problem 1   Retirement Remorse

Hilda retired too soon. As a result, she is drowning in psychological and emotional problems she interprets as financial. This could have been avoided with some preretirement planning.

299

Jane's statement, although dramatic, is an oversimplification of the problem. Hilda might benefit from part-time employment. Once retired, it can be difficult to return to a full-time position. Even if able to do this, Hilda would face the same problems at a later date. In my opinion, it would have been better for Jane to encourage Hilda to face the immediate challenge by getting help. It is never too late to solve problems and make the most of retirement.

Problem 2   Honeymoon Period

Marge's concern is justified because her husband has elected to ignore that he is going through a major transition. It's true that when his "honeymoon" period is over, he may find a satisfactory retirement lifestyle. In the meantime, he is needlessly putting himself and his spouse through a turbulent period. The danger is that he may miss out on the positive possibilities of retirement. Some people pay a severe price to reach retirement by working for years in a job they dislike and then failing to make the most of it.

Problem 3   Farewell to Challenges

The family concern is justified. Henry seems to want to retire to nothing. He seems to be rebelling against past standards set by others. He is not designing a retirement plan for himself. He forgets he is free to establish his own standards, activities, and challenges. Chances are good that Henry will eventually come to this conclusion.

Problem 4   Decision-Free Retirement

If Mrs. Henderson becomes too dependent on her son, she could wind up with less money than she needs to protect her lifestyle. This would cause a major loss of freedom. By staying in charge of her assets, Mrs. Henderson will remain a strong person and earn the respect of her son and daughter-in-law. She should demonstrate to everyone that she is in charge. She can seek the advice of her son but should resist turning things over too soon.

Problem 5   **Retirement Attitudes**

Each individual reflects his or her own background, philosophy, and personality. If the Major needs a daily wake-up list to function successfully, he should have one. If the day-at-a-time, no-planning pattern provides Mrs. Jason with an upbeat lifestyle, she should use it. If the limited planning works for Mrs. George, she is lucky. If a consuming mission is the only approach that will provide Mr. Shaw with a challenging retirement, he should find one.

Each answer is simplistic. Time utilization after retirement is more complex than people think. A time-utilization strategy is effective if it leads to a fulfilling lifestyle. I feel a combination of the suggestions proposed by Mrs. George and Major Valor would be the best approach.

Problem 6   **Plan A Success Formula?**

Mr. and Mrs. Payne could make their plan work providing they keep open minds and continue to try new activities until they find the proper mix. This seems unlikely because of the following dangers: (1) They may get so involved in activities that they will stop exploring, with the result being a mix that is out of balance and not fully satisfying. (2) They may discover they have different activity interests; and, unless they are willing to provide each other sufficient space, conflicts may arise. (3) They may tire of their "perfect mix" pursuit and spend too much time at home becoming overdependent on television and disenchanted with retirement.

Problem 7   **Plan A or Plan B**

Miss Ritter has an excellent Plan B. She is developing competency in a high-skill area where it should be easy to get a part-time job. She is placing herself in a position to augment her Canada Pension, which will supplement her teachers' retirement. Her preferences for theatre festivals and similar activities will require additional income. Finally, she appears to have the necessary discipline with which to protect her leisure hours. I feel she can make her Plan B work so her future Plan A will be even more successful.

Problem 8   A Case of Resentment

Mrs. Greer has nothing to lose by inviting Mrs. Adamson for lunch to attempt resolving the problem. If this does not work, she should discuss the problem with both ministers in a closed session. As a volunteer, she should not live with the problem and hope time will solve it. Mrs. Greer should also inspect the way she is treating Mrs. Adamson. Is she, without knowing it, demeaning in her approach? Has she created a meaningless conflict? Does Mrs. Adamson consider her a threat? Until Mrs. Greer determines that she may partially be at fault, the possibility of an improved relationship is remote.

Problem 9   A Decision for Mrs. Carroll

When it comes to exercising, Mrs. Carroll should stay within her comfort zone. She should continue to walk alone where it is safe and increase her efforts to find new colleagues. This may not be too difficult because there are probably others who share her interests. The friends who joined the exercise group may tire of their new routine and want to walk again.

Problem 10   Less is Better

Ronald is permitting Opal to intimidate him. He should take a firm stand and openly discuss all aspects of the problem. He should provide financial specifics when they spend money needlessly on food. He should also mention the importance of a more thoughtful diet on future health and happiness. Ronald should encourage Opal to state her views. Is she cooking to satisfy him or herself? It could be more of a challenge to prepare memorable meals on a lower budget. Ronald should believe that a change will benefit both parties and should not expect one discussion to settle the matter. Changes of this sort do not occur overnight. Opal needs time to see things his way. Once Opal begins to make progress, Ronald should provide positive reinforcement through compliments or, perhaps, a gift.

Problem 11   The Possible Connection

Considerable research is progressing in this area. At this juncture, however, any direct scientific connection between physical and mental wellness is speculation. This does not mean a psychological connection between the two is not real. If Frank believes staying active physically helps him mentally, or the other way around, he wins. As far as documentation is concerned, John's position is the easier to defend. To him staying in good physical condition while staying mentally active provides enough benefits without the necessity of a provable connection.

Problem 12   Gloomy Gertrude

Gus should face Gertrude and state emphatically that she must either change her attitude or he will insist she receive professional counseling. He should also inform her that he expects equal time when it comes to talking. Gertrude must understand she will ruin retirement if her behavior continues. Gus should not expect too much too soon, and he should provide positive reinforcement when the situation warrants.

Problem 13   Preretirement Emphasis

It is my opinion that preretirees who place undue emphasis on monetary matters may be short-changing themselves. For most retirees, a balance between financial and human concerns is necessary for an acceptable level of fulfillment. The idea that resolution of financial concerns will allow everything else to fall into place is erroneous. Problems of retirement extend far beyond having an adequate income.

Problem 14   Upset Plan

It is difficult to recommend the best alternative without better information on the lifestyle, values, and family orientation of Mrs. and Mrs. Brant. Still, I favor a slightly more liberal version of Alternative 3. Cindy must work out her own solution, but the grandchildren should not be denied essential economic and health care during the process. This probably means cutting into Mr. and Mrs. Brant's nest egg without drastically changing their retirement plans. Whatever solution is finally agreed upon, the more discussion the better. Mr. and Mrs. Brant should support any solution equally. Under no circumstances should they permit the problem to injure their own relationship or destroy their basic retirement plan.

Problem 15   Sid and Sarah

Sarah is gambling Sid will not find another partner willing to satisfy his needs. Sid is gambling Sarah will eventually see it his way. Because both parties enjoy each other so much, neither wants the relationship to end. Time will tell if they can work out the conflict.

Problem 16   A Devastating Surprise

Mrs. S should see a lawyer and discuss the many ramifications of her husband's decision. There is more involved than a simple division of property. Who will pay the legal services? What about the tax provisions? If children are involved, what about a will or a trust? Is the break reconcilable? In addition to a lawyer, Mrs. S should seek the advice of a friend to help her through the transition. If she is fully informed and has records on all properties, she may not choose to make the division of property a matter of contention. This, however, should be discussed first with her lawyer. More than at any previous stage of her life, Mrs. S needs to survive the emotional trauma and take charge in building a new life for herself.

Problem 17   Retirement Conflict

Mrs. Parker's irritation is understandable, but it may not be fully justified. The ideal situation is for spouses to work together after retirement, not against each other. Some give and take on each side is usually necessary. Mr. Parker's suggestion that they can enhance their retirement by saving in the consumer area and spending more for travel is fine if more travel is what they want. Mr. Parker should have worked more closely with his wife on her spending patterns before retirement. Now he needs to be more sensitive in his approach. He should provide some space for his wife in other areas so they can improve their spending habits as a team. Retirement often will force spouses to work more closely together. The better they become at this, the better their retirement should be. Postretirement conflicts of this sort are not uncommon.

Problem 18   Turnover

Mrs. Z's husband should have educated his wife about their investments earlier in their married life. At this time, she should invest conservatively to match her comfort zone. Perhaps a savings and loan association or a money-market account through a major bank would be best until she becomes more sophisticated. In the meantime, she should devote time to becoming more knowledgeable about investment opportunities. This could mean attending a course, joining an investment club, or working with a highly recommended investment counselor on a trial basis. Mrs. Z could turn out to be better at investments than her late husband.

Problem 19   Time Conflict

Mr. Trent may wait too long to enjoy the estate they have built. They could also fail to take advantage of income splitting with their children to reduce the family tax burden. A workable compromise might be to move the process up a few years by traveling or distributing their estate earlier. An immediate lifestyle change (a purpose of retirement) would still permit plenty of time for Mr. Trent to dabble with investments. Mr. and Mrs. Trent should have planned a retirement strategy much sooner, and Mrs. Trent should have been a full partner in this process. Hidden conflicts between spouses have a way of surfacing after retirement.

Problem 20   To Trust or Not To Trust

Mr. and Mrs. Laval should present their questions to an experienced lawyer and perhaps others to gain a better background on trust matters. Once this has occurred, they should discuss the matter openly with their children—especially their concern about the grandchildren in the event of a divorce. The more that primary beneficiaries are involved, the better—so long as control is not relinquished. If they eventually opt for a trust, they should hire a C.A. to design a tax-saving trust that will satisfy their needs. Once the trust has been established, Mr. and Mrs. Laval should devote their time to the pursuit of retirement happiness.

Problem 21   Too Much Versus Too Little

I believe Mrs. Grey has the right approach. She seems to be better at managing her risks. Mrs. Grey's policies appear adequate. It still might be a good idea for her to have a respected professional review her policies with some possible consolidation in mind. She may have a gap that is not obvious. Mrs. Starr is in desperate need of a good insurance agent. Her insurance portfolio needs a complete review, which can simplify her program and save her money. Also, despite her many policies, she may still have an obvious gap in coverage.

Problem 22   To Each His Own

Each individual should select the living environment that meets personal values and desires. It is obvious that Mrs. Krouse does not want to live in a retirement center. It does not fit into her comfort zone. It does, however, seem to fit that of Mrs. Henry. Mrs. Krouse's argument that being around older people can cause her friend to age faster is without merit. Attitude is the key factor. Mrs. Henry may actually stay younger and enjoy the many benefits of a well-managed center. She can have the best of both worlds—the protection and other advantages of a center and independent activities.

Problem 23   Master Senior Award Decision

Mrs. Reynolds is right. It would be unfair not to include Mrs. Harvey along with her husband. She is apparently wise enough to give Mr. Harvey the freedom he needs to build relationships on his own. She also appears to handle her physical handicap with grace by staying positive and not pulling her husband down. Although the case is presented for discussion purposes, in real life Mrs. Harvey may deserve the award more than her husband.

Answers to True/False Questions

Chapter 1	Chapter 7	Chapter 13	Chapter 19
1. F	1. T	1. F	1. F
2. F	2. T	2. T	2. F
3. T	3. F	3. F	3. T
4. F	4. F	4. F	4. F
5. T	5. T	5. T	5. T

Chapter 2	Chapter 8	Chapter 14	Chapter 20
1. F	1. F	1. T	1. T
2. F	2. T	2. F	2. T
3. F	3. T	3. F	3. T
4. F	4. T	4. F	4. F
5. F	5. F	5. F	5. T

Chapter 3	Chapter 9	Chapter 15	Chapter 21
1. T	1. F	1. T	1. F
2. T	2. T	2. T	2. T
3. F	3. T	3. F	3. F
4. T	4. T	4. F	4. F
5. T	5. T	5. F	5. F

Chapter 4	Chapter 10	Chapter 16	Chapter 22
1. T	1. F	1. T	1. F
2. T	2. F	2. F	2. F
3. T	3. F	3. F	3. F
4. T	4. F	4. T	4. F
5. T	5. F	5. F	5. T

Chapter 5	Chapter 11	Chapter 17	Chapter 23
1. F	1. T	1. F	1. F
2. F	2. T	2. F	2. T
3. F	3. T	3. T	3. T
4. T	4. F	4. T	4. T
5. T	5. F	5. T	5. F

Chapter 6	Chapter 12	Chapter 18
1. F	1. F	1. F
2. F	2. T	2. F
3. T	3. T	3. F
4. T	4. T	4. F
5. F	5. F	5. T

About The Author   Elwood N. Chapman was the ideal choice to write COMFORT ZONES. Author of more than a dozen books with combined sales of over one million copies, Mr. Chapman considers COMFORT ZONES his most important effort thus far. The book was developed during Mr. Chapman's own retirement following twenty-nine years of successful college teaching.

Over the years, Mr. Chapman has been extremely active as a writer, speaker, and consultant, and has traveled extensively. He is best known for his work in the field of human relations. His book YOUR ATTITUDE IS SHOWING has been read by hundreds of thousands of individuals, and is regarded as the best book available on attitude development.

Mr. Chapman is a graduate of the University of California, Berkeley and lives with his wife Martha in Ontario, California. He welcomes comments from his readers, and can be reached by writing Reid Publishing Ltd., Box 7267, Oakville, Ontario L6J 6L6.

ORDER FORM

QTY.	TITLE	PRICE	EXTN.
	THE FIFTY-MINUTE SUPERVISOR (93191-03-3)	8.95	
	EFFECTIVE PERFORMANCE APPRAISALS (11-4)	8.95	
	SUCCESSFUL NEGOTIATION (09-2)	8.95	
	QUALITY INTERVIEWING (10-0)	8.95	
	TEAM BUILDING: AN EXERCISE IN LEADERSHIP (16-5)	8.95	
	PERFORMANCE CONTRACTS: THE KEY TO JOB SUCCESS (12-2)	8.95	
	PERSONAL TIME MANAGEMENT (22-X)	9.95	
	EFFECTIVE PRESENTATION SKILLS (24-6)	9.95	
	BETTER BUSINESS WRITING (25-4)	9.95	
	QUALITY CUSTOMER SERVICE (17-3)	9.95	
	TELEPHONE COURTESY & CUSTOMER SERVICE (18-1)	9.95	
	RESTAURANT SERVERS GUIDE (08-4)	8.95	
	THE FIFTY-MINUTE SALES TRAINING PROGRAM (02-05)	8.95	
	PERSONAL COUNSELING (14-9)	8.95	
	BALANCING HOME & CAREER (10-6)	9.95	
	MENTAL FITNESS: A GUIDE TO EMOTIONAL HEALTH (15-7)	9.95	
	ATTITUDE: YOUR MOST PRICELESS POSSESSION (21-1)	9.95	
	PREVENTING JOB BURNOUT (23-8)	9.95	
	SUCCESSFUL SELF-MANAGEMENT (26-2)	9.95	
	FINANCIAL FITNESS: THE HEALTH OF YOUR WEALTH (20-3)	9.95	
	UNDERSTANDING CHEMICAL DEPENDENCY (27-0)	9.95	
	THE FIFTY-MINUTE CAREER DISCOVERY PROGRAM (07-6)	8.95	
	THE FIFTY-MINUTE STUDY SKILLS PROGRAM (05-X)	8.95	
	THE FIFTY-MINUTE FIND A JOB PROGRAM (06-8)	8.95	
	UNFINISHED BUSINESS: YOU & YOUR AGING PARENTS (19-X)	14.95	
	COMFORT ZONES (0-921601-00-X)	18.95	

	SUBTOTAL	
	*POSTAGE & HANDLING	
	TOTAL	

Prices subject to change without notice.
Please contact directly for quantity discount.

SHIP TO:

_____

_____

_____

_____

BILL TO:

_____

_____

_____

_____

* Individuals: Money order or cheque must
  accompany order. $2.00 per single book,
  $0.50 per additional book.
  Corporations: Orders will be billed.

SEND ORDERS TO:

REID PUBLISHING LTD.
Box 7267
Oakville, Ontario
L6J 6L6
(416) 842-4428